The Best Ski Touring in America

The Best Ski Touring in America

by
Steve Barnett

Sierra Club Books • *San Francisco*

The Sierra Club, founded in 1892 by John Muir, has devoted itself to the study and protection of the earth's scenic and ecological resources—mountains, wetlands, woodlands, wild shores and rivers, deserts and plains. The publishing program of the Sierra Club offers books to the public as a nonprofit educational service in the hope that they may enlarge the public's understanding of the Club's basic concerns. The point of view expressed in each book, however, does not necessarily represent that of the Club. The Sierra Club has some sixty chapters coast to coast, in Canada, Hawaii, and Alaska. For information about how you may participate in its programs to preserve wilderness and the quality of life, please address inquiries to Sierra Club, 730 Polk Street, San Francisco, CA 94109.

Library of Congress Cataloging-in-Publication Data
Barnett, Steve, 1946–
   The best ski touring in North America.

   Bibliography: p. 261
   Includes index.
   1. Cross-country skiing—North America—Guide-books.
2. North America—Description and travel—1981–
Guide-books.   I. Title.
GV854.8.N58B37   1987   917   87-4722
ISBN 0-87156-722-9

Cover design by Bonnie Smetts
Book design by Detta Penna
Maps by Nancy Warner
Printed in the United States of America
10 9 8 7 6 5 4 3 2 1

Contents

Desert Southwest 135

Far West 161

Welcome
to
Ski
Touring

Finding the Best Ski Tours

In this book, I present to both skiing and nonskiing readers the full breadth of a great sport. I want to make clear with concrete examples the tremendous range of pleasures, challenges, and experiences that it offers those who love the outdoors. To do this I present a collection of the best ski tours in North America. These trips all have a classic dimension—that special resonance between the skiing, the scenery, the weather, and the terrain that creates a great experience on skis—and they provide satisfaction so great that ski tourers will either repeat them or dream about them for years to come. The tours are found in nearly all parts of the country and cover all degrees of difficulty, from day trips skiable by anyone to difficult multiday traverses in deep wilderness.

Along the way I hope to convey the excitement, adventure, and beauty that make ski touring a great sport, especially to those readers who are not yet hooked. The attraction of ski touring stems from more than just the wind-in-the-face exhilaration of looking out over a wild, snowy scene. The very act of skiing is one of the most pleasurable of physical experiences, and it's normal for deep-powder skiers to end their day with uncontrollable ear-to-ear smiles. Cross-country skiing is a perfect sport for maintaining fitness because it exercises arms, legs, and the cardiovascular system equally and simultaneously. Furthermore, it doesn't jar and tear at joints. The motion itself is as graceful as ice skating, as economical of effort as bicycling, and as rhythmic as dance. The skiing environment is always pristine with new snow, no matter what it was like without snow, and is often much more than that—sublime, magnificent, spectacular, or gorgeous.

This book is also educational. Where appropriate I talk about the problems and techniques of touring particular to each area. This includes geography, climate, skiing history, and special safety considerations, as well as relevant equipment and technique.

The present time is one of great excitement among hard-core American ski mountaineers. Part of the reason is the continuing reverberation of the revival of the telemark turn and the attendant use of Nordic equipment and techniques for mountain travel. The European method of using alpine equipment with convertible bindings (the heels can be released and the whole boot pivots from the toe for uphill and horizontal stretches) had never seemed well-adapted to the wilderness skiing found on this continent. There were too many long approaches on the way to or from the mountains. The Nordic equipment, adapted as it was for traveling long distances on skis, made it possible for many skiers to comfortably complete trips they had thought of before but dismissed as being too long. With the telemark technique it is possible to use this same Nordic equipment for skiing steep slopes in difficult snow and to have fun while doing it. Thus the ideal of "anywhere there is snow I can go skiing" is brought much closer to realization.

The other half of the excitement in the ski-mountaineering community is the nature of the trips that are now being explored. Telemark or not, there have been many glorious new routes done in the last decade. Trips like the Redline Traverse in California, traverses of the Northern and Southern Selkirks in the Canadian Interior Ranges, of the Wind Rivers and Tetons in Wyoming, a traverse of the Canadian Rockies from the Ramparts to Lake Louise, traverses of the Waddington and Monarch icefields in the British Columbia Coast Range, the circumnavigation of Denali and Mt. Logan, long routes in the Arctic islands of Canada, along with other routes described in this book all combine boldness, mountain grandeur, endurance, and commitment. No wonder many skiers think this is a Golden Age for ski mountaineering in North America.

What distinguishes North American skiing from European skiing? More than anything else it's the extent of wilderness. Certainly the Alps are as magnificent as any mountain range in the lower 48 states, but they are a civilized range. Every valley has roads and towns in it, and many of them have ski lifts rising up from the towns to the timberline regions above. Even in those high regions of rock and ice the mountains are civilized. Huts, which are usually really hotels, are perched in the most improbable places as well as on trade routes. They give you the luxury of traveling with small packs, of spending the night in comfort in a bed, and of eating an excellent meal every evening of your trip. Such amenities are rare in North American skiing.

I've tried to include the best hut-to-hut trips here, but they are not at all typical of the most exciting skiing. North American mountains are still relatively wild, with many unpopulated valleys, large stretches with no roads, and almost no high-altitude facilities. The feeling of wilderness is magnified many times over in the winter. The prototypical American trip is one where you shoulder a heavy pack, complete with sleeping bag, tent, and meals for many days, and forge your way through the empty white mountains. On skis such travel is a throwback to the days of mountain men and voyageurs. The promise of that feeling of yesteryear is one of the sport's stronger attractions—and a barrier to its greater popularity. There are, of course, many excellent ski trips that are intermediate between these two extremes.

It's been a bit difficult for me to resist writing about all the bold wilderness traverses now being done and leave enough space for the shorter trips. These long trips often seem to be the culminating ski adventures in any one region. Any of them would be impossible in the Alps because that kind of unpopulated space doesn't exist there. They are harder work than the hut-to-hut alpine trips but offer in turn a sense of accomplishment, a profound feeling of isolation, and a sense of wonder as you penetrate into more and more unknown nooks and crannies of the mountains. To succeed on such a long tour takes a great deal of knowledge, experience, and determination.

The short trips in this book are classic ski trips in their own right. I've presented those that most retain the sense of pleasant surprise I've mentioned above, trips that show you wonders you didn't expect to see. One of the hallmarks of a classic trip is that while traveling you see four other trips that you dearly would like to do. This is a part of the sense of wonder that you have on a really good tour—that it makes the sport seem open-ended. You can pore over maps for a week and know a region really well and still come up with a ski route you didn't see before. Then it seems as natural as can be, and you can only wonder how you ever missed it.

WHAT MAKES A CLASSIC SKI TOUR?

It should come as no surprise that careful planning and preparation are essential ingredients of a successful major ski tour. Of course so is improvisation! How do you find the best route in a given area, the one with the classic dimension? It depends on what you are looking for. Let's start with the following list:

MAXIMUM SCENIC VALUE   The route should touch as many of the scenic highlights of the region as possible.

MAXIMUM SKIING VALUE   The route should have a mix of different types of skiing: downhill through open country, downhill with tight maneuvering, cross-country on rolling country, and cross-country on a scenic trail. Desirable for the downhill are long fall-line slopes with constant grade. Open bowls are always nice but so are forest slaloms. Variety in the form of rolls and counterslope turns are fun, while gullies to cross and constant sidehilling are much less so. Open forest is nice. Tight lodgepole, manzanita, or brush-filled Eastern forest is to be avoided.

For flatter cross-country skiing much the same terrain constraints hold. Sidehilling is usually less pleasant and efficient traveling than following a flat valley bottom, shelf, or ridgetop. Frequently no good ridge exists or, if it does and if it is above timberline, the snow will be blown off it, and cornices will overhang its edges.

The bottom of a broad U-shaped valley can be a delightful route of travel, especially if the forest in it is open. On the other hand, traveling along a thickly forested V-shaped stream bed is often an infuriating struggle with the standing brush, the downed trees, and the steep hillside, and is worth avoiding, even at the cost of considerable climbing or sidehill traversing.

Also to be considered are the exposures of the parts of a route to wind and sun. A good route at one time of the year may not be a good route at another time, so just looking at a map is not enough to find a classic route. It helps to have an intimate knowledge of a region's forest types, weather history, and snow conditions. For example, if you know that a forest in a given exposure in a given range is too thick for easy travel until you get to a certain elevation, then you should be looking for a road or trail to follow up to that elevation. From there you can leave the trail. Perhaps the best route then goes cross-country far from that road. Or you can try to find a route via a slope of a different exposure that climbs to the altitude where the forest opens or where the snow gets deep enough to bury the brush.

It's common in midwinter for north-facing slopes to have deep unconsolidated snow that is difficult to travel in, while south-facing slopes are better consolidated, safer, and warmer. In spring the situation changes and the south-facing slopes may quickly get too soft, too unstable, and too hot to be good routes, while the north-facing slopes are fine all day. Thus the best route changes with the season and the snow conditions.

SAFETY   It's all too easy while ski touring in the mountainous West to put yourself in mortal danger while you are having the time of your life. Ski touring is not like climbing, where fear is part of the experience and where there's never any doubt where the danger lies. There's no grizzly foaming at the mouth between you and her cubs, no foaming explosion of whitewater surrounded by razor-sharp rocks, no rain of rocks falling on you while you are hanging on to insignificant holds on a vertical mountain wall. No, there are, at first glance, only acres of sparkling, perfect powder that will exert an almost sexual attraction on the good skier. But the danger, upon closer examination, may be just as great as in other more obvious cases. A fatal avalanche may be patiently awaiting the touch of your skis. It will be quiet and motionless and then break into violent action at just the wrong moment. Careful route selection can help a lot to reduce that risk, and safety should be given just as much consideration as scenic value and skiing value.

Of course just those things that maximize skiing pleasure are what you should avoid to find maximum security: steep, open bowls with long continuous drops, steep couloirs, cornices to jump from into beckoning fields of powder, avalanche-cleared swaths in the forest that are easy routes for ascent as well as descent. Who wants to concentrate their skiing on wind-swept but safe ridges, or wind-blasted, windward slopes, or through thick forest, or to always avoid slopes steep enough to get you flying through the powder? Obviously compromises are in order, but they have to be heavily weighted toward safety rather than skiing pleasure. Fine judgment built from experience helps, as does the sense of the frailty of your judgment that experience also brings. It's a good idea to learn to enjoy skiing under more difficult conditions on routes that minimize avalanche danger. The technique is more stringent than and somewhat different from what you learn just skiing on lift-served slopes or in good powder, but it is not magic and can be mastered by anyone who has the will. Balancing these conflicting requirements is the art of finding a classic route.

Is your route simple or complex? If there is a storm or fog can you keep moving or will you be forced to sit tight? Obviously, if you are in a valley you can usually follow it no matter what, though even in that situation I've made gross mistakes where streams fork. A ridge route might not be so simple. Maybe there are cornices or cliffs along the ridge. Travel is usually possible in forests when there is bad visibility, but it is an entirely different situation above timberline. Can the route be navigated safely in a whiteout with map, compass, and altimeter, or are there potentially dangerous obstacles along the way or too many ways to get lost? If there is a storm, can you get trapped by avalanche paths both ahead of and behind you? This is a common problem with long western ski routes. Look carefully beforehand for potential escape routes, and consider their presence or absence as major factors for choosing or rejecting a trip.

ACCESS Some tours, like climbing Mt. Logan on skis, are really expeditions. Having to fly into base camp or to spend weeks hauling loads up glaciers is just part of the game. But for many otherwise desirable trips the necessity of skiing long distances just for access while carrying heavy loads limits the trip's appeal. Even the necessity of shuttling cars over long distances for many of the traverses in this book must be considered a flaw for otherwise perfect trips. A loop trip makes a lot of sense in terms of logistics and can easily be just as aesthetically satisfying as a traverse.

Put all these constraints together and you can see why it's hard—but not impossible—to find a classic route, even in a well-endowed mountain range. And, of course, a classic route does more than just satisfy a list of someone's requirements; it has an internal resonance of its own, a bit of magic that makes skiing it a totally satisfying experience.

Safety Guidelines
for Ski Touring

DANGEROUS TOURS AND
DANGEROUS TOURERS

Are some tours intrinsically less safe than others? At first glance it would seem obvious that this is so. Some areas, such as the Colorado Rockies or the Wasatch of Utah, for example, frequently have high or unpredictable avalanche danger. Take a tour like Mt. Superior with its steep but very attractive summit slopes and it seems natural to call it a dangerous tour—there is a much higher probability of getting into fatal problems on Mt. Superior than while skiing along a trail in Arches National Park. But there is also a much greater responsibility on the part of the tourer to be exceedingly more cautious on Mt. Superior than at Arches! Thus, I think it more useful to talk about intrinsically dangerous tourers than about intrinsically dangerous tours. There are ways to get into serious trouble on even the easiest of tours, even for experienced skiers, and the crucial factor in avoiding trouble is the margin of safety that the tourer habitually maintains on ski explorations.

I know a skier who made it a practice to ski as aggressively as possible in the wilderness. He always looked for the steepest slopes and even on easy slopes he either skied fast or made as many turns as possible. He was, he said, preparing himself for harder skiing elsewhere. Is it surprising that he shattered his ankle while touring? Aggressive skiing, as I will explain, has its place in certain wilderness skiing situations, but most of the time moderate skiing, with safety the first priority, is more appropriate. You should always be trying to reduce the probability of finding yourself later in a dangerous situation.

The consequences of getting into trouble differ according to who your companions are and the distance you are from help. If you are skiing close to civilization, where escape is relatively simple, and if you are skiing with others who could aid you in case of trouble, then you are perfectly justified in skiing more aggressively—faster, steeper, through tighter forest or cliff bands. If you go out skiing alone in the wilderness, however, then you must ski conservatively. If, for example, you start to fall when you are skiing alone, twisting in crusty trap snow, it is better sometimes to drop to the ground in control, with no stress on your limbs, than to fight to keep standing, as you might if you were skiing with others and were closer to help. Sometimes the better part of valor is to zigzag instead of trying to make turns or even to take your skis off and walk. Usually you will ski slower, avoid potential avalanche slopes even more zealously, and generally do what you can to reduce the chance of getting into trouble in the first place.

It's commonly said that skiing alone is inherently more dangerous than skiing with others. That's certainly true given equal behavior on your part, but your behavior is not likely to be the same in the two situations. A case can be made that the actual danger is about the same because you are keeping about the same margin of safety in both situations, always mindful of the relative consequences of trouble. Some of the really monumental ski trips of all time have been done alone, like Orland Bartholomew's Sierra Traverse or John Clarke's several long explorations in the British Columbia Coast Range.

Maintaining the margin of safety when skiing alone involves more than conservative skiing. You will probably need a larger pack than you would carry for an equivalent ski tour with a partner. Even for a day tour you should have enough equipment to survive a night out if the worst happens and you somehow injure yourself (see the story several paragraphs below). That doesn't necessarily mean that you will carry a full tent, sleeping bag, and stove, but may mean that you will add a shovel, a warm jacket, booties, and a bivouac sack to your standard day pack. Even in a party of several people out on a day tour there ought to be enough equipment between the skiers to allow one of them to spend a night out.

For example, if you are going to ski Mt. Superior you should check very carefully beforehand to see what the snow pack is like and what local professional avalanche controllers think about the chances of an avalanche accident. Even though this is an inherently more dangerous tour than most you can maintain a margin of safety by not considering skiing it except in periods of exceptionally safe snow conditions. Then when you do ski the tour you will carry the safety tools skiers use on avalanche-prone terrain: a radio locator beacon and a shovel. This behavior gives you the best margin of safety you can have. Of course to ski at all in this kind of terrain you must educate yourself as well as possible about avalanche prediction, avoidance, and rescue. That knowledge is a lot more valuable than any of your equipment.

Take in contrast a tour that most people would consider to be inherently safe, such as skiing along a set cross-country trail of only moderate difficulty. I know of a case where a skier on such a trail in Minnesota fell on a fast section, hit a rock exposed by a low snowpack, and cut a ligament in her knee, leaving her helpless. As it turned out, she was rescued by her husband who heard her screams, but had she been skiing alone, as would seem reasonable to most skiers, she would have faced a night out. Skiing alone on this trail wearing nothing but a racing suit would be safe on the weekend, when other skiers were present, but to make it safe on a deserted midweek day a skier should carry a day pack with extra clothing and a first-aid kit and let someone know where they are going. That is maintaining a margin of safety.

The point is that there is no tour that is absolutely safe and nowhere that you have license to be an idiot. The most dangerous situations are probably those that most lull you into complacency, for example, when avalanche danger is reported to be moderate and you are lured onto danger-ous pockets of unstable snow, or when good weather is predicted and you leave extra clothing and navigation tools behind in order to ski with a light pack and then are hit with a sudden intense storm. Anywhere skiing is possi-ble, hypothermia is also possible—including southern California and Baja California in Mexico. Maintaining a margin of safety means thinking ahead about the consequences of unexpected events and equipping yourself ap-propriately, and also maintaining an ability to improvise—to build a snow cave, to repair a ski or pole, to find an escape route in a storm, and to treat an injury. Maintaining a margin of safety demands that the skier has a good understanding of the particular dangers of the terrain, such as avalanche danger in steep mountains or crevasse danger on glaciers, knows how to navigate when not on a marked trail, and knows how to avoid hypother-mia. These topics will be covered in the following chapters.

THE THREAT OF AVALANCHES

Avalanches are the single greatest safety problem facing the ski tourer, greater even than getting cold, getting lost, or getting injured. The prob-lem is that the danger is insidious—you have to be either experienced or well-trained to feel fear when the danger is high. Too often you can step into mortal danger without realizing that anything is wrong. In fact it's often the most alluring slopes and conditions—open bowls full of fresh deep powder, for example—that present the greatest hazards.

To learn about the mechanics of avalanche prediction, avoidance, and survival it's best to take one of the courses offered in most mountainous areas and to read some of the excellent texts that have appeared in the last few years. I particularly recommend *Avalanche Safety for Skiers and Climbers* by Tony Daffern because it is oriented toward the practical prob-lems faced by ski tourers in the field rather than the somewhat different problems faced by ski areas and highway departments. Also very good is Ed LaChappelle's *The ABC's of Avalanche Safety*, which is a small, easily carried booklet. I won't duplicate the information in these books—they do a good and thorough job—but I will provide a quick avalanche primer.

To assess avalanche danger as you travel on skis, you must constantly try to understand the structure of the snowpack, which will be changing as you move from point to point. You may examine the snowpack both by digging a pit in it, which is thorough but time-consuming, or by frequently pushing your ski pole in as far as you can. Both methods allow you to look for layers in the snow, which can be identified by sharp discontinuities in the stiffness of the snow. The layers may be very weak, usually temperature-gradient hoar snow, or very hard, such as ice crusts caused by sun or rain. Snow over the discontinuous layers can slide if the slope is steep enough and an appropriate trigger (you or your friends) sets it off.

The most common weak layer is called temperature-gradient or TG snow. It is created by metamorphosis of the snow crystals when there is a strong temperature gradient, which is to say it forms when the temperature of the snowpack changes sharply from bottom to top. This frequently happens early in the season when the snowpack is shallow and there are very cold nights. The ground is always at the freezing point and the air at the snow surface is much colder. Since the depth of the snowpack is not great, the gradient (degrees per inch) will be strong. This kind of TG snow is called depth hoar and is very common in the Rockies. The TG snow takes the form of platelets or even scrolls, rather than the usual stellar (starlike) crystals. These forms interlock with each other much less than do the numerous points of stellar crystals. Thus they form a dangerously weak layer in the snow. In the high altitudes of the southern Rockies another form of TG snow appears in significant depths on the surface of the snowpack: it is called surface hoar. This is the wintertime equivalent of dew. It forms later in the season and is a good sliding surface for subsequent snowfalls.

I must stress that a little knowledge can be a dangerous thing. There is a real danger that after taking a course or reading a book you will feel that you can dig a pit and say, "This slope seems okay." You might be encouraged to ski a wider range of slopes than you might ski if you were equipped with a greater sense of danger but less knowledge. You will get away with skiing slopes that look to be both fun and potentially dangerous for a long while, and then you will get hit. You are perhaps even more likely to get hit at times of moderate danger because then you will be less cautious. You must remember that one safe-looking pit doesn't necessarily tell you what the snow profile is even a short distance away if that new area has a different exposure to the wind or sun, a different altitude, or different vegetation under or over it. All it takes is one relatively small pocket of deeper snow blown in by the wind over a hard layer to create a hazardous situation, even though most of the mountain snowpack is stable.

How do you get a good sense of what the snow pack will do? One way is the ski patroller's way: you get to see many avalanches actually happen and even participate in a few. That's not a possibility for most tourers, who must pick the brains of those more experienced, analyze recent slides, and keep track of the weather and snow conditions, always trying to relate the facts to avalanche possibilities on different slopes and at different altitudes.

Over the long run, of course, only strong conservatism will assure you a long untroubled life as a ski tourer. It helps to ski well enough to avoid the easy, fun run down the middle and to be able to stick to the edges, trees, and ridges that are safer. Even so you might be on a slope sometime, hear a "whoomp," and feel the snow around you disintegrate and start moving. It's like driving around a bend on a mountain road and suddenly seeing headlights coming at you in your lane. It helps to have thought ahead about what you should do if you get caught.

What do you do if caught in an avalanche? First you try to ski out of it, if the edge of the slide or such islands of safety as a clump of trees aren't far away. The distance you can go is limited. It's a good idea, if you're worried about slides, to try to ski from island of safety to island of safety, so that your distance from safety is always as small as you can make it. You should fight to stay on top of the slide. Swim up through the snow—if you are completely buried, your chances for survival are obviously much lower. Experience shows that you will have a much easier time staying on the surface if your skis are off. For downhillers that's not so much of a problem because the slide is likely to release their bindings. For Nordic skiers it is a greater problem, because their bindings don't automatically release. If possible choose bindings that you can release easily with a brush of the hand. Safety straps should be off when crossing potentially dangerous slopes. If you are getting dragged under, try to form an air pocket around your face with your hands before the slide stops.

The well-equipped mountain ski tourer is always equipped with avalanche gear: a shovel, a radio locator beacon such as a Pieps or an Echo, and, most important, an alert mind. You should always act as though you didn't have the shovel or the locator, which is to say, don't let their presence encourage you to do something you wouldn't do otherwise. They do increase the chance of survival, but they don't at all guarantee it and thus should be thought of as last resorts. More information about avalanche survival gear can be found in the chapter on equipment.

Regional Avalanche Guide

Each region of the country has its own characteristic "normal" seasonal history of snowfall, temperature, and wind. Each mountain range also has a distinctive topography. Put them together and you can say that each area has its own "normal" avalanche cycles. I say normal with quotes because there is another rule that says that normal weather is just a statistical artifact. The normal year is an average of a great number of past seasons, but in actual fact a normal year almost never happens. Still, as far as avalanches go each range has characteristic types of avalanches that fall at characteristic times (even if for ranges like the Colorado Rockies that characteristic might be the unpredictability of the slides).

Cascade Weather and Avalanches

The Cascades of Oregon and Washington with their enormous snowfall see many large avalanches. I think, however, that they present less of a problem to the ski tourer than the colder and less snowy ranges of the Rockies because Cascade avalanches are generally predictable. Furthermore, the danger is at its worst at just those times when nobody in their right mind is outside—in the middle of a bad storm with heavy wet snow or rain falling, often accompanied by high winds or thick fog. You'd have to be pretty desperate to be out on skis traveling or trying to have fun under such conditions. It's so temperate in the Cascades that the snowpack usually stabilizes quickly after a storm (the snowpack strengthens if the temperature is only a bit below freezing). Long-lasting depth hoar, a terrible problem in the Rockies, is rare due to the usual heavy and early snows and due to the fact that whatever depth hoar develops is likely to be cleaned out quickly by enormous snowfalls or heavy rains and the subsequent spontaneous slides.

A principal problem of winter travel in the North Cascades is that the range is so rugged that a heavy storm in midwinter could leave you pinned down with no safe exit. Such storms are frequent and sometimes last for weeks. Consequently, midwinter travel deep into the North Cascades is rare. Late spring is the best time. The eastern slope with lighter snowfall and gentler slopes is a lot better in this regard, but there is a tradeoff since it also has greater problems with depth hoar.

Sierra Weather and Avalanches

The Sierra tends to get large dumps of snow interspersed with long periods of sunshine. Temperatures are usually moderate to warm. Thus avalanche danger is very high during or right after storms, but the snowpack stabilizes rapidly. Large storms can continue well into the spring so you have to be prepared at any season to find a safe place and sit tight.

At the highest altitudes, temperatures are lower. It is possible in mid-winter that north-facing snowpacks could have deep weaknesses (TG) that remain dangerous long after the last heavy storm.

Generally, though, the Sierra is a relatively safe range to ski in. The avalanches are usually predictable, running during or just after the storm, or during a sharp thaw.

The best strategy for avalanches—to sit out the storms and wait a day or two for the snow to stabilize—also is the best strategy for travel. Right after one of the big dumps travel will be very difficult. There might be four feet of unconsolidated snow on the ground, and the ski tourer will be plowing a trench almost that deep. There's no way to do that and enjoy the thrill of gliding on skis. Just a few days of waiting, though, and the snow will settle enough that travel will again become easy and downhill skiing both fun and safe.

As in the Cascades there can be depth hoar on the drier, colder, eastern slopes of the range. It's a potentially more severe problem in the Sierra than in the Cascades because the eastern slopes are the longest, steepest, and most accessible of Sierra slopes.

Rockies Weather and Avalanches

The Rockies and Intermountain Ranges are the most dangerous places in the United States and Canada with respect to avalanche danger. Take Colorado as an example. Its mountains are the farthest east of all the western ranges. Thus they get a lighter snowpack than the coastal ranges. The continental climate is much colder than the maritime climate of the Pacific coast. The altitudes where most of the skiing is done are relatively high, making the air temperatures even colder. Thus you have all the necessary ingredients for the formation of a deep layer of TG snow early in the season. Only in an exceptional year will there be a snowfall right at the beginning of the snow season heavy enough to keep TG formation to a minimum. Once the TG layer is formed there is little likelihood it will be cleaned out before spring. In this climate it will almost never get very warm, let alone rain heavily as it might in the coastal mountains. The weak layer will be in the snowpack all winter. A very heavy snowfall might trigger a slide on it, and so might a skier traveling over a wind-deposited pocket at the top of a bowl full of luscious-looking powder. Thus there might be dangerous pockets of snow, ready to slide, long after the last heavy storm.

You can almost never take stability for granted in the Rockies. Surprises are frequent. What do you do? Unless it's one of those really exceptional years when the whole snowpack is strong (determined by keeping track of the weather from fall onward, by digging frequent snowpits, and by relying on the experience of ski patrols and other tourers throughout the winter), you always travel with beepers and shovels, always pick the safest route possible, and frequently say no to slopes that look suspicious. Even small slopes can be dangerous, such as the wind-loaded sides of gullies, and it's all too easy to relax for these.

In the spring the situation changes, and the danger becomes much more predictable. Then, as long as the nights are cold, the snowpack freezes solid overnight and the skiing is safe until the snow thaws. Late in the afternoon it may become very dangerous, but you will be well warned by the deep, soupy snow. South-facing slopes, which consolidate faster in midwinter, in spring become more dangerous. At some point in the spring the snowpack will thaw all the way through and the biggest avalanche of all becomes possible, the climax slide, which cleans out the entire snowpack right down to the ground. Safety at this time means traveling early, skiing the south-facing slopes first and the north-facing ones later, and late in the day avoiding entirely those avalanche chutes and steep bowls where such slides have happened repeatedly over the years. You should be planning your descents for that delicious time when the sun has just warmed the surface of the snow while it is still frozen underneath and skiing down is effortless joy.

It's ironic that the very same meteorological facts of life that make backcountry travel hazardous also create ideal conditions for downhill ski areas. The Colorado Front Range has the largest concentration of such areas in the United States. The juxtaposition of large numbers of skiers—many of whom are from out of the area and not familiar with local conditions—and high avalanche hazard is obviously fraught with potential for disaster. That's why the Rocky Mountain states have tough laws regulating out-of-bounds skiing for lift-served skiers at downhill areas. While we can't agree with the letter of these laws, it's impossible to deny that there is a problem. Out-of-bounds skiers have to be responsible for themselves and take the utmost precautions to avoid becoming part of avalanche statistics.

Most encounters between man and avalanche in North America occur in the great ranges of the West described above. Yet any steep slope anywhere that snow may fall has potential as an avalanche site. Avalanches can happen in peculiar and unexpected places. They have occurred on slopes of man-made snow at ski areas in the East and Midwest to the total amazement of the local skiers. They have occurred in gullies in wooded Eastern hillsides, and they certainly are a serious danger on the wind-loaded slopes above timberline in the White Mountains of New Hampshire or in the Chic-Chocs of Quebec's Gaspé Peninsula. They have happened to campers digging snow caves at exactly the wrong stress point on a wind-loaded slope, to people enjoying a quiet night before the fireplace in their cabin, to skiers sunning themselves at lunch at the ski lodge, and to experts who have checked and rechecked slopes only to have them let loose when they actually skied them. Cascade avalanches have been so wet they literally have washed victims down-mountain before drowning them. Sierra avalanches have cracked with 30-foot fracture lines, and one famous Rockies avalanche killed a cinematographer in a bombproof location miles from the start of the avalanche.

Avalanches have just as many peculiarities as eccentric humans, and you just can't take them for granted. Take a course, read books and articles about avalanche accidents and safety procedures. Read the sobering annual publication *Accidents in North American Mountaineering*. You can learn to recognize what danger looks like.

GLACIER SKIING

Compared to Europeans, American skiers do comparatively little glacier skiing. Our highest and most frequented ranges, the Colorado Rockies and the California Sierra, have only the feeblest excuses for glaciers, so small that special equipment or precautions aren't really needed. The Wind River Range of Wyoming has a few glaciers of more than token size, but these are so remote that they are rarely visited even though a trip through them is reputedly a first-class ski mountaineering tour. Most U.S. glaciers and most U.S. glacier skiers are found on the peaks of the Cascades of the Pacific Northwest. Mountains such as Mt. Rainier and Mt. Baker are literally sheathed in ice (48 sq. mi. and 24 sq. mi., respectively). Western Canada is also a center for glacier skiing and, of course, Alaskans have no trouble finding glaciers close to their homes.

The primary hazard facing a glacier skier is that of falling into a crevasse. As the glacier moves downhill it must follow the uneven contour of the bedrock underneath. The lower layers of glacier ice are under enough pressure that they flow like a liquid and don't crack as they move over and around obstacles. The upper layers, however, are not under such great pressure and they crack as they move unevenly. These cracks are crevasses, and they can be deep enough that you can't see the bottom. When snow falls on the glacier a lid of snow can form over the crevasse, hiding it from view. This is especially true if there is wind along with or just after the storm. Skis make glacier travel much safer because they spread the skier's weight out over a large area and are much less likely to break through a snow bridge than boots alone. Still, a fresh snow bridge may not be strong enough to hold the weight of a skier. In the Alps there are deaths every year from skiers falling into weakly bridged, hidden crevasses.

In the Pacific Northwest this is not much of a problem because there is very little glacier skiing in early or midwinter when fresh snow and wind create crevasse traps. Unlike the Alps, there are few ski areas that offer glacier skiing or easy access to glaciers with such exceptions as Mt. Hood, Oregon, and Blackcomb, British Columbia. Most tourers don't get out onto the larger peaks until the spring. By then the snow bridges are thick and the regular cycle of thaw and freeze has made them very strong. I have never even heard of a skier falling into a hidden crevasse in the Washington Cascades in the spring. A common procedure there is to rope up for the ascent and ski down unroped. It is just as common to leave the rope in the pack, keeping it available for emergencies.

The situation is different early in the season (October or November, for example) in the Cascades, glacier skiing in Alaska, and anytime in the Canadian Rockies. Then snow bridges may be weak and the rope must be used more often.

With or without the rope, prevention is the best cure for glacier problems. Few snow bridges are hidden so completely that they don't leave any clues. If you see a slot or a row of holes, assume there is a crevasse underneath that extends well beyond the visible signs. Extrapolate from those signs where the crevasse might be, and as you get close to the presumed location start probing with your ski pole. Careful observation and diligent probing are your first line of defense.

Even if the chances of falling into a crevasse are small, the consequences are so serious that you should carry a rope on any trip that crosses glaciers large enough to have many crevasses. An 8 mm perlon rope is recommended. Some have used even lighter ropes such as a 6 mm Kevlar one that is stronger than a 9 mm nylon one. It's not suitable for climbing since it has about as much stretch (and strength, too) as a steel cable but it is fine for glacier travel where the shock forces are low. It's very light, about 2 pounds for a length of 120 feet. The one problem is that like a steel cable it can be fatigued and weakened by the repeated tying and untying of tight knots. Knots should be left in such a rope, and locking carabiners used to attach it to the skier's harnesses. It may be wise for every member of the party to carry an additional 50- to 60-foot piece of such rope since these can aid greatly in rescues and are handy for other purposes as well.

Along with the ropes all skiers have to carry prusik loops, which will enable them to climb a rope. These are lengths of rope tied in a special knot around the main rope. The prusik knot slides freely along the rope when it is loose and grips the rope when it is under tension. Thus a pair of prusik knots tied to loops for your feet and your climbing harness can be used to climb up the rope if you are unlucky enough to fall into a crevasse.

Prusiks should be made of 5 or 6 mm perlon. These prusiks are so small that you can leave them stuffed in your pockets while you ski. A complex climber's harness isn't really necessary for glacier skiing. Chouinard Equipment makes a light, cheap harness, the Alpine Bod Harness, that can be put on and removed while wearing skis. A simple swami belt, a length of 1-inch webbing wrapped several times around the waist and tied with a ring or double fisherman's knot, along with one or two leg loops of light webbing are sufficient and light in weight. The leg loops keep you from suffocating if you should be so unlucky as to have to spend some time hanging from a rope. It's a good idea also to have some kind of simple chest harness (a figure eight of light webbing will do) to keep yourself from hanging upside down, helpless, in the crevasse. For details of crevasse rescue techniques read *Mountaineering: The Freedom of the Hills*, published by the Mountaineers of Seattle.

It's important not merely to own the crevasse rescue equipment but to try it out beforehand. Nearly everyone who does a crevasse rescue practice for the first time finds it remarkable how much harder it is to do than it sounds in theory. The hardest part is usually getting over the lip of the crevasse, where the rope has dug itself into the snow. This is where the extra pieces of rope carried by each skier or, failing that, the tail end of the glacier rope comes in handy. The rescuers can lower the extra rope over the lip and keep it from digging in by running it over a ski or pack. The rescuee can then transfer from the buried rope to the free one. An extra prusik and extra carabiner can make this transfer easier.

You should think carefully about the procedure you will use in case of an accident. This may not be covered in enough detail in climbing instruction books. For example, how will you stop the fall? Usually the rope will dig into the lip of the crevasse adding welcome extra friction. Can you throw your skis across the fall line? Or do you have self-arrest grips on your poles? Or is the snow so soft that all you have to do is fall down? Then how will you tie the rope to an anchor so that you can get yourself free to aid in the rescue? Using your prusik loops might be a good way. Obviously it will be easier if there is more than one ropeful of people in the party. How many people should be on a rope? Having only two on the rope is sometimes inescapable, but does provide less margin for stopping a fall and for implementing the rescue. Four on the rope is too clumsy to ski anywhere but gently uphill. Three seems optimal.

Skiing downhill while roped to other skiers is not trivial. Often it is comic. Somehow you must synchronize turns to keep the rope reasonably taut at all times. As often as not it seems that the rope creates as much hazard as it eliminates. That's because one skier or another gets out of sync and tries to pull everyone else into a crevasse. If the situation is really dicey it's probably best that only one skier at a time skis while the others belay that skier, using ice axes or skis jammed vertically into the snow. In loose snow, if a really solid belay is needed, the best tactic is to bury a ski horizontally and stamp the snow around it until it is good and solid.

While the possibility of mortal danger always hangs over a glacier, even a seemingly benign one in the Cascades or Canadian Arctic, there's a tremendous reward in glacier skiing, too. The architecture of those very hazards that threaten you, the yawning bottomless slots, and the seracs towering overhead give glacier skiing a touch of the fantastic, a dreamlike quality that can lead you to do it again and again. It's one of the most otherworldly landscapes you can find on Earth. Also, of course, glacier skiing is the key to the best of summer skiing and is an inescapable part of skiing any of the great peaks of Canada or Alaska.

KEEPING WARM

The trips in this book have all been chosen because they are likely to give the ski tourer an exceptionally rewarding experience. Still, many of them involve long excursions into potentially hostile environments. Some are trips of several days, one is a trip of several weeks. Despite the clear glory of standing on a high snowy peak in the middle of a great wilderness, the difficulties—real and imagined—of living in a wintry environment ensure that the sport of wilderness ski touring is still a small one. Certainly the fear of long cold nights spent miserably, awake, shivering, pulling apart the frozen clumps of down in your sleeping bag feather by feather, and of desperate forced marches on numb feet trying to reach camp before frostbite sets in must be a big factor in keeping these trips from becoming highly popular. How solidly based are these fears? Solidly enough that most ski tourers who go camping have had these bad experiences in their early journeys. At the same time they are avoidable enough that most of these same skiers rarely have trouble once they have a little experience.

Hypothermia stands right alongside avalanche danger as a danger facing ski tourers, but unlike avalanche danger it is a possibility anywhere people ski. Hypothermia occurs when a person's body temperature falls below a level that permits proper mental and physical functioning. It can happen insidiously, with the victim denying to the last that anything is wrong. It also is completely avoidable. To learn about the diagnosis and treatment of hypothermia read *Hypothermia: Killer of the Unprepared* by Lathrop.

Keeping warm in a cold environment is a function of both your behavior and your equipment. The two are related. You have to realize just what your equipment can and can't do and meticulously respect those limits. No equipment, no matter how technologically advanced, is so miraculous that it will keep you at a comfortable temperature whatever your behavior or situation, whether you're working hard climbing a mountain or sitting quietly by your tent at nightfall, whether it's 33° F. and raining or −10° F. and snowing.

There are some simple rules to follow to maintain your body's ability to keep itself warm:

1. When your feet or hands start getting cold, take action immediately. If your whole body starts getting chilled take action immediately. Don't tough it out and wait.

2. To get warm, put on dry clothes, either over the wet ones or replacing the wet ones. Always keep dry clothes in reserve. A hat, especially, helps keep you from losing body heat. Once dry clothes are on, start exercising. For example, run or jump in place, shovel snow, put skis on and run around the area. If you are already exercising and you are still getting cold, you've got a problem. Put on as many warm clothes as you can, and stop and eat. Then exercise.

3. To get hands warm, put on extra gloves or mittens and shake your hands vigorously downward, which drives warm blood into them.

To get feet warm if you've been inactive, start running, jumping, or skiing till they warm up. Or put on insulated booties. If your feet are cold while you are active, change into dry socks and put overboots on, if you have them, over your boots. Getting cold while you're active indicates that the body core is getting chilled and it's time to put more clothes on the whole body.

4. Match your activity rate and your clothing. Read the chapter in this book on equipment and clothing. If you are climbing, you will almost certainly be warm, no matter how cold it is. There's no reason to sweat a lot and get clothes unnecessarily wet. Take off layers. If possible open up the ventilators and take off your hat and your gloves. One experienced skier I know takes off his shirt while climbing, even in snowstorms. Then when he stops, his dry clothes go on in a millisecond. His behavior seems extreme when you see snowflakes melting on his bare skin, but he seems to keep at least as comfortable as anyone else. If there's a breeze, it's a good idea to wear a light anorak with just a thin layer underneath to keep from getting chilled without also getting overheated. Then as soon as you stop put on a warmer layer and your hat. The idea is to keep your body core at a constant temperature, which makes it easy to keep your feet and hands warm, too.

Body heat is generated by the slow combustion of the food you eat. When you get cold, one good response is to eat some easily digestible snacks. Another helpful step for keeping warm is to maintain a steady intake of liquids. Dehydration is subtle. It can easily be severe enough to weaken you after a long climb without giving the warning signal of thirst.

If your core gets chilled the body automatically starts cutting off the blood flow to the extremities. Thus one way to keep the extremities warm is to keep the core warm—but keep it too warm and you'll soak your clothes with sweat. That's why the layer system is effective: it gives you the versatility needed to adjust your clothing to both your metabolic output and the environment. Cold extremities can also be caused by clothes that are too tight and restrict the blood flow to the hands and feet.

Inevitably some of your clothing will get wet, whether from snow or rain or from sweating. Wool will hold warmth somewhat when wet, though it may itch or feel clammy. Cotton is useless when wet and hard to dry, and you'll be colder with it wet than without it. Some of the new synthetic fibers, such as polypropylene, polyester, or nylon (polyamide), have nearly ideal properties. They stay warm when wet, are comfortable, and absorb so little water that they are easy to dry, even with just body heat. Pile or bunting jackets can be dried sufficiently to keep you warm by spinning them so the water flows to one end and then wringing that end out. In any case, keep some extra dry clothing in your pack at all times so that you can warm yourself or someone else if you or they get wet and chilled.

Protecting Your Feet from Cold

Fortunately, serious frostbite is rare for ski tourers. But even the discomfort of cold feet is enough to seriously mar an otherwise enjoyable trip. Careful preparation and choice of the right equipment will keep your feet warm in any winter environment.

Fit the tools to the job. Obviously you have to plan much more seriously for cold on a trip to Mt. Logan in the Yukon than for spring skiing in the Sierra. But even in the Sierra you have to have much more serious equipment for skiing the entire Sierra Crest than for skiing short day trips that never go more than a few hours from your car.

Boots should be roomy at the toes and roomy enough for you to wear two layers of socks. Too many socks in too tight boots can restrict circulation and leave your toes as cold as no socks at all. For very cold climates, double boots and insulated overboots are good protection against the cold. Damp socks will cause feet to be cold, so vapor barrier socks or neoprene wet-suit socks also help keep feet warm. Gaiters keep snow from melting on the socks, wetting them. Sometimes cold seeps in through the soles of ski boots. An insulated insole will prevent that.

Wet climates can be as hard on your feet as very cold ones. Overboots effectively keep boots from getting wet, and vapor barrier socks and neoprene socks help keep feet warm even if the boots are wet. Waterproofing compounds will protect boots if they are religiously applied every day. In any case, for a long trip carry spare sets of dry socks. You might alternate socks from day to day, drying out each wet pair in your sleeping bag, in the sun, or over a fire.

Staying Warm Overnight

What kind of sleeping bag should you have? How heavy should it be? Again it's a matter of fitting the tool to the job. Synthetic-filled bags are relatively heavy and bulky but do work when wet. Down bags are exceptionally comfortable, are light, and stuff into small bundles. On the other hand, they must be cared for meticulously to keep them from getting wet. Therefore, for winter camping in a wet range such as the Cascades, the synthetic bag seems a better choice. The Sierra is sometimes wet, but the sun there is strong enough to dry down bags in winter, so the choice seems a toss-up. In Montana, Wyoming, or Colorado, dry cold is the rule and down seems very reasonable.

Both types of bags have been improved in recent years. Gore-Tex covering for down bags greatly improves their resistance to moisture from outside. They can still slowly collapse, however, from condensation freezing on the inside in extremely cold temperatures. Synthetic fibers have become lighter and softer.

A good approach is to use a layer system for sleeping gear as well as for outer clothing. A medium-weight Gore-Tex down bag would be the foundation, one weighing about three pounds. Such a bag in a premium-quality grade is quite expensive but lasts a long time, is luxuriously comfortable, and has such a wide temperature range that it can be used in other seasons as well. If it costs too much, settle for a good medium-weight synthetic bag. For extreme cold, a lightweight or medium-weight synthetic bag can be placed over the down one. That will keep moisture from freezing in the down bag, and it also can be used by itself for a warmer, wetter climate. If light weight is paramount, use one of the light bags and drape your down parka and other clothes over it to provide extra insulation.

In theory your clothes will be chosen to be adequate for most activities in whatever environment you are in and the sleeping bag only has to take care of the difference between day and night. This is true if you can avoid exhaustion, keep your clothes dry, and if you want to sleep in them or with them draped over you. If not, or if you want to maintain a greater margin of warmth, you need a heavier sleeping bag. In any case, meticulously keeping your clothes and sleeping bag as dry as possible will go a lot further toward keeping you warm than just spending a lot of money on equipment.

Equipment and Clothing

Humans are the toolmaking animals. They certainly seem to have an innate fascination with gadgets. With that in mind, remember that some of the greatest ski trips ever done, such as Fridtjof Nansen's 1889 crossing of the Greenland icecap and Orland Bartholomew's 1928 solo traverse of the Sierra Crest, were done before the advent of any "miracle" fibers or ski-building materials. Even such miracle materials as polypropylene for clothing or fiberglass for skis have their limitations. They don't guarantee warmth, and they don't guarantee against equipment failure. As was the case for Nansen and Bartholomew you, the skier, must know the limitations of your equipment and observe those limits. It's like what happens to many drivers when they get a vehicle with four-wheel drive: they get stuck as often as they would have in their former cars; they just do it in worse places. The use of modern materials does mean that your pack can be lighter than it ever would have been in the past and your skis and boots can perform at a higher level than was possible with the older materials of wood and leather, but that's not to be taken for granted. It's perfectly possible to make a lousy ski or an unusable boot with materials that would put the Space Shuttle to shame, and many manufacturers have tried. But if you choose carefully, reading equipment reviews, talking to other skiers and to several shops, and trying before buying, you will have a big head start, in gadgetry at least, over the pioneers of skiing.

MAP, COMPASS, AND ALTIMETER

Your basic navigational tools for ski touring are the topographic map, the compass, and the altimeter.

Map

The topographic contour map represents a three-dimensional landscape on a two-dimensional piece of paper, using a system of contour lines—

concentric lines that never cross each other. Each line represents a contour of equal altitude; that is, every point on a contour line has the same altitude. Any two lines represent points separated by a fixed vertical distance. On USGS maps that is usually either 40, 80, or 100 feet, and the contour interval is specified at the bottom of each map.

How do you interpret the contour lines? If a series of lines is crowded tightly together at some point, there is a lot of vertical drop in just a short horizontal distance—in other words, there is a very steep slope there. If the lines are so tight that they actually touch or merge into each other, then there is a near-vertical cliff indicated. If the lines are spaced well apart then they represent a gentle slope. If there is a large area with almost no contour lines in it that area is nearly flat. A long series of v-shaped lines stacked one after another means either a valley or a ridge: to decide which, you have to see if, as you cross the feature, you cut across lines of higher altitude (which means the feature is a ridge) or of lower altitude (which means there is a valley or canyon).

The way to learn to read the map quickly and usefully is to stop frequently while ski touring, pull out the map, and try to match it to where you are and to natural features that you can see around you. Even if you are experienced, it's a good idea to do this occasionally because a big part of not getting lost is constantly keeping oriented. Yes, people who do know what they are doing sometimes get lost, and it is usually because of smugness combined with bad visibility. They are too proud or lazy to keep checking the terrain against the map, compass, and altimeter.

As you get experienced at reading a contour map you will find yourself frequently looking at the most minute details on it, either to decide exactly where you are, or to decide exactly what the best route will be, taking into account such factors as snow conditions, avalanche danger, the types of forest, the skiing ability of the skiers, and the eagerness of the skiers to climb or to ski downhill. There is a lot of information packed into these maps. I have spent hours poring over one quadrangle (map sheet) trying to find a perfect ski route and still missed the one that later seemed perfectly obvious.

Compass

The compass is a freely floating magnetic needle that always points north—except that it doesn't. The north magnetic pole is not exactly the same as the geographical north pole, and the compass doesn't, from most places in the world, point exactly north. The difference is especially great if you live on the Pacific Coast or in Alaska. How do you compensate for this difference between the magnetic and geographic poles? At the bottom of any USGS map there are two arrows connected like the hands of a clock. One always points directly up to the top of the map. That represents true geographic north. The other is at an angle to the first one and represents magnetic north. The angle between them is called the declination and is the amount you have to adjust your compass reading to be geographically accurate. The trick is not to make a mistake and actually be twice as far off as you add the declination to the wrong side of the compass reading. For example, the declination in Washington State is about 20 degrees. A mistake could put you 40 degrees off of north, which is catastrophically incorrect. A good way to remember what is right is to remember that the line of 0 declination, where the compass gives correct readings, goes through Cleveland, Ohio. If you are west of a line running north to south through Cleveland, then your compass needle will point east of true north and you must add the declination to the reading; that is, if you align your compass with magnetic north and sight a distant landmark, then to get its true heading you must add the declination to the reading from the compass. If you are east of that line through Cleveland, you must subtract the declination from your compass reading.

How can you use the compass? Well, you can use it to find where you are on the map in relation to prominent landmarks. You can use it to find out if you are in the correct drainage or are climbing the correct ridge. If you are above timberline and the visibility deteriorates into a whiteout where you can't even tell the snow from the sky, you can continue traveling if you follow your compass heading toward your destination. If you have been constantly keeping oriented, you should be able to determine that heading from the map. Have the person with the compass stay behind a partner, constantly keeping the partner in line with the desired heading.

Altimeter

The altimeter always gives you a correct reading of your altitude above sea level—except that it doesn't. It works by reading the barometric pressure, which changes in a regular way with altitude. The pressure changes, however, with the weather as well as with the altitude, and that can throw your readings off. It also means that you can use your altimeter to predict, to some extent, the coming weather. To do that you have to keep as accurate an idea of your true altitude as possible. That means that whenever you reach a spot that is clearly marked on a map, such as a lake, summit, or pass, you should reset your altimeter to the altitude shown on the map. Then you can see if the pressure is changing from factors other than your own traveling. If the pressure goes up (indicated altitude goes down), that usually means good weather is on its way. If the pressure goes down (altitude goes up), that usually means that a storm front is coming.

The altimeter helps with navigation by showing you what contour line you are on. Then, in thick forest or in a whiteout you can try to correlate that contour line with features like creeks, the steepness of the slope, or the direction of the slope (determined with the compass) to find out exactly where you are. In bad visibility it can also help you get to a destination by letting you make a decision, for example, "We'll follow the 7500-foot contour until we get to the second creek, and then we'll follow the creek down to camp." This illustrates another good rule, which is to plan your navigational errors so they make it easy for you to get to where you want to go. That is, if you are aiming for a camp on a creek or a ridge, make sure that you aim just a bit high so that you will be sure of being able to find it by skiing down following the creek or ridge. If you tried to be exact and still missed the camp, you might not know whether you were above it or below it.

NORDIC VS. ALPINE: BOOTS, SKIS, POLES

To start, you have to make a choice between alpine touring equipment and Nordic, cross-country equipment. The first consists of short, alpine-width skis mounted with bindings that have a mechanical hinge at their fronts and that can be locked down at the heels to allow normal downhill-type skiing with rigid boots. The second uses narrower, lighter skis, with or without metal edges, and very simple bindings that just hold the toes of flexibly soled touring boots. There are some tours in this book that are totally unfit for the heavier, clumsier alpine touring equipment. These are the tours that use cross-country trails or that have substantial lengths of horizontal travel on them. You might as well try running a mile in downhill ski boots. But if the tour involves mostly climbing up and then skiing down, alpine touring equipment is a viable way to go. Also, if you are an accomplished alpine skier and don't want to take the time to learn a new and quite different technique, then alpine touring makes sense for you—you can just step into the skis and go. The trip is most important, not the tools you use—as long as they don't get in the way too much.

With that said it must be admitted that I have a strong preference for the Nordic approach on nearly all ski tours. It's simple, aesthetically pleasing, and kinesthetically pleasing, too. Nordic equipment simply feels good while skiing across, up, or down. You don't have to clank like a robot while skiing, nor do you have to carry a small machine shop to keep things properly adjusted. I can also say that Nordic is more reliable than alpine touring gear when the equipment is carefully selected. Therefore, from here on I will discuss only the Nordic equipment. To find out about alpine touring equipment you can search the magazines for reviews of this gear, which is constantly changing, and consult equipment vendors.

Glissade double boots. Photo by Steve Barnett.

Boots

The right choice of boots is essential for comfort on a ski tour as well as for control over the skis. It's not enough to have a good boot, though; you must have compatible bindings and skis, too. Don't assume that because there is a "Nordic norm" that any binding works well with any boot. It's not true! Even good boots must be matched to skis. Only then is it possible to have a system that's trouble free for long periods and that works so well it doesn't force you to notice it.

You want from your boots a combination of absolute control over the edging and direction of the skis, enough flexibility that you can run like a racer, total warmth no matter how wet or cold it is outside, such comfort that you could go to sleep with your boots on, and the durability to last forever. It wouldn't hurt if they were free, also, but of course you will have to make some compromises.

Most of the tours in this book can be done in medium-weight boots. Light racing-system boots and racing skis are best on prepared tracks. But off those tracks, even on easy tours, they won't be as good as the new generation of medium-weight boots pioneered by the Asolo Glissade series. Heavy telemark boots with strongly reinforced uppers are excellent for long, steep downhills. Thus they will be good for tours like Mt. Shasta or the San Juan High Route. They are not particularly good for gentler terrain and longer traverses. The Glissade type of boot with internal plastic reinforcement for its sealed sole has adequate control for even the hard downhill-oriented tours and also has good comfort and forward flex for the long cross-country tours. They are light in weight, are easy to waterproof, dry relatively quickly when wet, and are warm. They don't seem to break down and lose control with use. Early problems with the toes breaking on these boots have been completely solved. One of the nicer advantages of these boots is that they are easy on bindings because of their thin soles and good forward flex, making the combination of boot and binding more reliable. There have been many problems with reliably matching the heavier telemark boots with heavier bindings. One or the other or both become overstressed and break. Ask several dealers about problems before you buy, and make sure that the boots have a good warranty.

If you are going to be skiing in extremely cold conditions, double boots are worth looking into. They are inherently warm, and the inner is easier to dry than a whole wet, heavy boot. The inner is also useful for walking around a hut or tent.

The medium-weight sealed-sole boots should be used with such medium-width skis as the Karhu GT or Fisher 99 or other backcountry-oriented, metal-edged touring skis with 52- to 55-mm waist diameters. If you use a wider ski, such as the Karhu Extreme or the Atomic Telemark O-T, then you should use as heavy and strongly reinforced a boot as you can get. You need the extra control to handle the extra leverage of the edges on the wider skis. The combination of strong boot with wide ski is best where downhill-skiing power is your goal—on those tours where there are long and steep downhills and little traversing.

Skis

Middle-of-the-road, mid-width (52- to 54-mm waist diameter), metal-edged, fiberglass skis are the best compromise for most of the tours in this book. A good example would be the Karhu XCD GT. Narrower, edgeless, light touring skis, such as the Epoke 900 or Karhu Gazelle, are good for tours that involve some set trail skiing, such as those on the North Shore of Lake Superior or in the Boundary Waters Canoe Area. Wider, single-cambered skis, such as the Swallow TRS, the Atomic Telemark, the Karhu Supreme, or the Rossignol TRS, bend into a clean arc when you press in their centers while holding the tip and tail. They are more specialized for downhill performance and are good for tours that have steep long downhills. They are less good if there is a lot of nearly flat traveling. The widest skis of all, including the Karhu Equipe, the Atomic Telemark O-T, Chouinard Toute Neige, and the Swallow Rainier, are wonderful on the downhill, but also not so good for long tours. An exception is on expeditions where they are used with skins to haul heavy loads on sleds and then used skinless for the run back to pick up another load. These skis are popular in areas, like the Wasatch, where there is a lot of deep-powder skiing down long, steep runs.

Wax or waxless? Cross-country wax has two seemingly contradictory functions. One is to lubricate the motion of the skis over the snow and the other is to allow the skier to climb. In cold weather wax works very well and there's no reason to use waxless skis. The appropriate waxes—green or blue hard waxes or their variants—are easy to apply and easy to handle. Also, a well-waxed ski will always be faster than a waxless one. In a climate where the temperature hovers around the freezing point, applying a wax that both slides and grips is difficult. Even if it's done correctly, slight changes in the snow's temperature or moisture content can necessitate stopping and readjusting the wax.

Waxless skis make sense in such conditions. Even when they aren't working well, a slight grip lets the skier maneuver more easily around obstacles or on a flat surface. Waxless skis that can be waxed in colder weather would be ideal, but these have always been commercial failures.

Poles

Lately, telescoping variable-length poles that also can be used as avalanche probes have become popular. Some of these lock with a twist-lock, others with push-button locks. Both seem to work well in the latest versions. The idea is to use them shortened for the downhill and lengthened for touring. The probe feature may be more valuable than the variable-length feature. There's nothing really wrong with using a long fixed-length pole of moderate cost. The lower-cost alloy is more likely to bend than break as compared to an expensive high-tech alloy, and the long pole is ideal for touring. It's quite possible to learn to use long poles for downhill as well. Keep them pointed back and learn to use uphill and double-pole plants as well as the normal alpine plants. It's much worse to use short poles for touring than long poles for downhill. The short ones are just about useless for the normal cross-country moves of the diagonal stride and the double pole. You can wrap friction tape around the long poles at mid-height and grip them there if need be on a steep traverse or on a steep downhill run. Several companies make self-arrest grips for variable-length poles that can give you some peace of mind on very steep and exposed terrain (where a fall could have bad consequences). These have hooks sticking out of the handles that can be immediately shoved into the snow in case of a fall. They can stop a fall and should be useful for roped glacier skiing as well since they give you a chance to arrest your partner's slide into a crevasse. They are good tools for ski mountaineering.

CLOTHING

To facilitate your choice and use of equipment and clothing for ski tours, let's look at a typical well-prepared ski tourer, strip him, and then plunder his pack. Of course this is just one skier's choice of clothing and equipment, and you will find that no two experienced tourers have exactly the same gear.

This well-prepared skier, you will find, is a devotee of the layer system. Why? Because it is flexible enough to cover comfortably for a wide range of conditions: cold and dry, cool and wet, working hard on a climb, skiing in windy weather, skiing in frigid weather, or skiing in spring sunshine. Also, it is a durable system in the sense that if any one garment is ruined or lost, you probably will have enough to get along without it. For the same reason, you may not want to get the absolutely lightest-weight system you can. You want a system just a little heavier and a lot tougher, with just enough extra to help you or someone else if there is an equipment or accident problem where extra clothes are needed.

You also want comfort, durability, freedom of movement, and flexibility. You've got to use the clothing you carry while you are climbing up a mountain, putting out a tremendous amount of heat while you are climbing up a trail in a wet snowstorm with a humidity of 100 percent, while you are standing on a summit with an Arctic wind trying to suck all of your body heat away in minutes, and while you are sitting around in camp, metabolism near zero and the air temperature dropping like a rock. The way to get all of this in a load you can carry without pain is by using a number of thin, moderately lightweight layers that can be mixed in different combinations to handle nearly any condition.

From inside out and top to bottom, here is what our well-prepared skier is wearing.

POLYPROPYLENE PULLOVER AND LONG JOHNS   These are wonderful and have deservedly become very popular in the last few years. They keep you moderately warm when they're wet, don't itch, stretch to let you move completely freely, absorb almost no water, and dry quickly, even with just body heat. Lately a few variants have appeared that are said to wash more easily and to smell less after several days of hard sweaty work.

PILE OR BUNTING JACKET   These are just as ubiquitous nowadays as poly-propylene underwear. Good ones let you move freely, keep you warm when wet, are lightweight, and dry fast. If a pile jacket gets soaked and there is no external source of heat, such as a fire, to dry it, you can just wring it out and it will be useful. Their only disadvantage is that usually the wind blows right through them. The next layers should take care of that. When there is a good chance of wet weather and little chance of extreme cold, skiers sometimes use two of these or even two plus a pile vest instead of a down jacket. Springtime is a good time to replace down with pile.

LIGHT POROUS ANORAK OR JACKET   A light anorak can be found for as little as $25 and still be one of a skier's most useful pieces of clothing. A light jacket with zippers will cost a little more and be a bit heavier. Either should be light enough to be stashed anywhere in a pack and light enough not to interfere with movement. For hard climbing or track skiing a light anorak seems to be much more porous and comfortable than an equivalent Gore-Tex parka. If it gets dirty, there's no problem cleaning it, as there is with Gore-Tex. By using something similar most of the time, you can save your Gore-Tex for when you really need it. Experience shows that zippers are the weak points of most parkas, and the anorak design avoids this problem.

LIGHTWEIGHT GORE-TEX PARKA   A well-prepared skier keeps an ultralight Gore-Tex parka stashed in the pack. Like the anorak it can be stashed into a very small space in the pack and weighs so little that there should never be any hesitation about carrying it and the anorak at all times. It is saved for when Gore-Tex's special properties are needed—and by saving it you can count on it working when you need it. It is useful for two situations, wet weather and high winds. Gore-Tex is almost completely windproof, yet still breathes, and it is a lifesaver on a high summit in Arctic conditions. This windproofness is even more valuable than Gore-Tex's waterproofness since you seem to get wet anyway, no matter what, if it's a real Cascade rainstorm. There's no problem using the Gore-Tex parka right over the anorak whenever the wind starts howling or wet snow starts pouring down, and that's good for an instantaneous shot of extra warmth.

OVERPANTS   The layer system continues over the skier's legs, too. Light long johns are topped by light pants or knickers. Stretch fabric is preferable since it moves better with the skier. Also, it lasts much longer since the seams are not stressed as much during extreme movements. Over these two layers go overpants. Here is one place where zippers are definitely worth their problems, since they allow the pants to be put on over boots. Gore-Tex pants aren't bad but aren't the only choice. Polypropylene-lined pants are warm and dry quickly. Whatever the material, make sure a rugged zipper is used and that the design isn't so bad that the pants will open while you are skiing and fall down around your ankles (no joke, it happens!).

GAITERS OR OVERBOOTS   Insulated overboots are a good way to get additional warmth for your feet in cold or wet conditions. They are expensive but worth it. Even without insulation they keep the boots dry and still add a considerable amount of warmth. Gaiters keep the snow out of your boots and should be chosen both for how well they actually do seal your boots from snow and for how easy it is to put them on over your boots. Waterproofed uppers usually seem uncomfortable. Gore-Tex uppers are okay but not necessary.

HAT   It's so simple but so important that you carry a spare in your pack. Put it on whenever hands or feet get cold or when you stop and start cooling off.

GLOVES AND MITTENS   The layer system is used here, too, with a windproof shell over an insulating mitten. This can be either an integrated assembly or separate pieces. Thin glove liners are also carried, usually of polypropylene, but wool will do as well. When possible, just the liners are worn, other times just the mittens, and when it is really cold the mittens are worn over the liners. The mittens can be whipped off when there is some job requiring delicacy, such as tying bootlaces or using a camera. Because mittens frequently get ripped, lost, or wet, a spare pair of mittens is carried in the pack.

WARM DOWN JACKET   The heavy down jacket is the exception to the rule of layering with light layers, but it is such a luxurious addition to your load that it's hard to do without it in cold weather.
     A high-quality down jacket has one outstanding virtue over all your other clothing: it virtually guarantees warmth no matter what your condition. You might be soaked, cold, and exhausted after a hard day on skis, without enough energy to have a prayer of warming even your fingers, let

alone your whole body. Put on that jacket and you'll be warm. It's true that the two parkas and several pile jackets probably have enough insulating value for most trips, but they don't have that guaranteed extra warmth that the big down jacket has. It is expensive to buy (more so if it's covered with Gore-Tex, which I highly recommend), hard to clean, and it must be kept dry, but it's hard to think of any single item that adds so much to camping comfort in the winter. It need not be a great extra weight to carry, either, since it permits you to carry a considerably lighter sleeping bag. You can sleep with it in a bag for tremendous extra warmth, or if you have a very narrow sleeping bag you can drape it over the top. It works.

THE DAYPACK

Now let's take our sample skier's daypack apart, the one used for a backcountry day trip.

Emergency Kit

This contains all your first-aid supplies as well as those odd materials that you think can be used to patch a failure of your skis, boots, poles, pack, or clothing. First aid is well covered in many books, which will give you a list of what to carry. A good one is *Mountaineering First Aid*, published by the Seattle Mountaineers. A small first-aid kit should include several types of tape (waterproof adhesive tape, fiber tape, and duct tape), sterile pads, a butterfly closure, and moleskin and other blister treatment aids. A patch kit should include the following items.

NEEDLE AND THREAD   There should be both lightweight thread for patching clothing and a very heavy needle and thread for serious repairs. Some people use dental floss as an extra-strong thread. In the last few years Patagonia has marketed an excellent small emergency sewing kit with just what you need in it.

A SMALL SWISS ARMY KNIFE   This is in addition to the one you carry in your pocket. The Tinker model is a small one that has most of the tools you will need.

TAPE   This is the most important fix-it material. Our skier carries a small roll of filament strapping tape and some duct tape as well. These can be used for patching poles, (described below), skis, boots, clothing, packs, or for first aid. Carry lots; it gets used frequently.

POLE PATCH KIT   Our skier carries two curved-back aluminum tent stakes, which are perfect for making pole splints. Just tape them thoroughly around the break in the pole and you will have a pole just as strong as new, even if it's a bit clumsy. They can also be used to patch skies. If a tip breaks, tape them over the break, making sure that the joints of the taping point backward like a snake's scales. If the tip is broken off clean, then tape the stakes to the rest of the ski over the broken tip. It's clumsy but it should work well enough to help you get out.

WATERPROOF MATCHES AND/OR PLASTIC LIGHTER   Carry these in their own plastic bags to keep them dry.

NYLON CORD   Carry 50 feet or so of this. It's useful for runaway straps, tying ungainly loads to your pack, first aid, rigging a sled stretcher if you need it, drying clothes over a fire, and any of a hundred other purposes.

A SPARE BAIL FOR YOUR BINDINGS   Some people even carry a spare set of bindings. With some bindings the bail can be detached in a fall and lost in the powder. You can, of course, tie the bail to the binding beforehand, as well as carry a spare. In other bindings the bail is fixed but the rivets holding it on can wear out and break, and for these you can carry spare bindings or carry small nuts and bolts to make temporary repairs.

POSIDRIVE #3 SCREWDRIVER   This is needed to tighten or replace binding screws if they loosen, as frequently happens. If the Posidrive is hard to find a Phillips #3 with the nose filed down will do. Some clever folks just carry the proper bit and use a ski pole or pliers that they are carrying anyway to drive it.

GLUE   Loose binding screws are a frequent problem. They can easily strip out the hole and leave you with a damaged ski and a difficult repair. It's better to prevent the process before it starts and glue the screws to the hole and the binding to the ski. In the field you want to be able to tighten an errant screw and then glue it in place. A quick acting cyanoacrylic glue (like "Krazy Glue") will do this without necessitating mixing and will set quickly. It also will leak in your emergency kit unless you are careful about how you pack it. It's still worth carrying.

AN ASSORTMENT OF SCREWS   This should include binding screws, but it's also good to carry some smaller ones as well. If absolutely necessary the screws can be used to remount a binding at a place other than where it was. This might happen if several of the original holes get stripped and the screws lost or stripped. Also, if you break a ski in half you can remount the binding on the front half and limp out. You can use the awl from a Swiss Army knife or equivalent to drill the holes. The small screws can be used, along with the glue and tape, to patch a delaminating boot.

Arranging Items in the Pack

IN THE EXTERNAL POCKETS   In an external pocket or top pocket our skier carries those things that might be wanted quickly: sunglasses, sunscreen, lip protection, toilet paper, ski waxes, compass, altimeter, and map.

Also carried on the outside of the pack is a small foam pad for kneeling or sitting in the snow and, if necessary, for a bivouac in case of trouble.

INSIDE THE PACK   Inside are the emergency kit, flashlight, water bottle, wax kit, food, spare hat and mittens, spare socks, warm outer layers, such as another pile or down jacket, and the ultralight Gore-Tex parka.

EXTRAS FOR CERTAIN CONDITIONS

GOGGLES AND FACE MASK   These are important if you are traveling in winter in an area exposed to wind, such as above timberline or on large frozen lakes as in Minnesota. If you wear glasses you will have a problem with them fogging inside the goggles. I don't know of any sure solution to this. Goggles with fans, goggles with ventilators, and antifog compounds for glasses all seem to work sometimes but not all the time. Write me when you find a solution.

SKINS   If contemplating a long, steep climb, include climbing skins in your pack. These used to be made of long strips of seal skin with the hair pointing backward. They allowed the ski to slide forward but not backward. Skins still allow skiers to climb steep slopes without worrying about waxing or changing snow conditions. Most mountain skiers consider them indispensable.

Nowadays skins come in two popular versions. Both are satisfactory. One is a synthetic fur on a cloth backing that is covered with a sticky gluelike substance on its other side. These are pressed onto the ski. The best of the new stick-on skins (like Pomoca Synthex) work very well, absorbing little water, resisting freeze-up, and sliding forward with little friction. The main problem with them is with the glue. It can give trouble if the ski base is wet, if it is extremely cold, or if the glue gets contaminated with snow. You have to care for skins meticulously, keeping them dry and free of snow and, after putting them on, rubbing them down with the side of a ski pole to make sure they really stick.

The other type of popular skin is a completely synthetic one made of polyurethane slit into scales that attach to the ski with polyurethane straps. This type doesn't work quite as well as the other once on the ski (it has almost no forward glide and the straps interfere somewhat with the ski's edging), but you don't have to baby it at all. This type is cheap and so nearly indestructible that you can walk on rocks without hesitation—which may be more useful than you might imagine.

ESSENTIALS FOR AVALANCHE RESCUE

Avalanche Locator Beacon

An avalanche locator beacon is an electronic device that permits rescuers to quickly locate a body buried by an avalanche. Whether the body when found is dead or alive depends both on luck and on the speed with which it is found. The locator by no means ensures survival, and it should not give the skier any greater confidence about skiing dangerous slopes, but by permitting faster rescue it does increase the probability of the victim being found alive.

Locator beacons are turned on at the start of the skiing day and left on. Skiers wear the beacon inside their clothes where it cannot be ripped off by an avalanche. Skiers should occasionally practice finding buried beacons so that if an accident happens they can respond quickly and efficiently (doing an efficient search is not simple). There are books about avalanches listed in the Bibliography, and they give detailed descriptions of how to organize a search.

The locator beacon should be considered a mandatory piece of equipment for the mountain skier in the American West. There are two frequencies in use worldwide, which raises the possibility of confusion and tragedy in rescues. Fortunately, only one is used in North America, the low frequency of 2,270 hertz.

Shovel

The other principal piece of equipment for avalanche rescue that should be carried by all western mountain tourers is a shovel. Several types are sold by small, mountaineering-equipment businesses. Make sure that the blade is sturdy enough to be used in hard, compacted avalanche debris and that the blade is big enough to actually do some good when you are trying to dig someone out in a hurry. A longer handle, possibly one that telescopes, makes digging easier. The shovel is also useful for camping, when it can be used to level tent platforms, to dig water holes into buried streams, and to build wind-protection walls and elaborate kitchen and dining areas.

Ski Touring Technique

Good ski technique rates well behind avalanche knowledge, navigational skills, and camping skills as something you need to know to ski most of the tours in this book. Experience proves that it's possible to enjoy serious ski trips with only a minimum knowledge of skiing. The famous Haute Route in the Alps was first done in 1903 in the days of wooden-edged skis and a single long pole. One skier I know did a thirty-day ski trip in the Sierra on his first time out on skis and enjoyed every minute. He says, "It never occurred to me that making turns on skis had anything to do with touring." Your first lesson is this: There's always a way to get down. It might be zigzagging, or it might be glissading down with the ski poles as a brake, or it might be keeping the skins on for a descent, or it might even be taking the skis off and walking down. That seems backward—skiing up and walking down—but people do it and enjoy their trips. The main objective isn't the downhill—it's being out in the beautiful white, wild mountains.

With that said it's still true that being able to ski down in control and with style adds another dimension of pleasure to any mountain ski trip. Mountain skiing is both easier and harder than skiing at a ski resort. On one hand you don't have to worry about style, and speed is not an important consideration. Thus you will find a lot of older ski mountaineers who have skied happily for decades on serious high-mountain trips who have a rough and ready style so primitive—based, for example, on a bombproof stem christie—that it would draw scorn at a modern ski resort.

On the other hand mountain skiing is much harder than modern resort skiing because you have to ski the snow that God puts down, not what is reprocessed with power tillers, grinders, and groomers. Snow is an incredibly variable medium, and to ski all of its forms well requires a long apprenticeship and much dedication. I think it's safe to say that few skiers show mastery over the whole range of natural snow conditions.

The variety of the snow that you must face while touring is one of the most interesting aspects of the sport. It creates difficulties, and at the same time it creates a challenge that, if you can meet it, will give you profound pleasure. Then you will feel really at home with your skis in the snow. Sometimes that challenge is an intellectual one, one of understanding the snow and the mechanics of skiing, other times it is simply a brutal challenge of strength and determination. Sometimes the challenge calls for delicacy, sometimes for discretion, and sometimes for courage. Experience shows that virtually every snow condition can be skied with complete turns through the fall line with Nordic equipment, including the full range of wet snows, stiff snows, and breakable crusts. The only condition the author has not seen solved by a telemark skier is *neve penitentes* (needles of snow up to three feet high that are the ultimate stage of suncups), which is a snow condition that the North American tourer may never see in a lifetime.

Learning to be a good skier in many snow conditions takes considerable time and effort. You might start out by learning survival techniques that will get you down hills without much skiing skill. Then you can go out right away on mountain tours.

For more details and instruction about learning to mountain ski on Nordic gear, the best strategy is to take a lesson as soon as you get your equipment so you can learn good technique from the start without having to unlearn years' worth of deeply ingrained bad habits. There are also several useful books about learning to ski downhill on Nordic equipment. The list must start, of course, with my own *Cross-Country Downhill* but should also include Ned Gillette's *Nordic Skiing* and Lito Tejada-Flores' *Back-Country Skiing*. The first book concentrates more on skiing harder backcountry conditions. The last two are more general texts that go into all the techniques you need to ski comfortably in the mountains.

GETTING STARTED

To become an advanced mountain skier—able to ski a wide variety of mountain conditions comfortably—you must start with the basics. Advanced skiing skills are developed by applying the basics to more and more unnerving situations.

Start on a flat surface. The basic moves on Nordic equipment are straight running, diagonal stride, skating, and the telemark position. With each maneuver you try to find the strongest, best-balanced, and most agile position, a position that is determined not by fiat from above but by experimentation on snow. Then you learn to use these same maneuvers in two dimensions to make turns—strided turns, skate turns, turns on the edge of a running ski, and telemark turns. You must always experiment to find and teach your body in a reflexive way the strongest, most agile position, and you must learn to move instinctively when you get out of balance or control. The position from which you can react the fastest, and which is the most stable, is the basic athletic position of knees bent, facing the action, shoulders loose, arms loose and low, lightly bent. It's easily determined by trying different positions and trying to have someone knock you over.

You'll see soon enough what's style and what's really strong. Plan to take two steps forward and one step back. Work some moves out on an easy slope in easy snow, then try to apply them to more and more difficult situations until you feel your skiing fall apart. Then go back to the easy situation and try again to get the basics straight.

The two basic turns for skiing mountain conditions are the parallel and the telemark turns. Neither is used all by itself, but both incorporate pieces of other techniques like step, skate, and snowplow turns, as well as pieces of each other. Following are tips for using telemark and parallel turns in a variety of natural snow conditions.

LOVE THE FALL LINE

Learn to love the fall line. Everyone's instinct is to pull back from the fall line. It's part of the general fear of falling, which is a strong reflex even for a newborn child. Skiing is anti-instinctual. That's part of the thrill. You must always be facing the fall line, concentrating on the fall line, ready to move into the fall line. Why? One reason is simply that that's the way down the hill. That's where you must go, and you must face toward your next turn to be ready for it, even though instinct makes many skiers face away from the fall line, especially at the ends of their turns when they should most be preparing for the next turn. Another reason is that the fall line lies in the direction of the greatest forces on the skier and by facing it, bending the upper body toward it, you are best positioned to respond to those forces as you turn and as the snow changes. Third, if you are running straight down the fall line you may be in a position of psychological instability, but—momentarily at least—you are in the most stable position possible. The force of gravity pulling you to one side or the other is minimized, and if you are composed you can recover your balance and find a strong position even in horrid snow conditions. Then on with the turn. The steeper the terrain the more important this is. To maintain control and to keep your speed down you must be willing to hurl yourself straight into the fall line. One of the principal sources of problems for skiers on steep slopes is that they are absolutely unwilling to stay in the fall line for as much as a millisecond. They hold their upper bodies back and try to hurl the skis around as fast as they can. Wrong. The skis just get tangled or else accelerate away from that reluctant upper body. By getting into the fall line decisively you avoid a long indecisive period of acceleration and stay in control of your skis. By hanging in the fall line for just an extra moment you can position yourself to use a really powerful telemark or parallel to finish the turn.

THE TELEMARK AND THE PARALLEL

Let's compare the telemark position with the parallel position. The telemark position has much stronger fore and aft balance, and if the front and back skis are kept at a slight angle to each other then they will turn, even in snow the consistency of setting concrete. Thus the telemark is great for situations when you need fore and aft balance and when you need strong turning power. It works well in breakable crusts, uneven windpack, deep wet snow, and deep powder.

The telemark is awkward compared to the parallel when it comes to strength and flexibility in angulation or in absorbing bumps. Because of the movement required of the two legs, it takes more time to get into and out of the telemark. The parallel, with good downhill-oriented skis, is better for hard snow, shallow powder, or most conditions where the snow's surface is uniform (which makes fore and aft balance easier). It is especially good when there is a hard base underneath a layer of softer snow.

Find a Strong Telemark Position

Learn a strong telemark position so well that you automatically strive to reach it and don't settle for a weaker version. The strong position will be with skis nearly parallel, weight on the front ski and on the ball of the foot of the rear ski, upper body leaning toward the fall line, lower body leaning into the hill to edge the skis. The position should be agile enough that you can instantly move all your weight onto the front ski or onto the rear ski. How do you control where your weight is? Not by leaning your upper body forward or backward! It should always be bent toward the fall line, limber and ready for what is coming. You should control your weight by moving your hips over the telemark. If your hips move forward over the front foot, then your weight will be over the front foot. If your hips twist back over the rear foot the weight will move onto that foot. The correct motion as you complete a turn is for your hips to twist back into the hill and over your rear foot. That happens as the skis turn and your upper body continues facing downhill. You should have considerable power from your hips over that rear ski. Experiment with the position till you find a turning motion that feels strong over that rear foot. You should be sinking slowly over that ski as you turn. The motion might be described as a gentle settling of your whole body—arms, upper body, and especially legs—as you finish the turn. That settling soaks up the turn, reduces the forces on your knees, increases your edging, readies you to spring into the next turn, and adds power to the turn. Control of the rear ski from the ball of the foot is the key to a powerful telemark.

MOVE INTO THE FALL LINE, THEN TELEMARK The telemark is a way to finish a turn in difficult snow. Telemarking into the fall line is sometimes awkward, especially at slow speeds. The rule is this: Get into the fall line, then use the telemark to finish the turn. How do you get into the fall line? There is no one best way to initiate a turn, so a short but incomplete list of possible initiations follows:

1. Step into the fall line.

2. Snowplow into the fall line. This is very easy for beginners to do and is good at low speeds.

3. A wide wedge and a weight shift onto the outside ski will put you into the fall line.

4. Unweight (up-and-down motion that momentarily takes the weight off your skis) and skid your skis into the fall line.

5. Carve your uphill ski into the fall line by weighting and edging it. Step with the uphill ski somewhat into the fall line. As you step onto it let your leg fold low. Then rise up while your upper body is twisted into the fall line, pressing the ski into the snow and at the same time twisting it into the turn. The pressed-out ski will bow into the snow, and when put on edge it will turn.

6. Jump your skis into the fall line. This is often done while simultaneously moving into a telemark so you land fully telemarked and ready to go.

7. Telemark into the fall line. In a similar manner to number 5, start in a low position and extend your legs as you turn into the fall line, which keeps the skis pressed into the snow. Most of your weight should be on the front ski. This is good at higher speeds, since you are never far from a strong telemark position.

Once in the fall line you have to get into a strong telemark. One way, if the snow isn't too deep, is to pick up the rear ski a bit and just place it correctly in the strong telemark position. Another way is to stay in the fall line for a split second and slide the skis together into the strong telemark. The skis will naturally move almost parallel with each other if you wait only a ski length or two. Then all you have to do is settle into a good telemark and let your hip fall into the turn, edging the skis. It does take composure to wait the time required to get the telemark position correct while pointing straight downhill. Rushing it, though, is likely to get you struggling awkwardly with a weak telemark position, which usually means that you are avoiding the fall line and leaning back.

ANGULATION   You always want your skis to be edged away from the fall line so that the sidecut on them makes them turn and so that they don't slip. You can do that by leaning your whole body into the turn. That works well enough on good corn snow or easy powder, but since your upper body is not facing into the fall line it does not give you much agility to react to uneven snow conditions or to make fast moves into the fall line. Ideally, you always want your upper body to be leaning into the fall line. Combine that with your edged skis and you have angulation: your body is articulated at the waist so that the lower body from the hips down is bent into the hill and the upper body is bent downhill. This doesn't feel instinctive at all to the nonskier, but it is something you'll have to experiment with till it feels natural. It's part of learning to love the fall line. Providentially, the angulated hip seems to give the position with the most power over the rear ski of the telemark.

RECAPITULATION   Again, here are two tips for telemarking in difficult snow:

1.   Get into the fall line. Then use your telemark.

2.   End the turn with your weight moving strongly onto the rear foot of the telemark. The worse the snow, the more you'll have to accentuate that weight shift. Without that shift in soft snow, you will plunge your front ski into the snow and come to a stop or do a somersault. Without it on harder snow, you will lose control of your rear ski.

The Parallel Turn

The parallel turn for mountain skiing is similar in many ways to the telemark. Only the ending is different. As you finish the turn, moving out of the fall line, you settle onto the edge of just the downhill ski. Except in deep snow, the inside ski is relatively unweighted. Your upper body still faces downhill, and the ski is still edged into the hill, meaning that your body must be bent at the hips. The trick is to stay centered over that ski as it turns under you. Sometimes, in sticky snow conditions, as you end the turn you want to apply just a little pressure to the uphill ski, with it forked away from the main, downhill ski, and moved ahead. Then it acts

Parallel turn. Photo by Steve Barnett.

like a reverse telemark and pulls the turn around. It also adds a bit of stability to the finish of the turn. That is the open or scissors turn, which is really just a variant of the normal parallel.

In theory then the parallel turn is simpler than the telemark; all you have to do is stay centered over the edge of one ski. In practice, in any but ideal skiing conditions, that simple task takes a great deal of skiing skill. In theory, if you can keep a steady, smooth pressure on the edge, the ski will turn smoothly too. But you have to keep that pressure on the ski as it goes up the hill out of the fall line and down the hill into the fall line while you are turning. A lot of balance is required to stay over that edge as you turn, especially if the snow is a bit "catchy." You need to have a lot of flexibility in your legs (like a rubber band) to control the pressure on the edge, and you have to have good timing too. A slight change in the timing of your legs extending and contracting as you turn the skis completely changes the timing of how your body weight pressures the skis and in turn completely changes how they turn. Sometimes you want a sharp check at the end of the turn—a sudden little blip of pressure and edging that ends a turn and bounces you into the next one. Sometimes you want the transition from one turn to the next to be so smooth as to be unnoticeable. These subtleties take time on skis to learn. It's worth it though to add such a powerful tool to your repertoire.

It's intriguing how every small change in the snow condition requires a small change from you. That's why you should try to build up a "toolbox" of different techniques that you can combine as needed to handle the snow. There's not necessarily one best way to handle any one condition. It's fun to find different ways to ski even a very difficult snow like a breakable crust. Following are some common snow conditions and some effective ways to ski them. Now we can put theory to work in real snow conditions.

SKIING SOME COMMON SNOW CONDITIONS

CORN SNOW   This is the easiest of all conditions. Your skis slide across the surface with a wish. Any technique, good or bad, parallel or telemark, works like a charm here. On very steep slopes the top layer may shear. Then, keeping your upper body from leaning into the hill and using your ability to stay centered over your skis throughout the turn will keep you from losing control of the skis as they slide an extra distance downhill with the shearing upper snow layer.

DEEP POWDER   This is the most exhilarating of all snow conditions. Both parallel and telemark work fine. It's easiest to ski powder with both techniques by using plenty of unweighting. Rise up as you enter the fall line and then settle down, pushing the skis across the fall line to check your speed. It's best to ski powder right down the fall line, making quick turns to slow your speed and then getting right back into the fall line. The deep snow keeps you from accelerating very quickly, so you can spend most of the time right in the fall line.

DEEP WET SNOW   Now we start getting into difficulties. Unweighting might not get you anywhere here, because even the top layers of the snow might be sticky enough to make it hard to get your skis into the fall line. You'll have to end each turn well on the rear ski and then move it forward, slithering it into the fall line. Wait until the skis pull up parallel and you can get into a strong telemark. You can afford to wait a bit in the fall line because the heavy snow will keep you from accelerating quickly. Cock your hip into the turn and power it with as much rear ski as you need. Don't try to push the turn around by swinging onto the front ski; that will bury it and throw you face first into the snow.

SHALLOW WET SNOW OR POWDER OVER A FIRM BASE   This is much easier than deep wet snow. It's possible to ski a sinuous "carved" line through this snow, keeping a steady pressure on the skis' edges, which (if they are modern mountain skis with a good sidecut) will keep them turning smoothly. You can start by stepping your uphill ski toward the fall line and moving your body over it so you are balanced on the ski, with the leg compressed and ready to unwind. Then extend the leg, twisting your upper body into the fall line. As your legs straighten, the ski is pressed into the snow, forcing it to bow outward, and since it is tilted on edge toward the fall line, it will turn into the fall line. Because of your compression previous to the turn, you can keep the ski pressured even as it turns into the fall line. Otherwise turning into the fall line would relieve the pressure on it since as it turns from across the hill to down the hill the ground is dropping away from it. Once in the fall line, move your rear ski into position and settle into a strong telemark to end the turn. You may also dispense with the telemark and just settle onto that inside edge of the outside ski and make it turn to the finish. There's really not so much difference here between telemark and parallel. In either case the solid base underneath the shallow snow makes it easy for you to put pressure on the skis by extending your legs.

Notice that the up-and-down motion here doesn't seem so different from that of the deep-powder turn. What's different is the timing, and that difference makes the turns completely different in feel and application. In deep powder you unweight by rising up and then turn into the fall line; in shallow wet snow or powder you turn into the fall line as you rise on the skis. In deep powder you turn skis into the fall line with less weight than normal on them; in shallow wet snow or powder you turn with more pressure than normal on them. Thus your "toolbox" should include the ability to vary the timing of the extension and contraction of your legs to produce different effects.

BREAKABLE CRUST   Here's where you need a well-equipped "toolbox." Many people would say that breakable crusts are the most difficult of snow conditions. Some books even say that they can't be skied well and that you should give up trying to make real turns in them. But breakable crusts can be skied. There are a million different kinds of breakable crust though, and each variation seems to require a different mix of tools to ski it successfully. There are breakable crusts with soft crusts, which you break through early in the turn, and there are breakable crusts with hard crusts, which you break through only at the end of the turn. There can be deep snow beneath the crust, and there can be shallow snow beneath it. The crust can be so thick that it totally traps your skis, or it might be thin enough that you can deform it relatively easily. And the variations of breakable crust—one of the most common high-mountain conditions—go on and on. I'll give a couple of examples.

SOFT CRUST, SHALLOW UNDERNEATH   Here a variant of the carved telemark discussed for shallow, wet snow might work well. With a good ski and steady pressure on it, you can make the front ski of the telemark-to-be carve into the fall line. Then a strong telemark with the weight moving back onto the rear ski will cut a clean finish to the turn. It's very important here to wait until you are in or even beyond the fall line before powering that telemark. Only then can you angulate and drive the rear ski with your hips. Sometimes, surprisingly, the compression parallel will work well in this type of crust also, but it calls for good balance and quick reactions.

HARD CRUST, SHALLOW UNDERNEATH   This is much more difficult. The skis don't break through till the end of the turn, and then they do so unpredictably. One effective way to start the turn on a low-angle slope is to do a series of steps into the fall line and then use a telemark to finish. On a steeper slope you might unweight vigorously (rising motion before the turn starts) and then skid the skis along the top of the crust into the fall line or beyond it. When the front ski starts to break through, shift your weight hard onto the rear ski of a strong telemark and crack the crust with that. Even if the ski sticks in the crust, you can shift the relatively unweighted front ski to maintain the slight angle between the skis necessary for the turning telemark and to keep the turn going steadily. It's a slam-bang technique, but it works in an impossible situation.

Of course this short list isn't exhaustive of the infinite variety of possible snow conditions and of how you must adjust to meet them, but I hope it will give you some idea of what should be in your toolbox and how you can select and mix your tools to meet the different problems.

East and Midwest

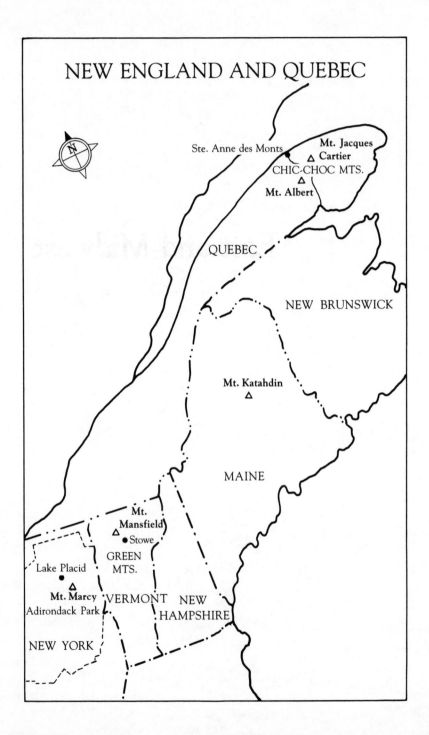

NEW ENGLAND AND QUEBEC

Ste. Anne des Monts
Mt. Jacques
△ Cartier
CHIC-CHOC MTS.
△
Mt. Albert

QUEBEC

NEW BRUNSWICK

Mt. Katahdin
△

MAINE

Mt.
Mansfield
△
● Stowe
GREEN
MTS.

Lake Placid
●

△
Mt. Marcy
Adirondack Park

VERMONT NEW
HAMPSHIRE

NEW YORK

Quebec

Chic-Choc
Mountains

TOUR   Skiing the Chic-Choc Mountains, Gaspé Peninsula of Quebec.

IN A NUTSHELL   The Chic-Chocs are a line of steep-sided plateaus that rise right out of the water on the north coast of the Gaspé Peninsula. The tops of the plateaus are near or above timberline and offer a variety of long wilderness trips.

WHAT MAKES THE TOUR SPECIAL   This area has the most reliable snow in the East. It also has the greatest expanse and variety of alpine terrain in the East with everything from rolling cross-country areas to extreme couloirs. There is good fall and summer skiing.

LEVEL OF DIFFICULTY   There is every level of difficulty of slopes. You don't have to be a good skier to enjoy a trip there.

BEST TIME TO GO   April and May are the best months. October or November trips are possible when there is no snow anywhere else in the East. It is also a good place to go during midwinter snow droughts.

HOW TO GET THERE   From the United States, drive north on I-95 along the coast as far as you can. Then take US 1 to Van Buren, Maine. From there, follow New Brunswick 17, and then Quebec 132 to New Richmond. Quebec 299 then heads north across the peninsula and will take you through the mountains.
From Montreal or Quebec, follow Canada 20 to Rivière du Loup, and then Quebec 132 along the coast until you get to Ste. Anne des Monts. Quebec 299 then takes you south into the mountains.

SPECIAL EQUIPMENT   Be prepared for bad weather. In winter carry windproof garments, face mask, and goggles, and use extra warm boots. Also carry a map and compass. It would be easy to get lost in a storm on the relatively featureless plateaus.

MAPS   Matane 22B, Gaspé 22A, Cap-Chat 22G, Port-Menier 22H. These are available from the Canada Map Office, Department of Energy, Mines, and Resources, Ottawa, Ontario.

LODGING AND SUPPLIES   Ste. Anne des Monts, Quebec.

There is a wide variety of ski touring in New England, much more than most tourers, even local ones, imagine. Even the cognoscenti, however, would have to admit that there are no tours with the wide open spaces, the wilderness, the deep snowpack, the long season, and the spacious forests of the Western mountains. Just outside New England's boundaries in Quebec, however, at the very northern tip of the 1,500-mile-long Appalachian chain is a mountain range that has all the attributes listed above. The Chic-Choc Mountains of the Gaspé Peninsula have a vast area above timberline, long miles of wilderness, deep and reliable snows that start in October and last well into summer, steep chutes and bowls for downhill thrills, rolling plateaus perfect for long-distance cross-country, and an open conifer forest unlike any in New England. It's even possible to do a week-long high-altitude traverse through these mountains. Through the whole of this range there is only one main road and hardly any population. These are the most alpine and dramatic mountains in the East. Not only are the mountains different, but the Gaspé region is culturally so distinct that it might as well be in Europe instead of in English-speaking North America.

The Gaspé Peninsula is the easternmost extension of the province of Quebec. It is bordered on the north by the Gulf of St. Lawrence, on the east by the Atlantic, and on the south by the Baie des Chaleurs. In many ways the Gaspé is similar to Washington's Olympic Peninsula. Both are surrounded on three sides by water. This causes extraordinary precipitation in both regions. Both have interior mountains that get heavy, long-lasting snows. The Chic-Choc Mountains of the Gaspé get far more snow than any other part of the Appalachian chain, and Western-like snowpacks of 10 feet are not uncommon. Summer skiing is the rule, with some snow-patches lasting into September.

The Chic-Chocs rise straight out of the water on the north (the St.

Skiing on the Gaspe Coast at Riviere-au-Renard, Quebec.
Photo by Steve Barnett.

Lawrence side) and then settle down to form several huge plateaus. Gentle domes rising from the plateaus form the highest peaks. The highest point in the range, Mt. Jacques Cartier, is only 4,160 feet tall. Due to the northerly location and the heavy precipitation, that elevation is equivalent to much higher altitudes further to the south. Jacques Cartier stands about 1,000 feet above timberline. Huge areas of the plateaus, especially the one around Jacques Cartier that is called the McGarrigles Plateau and the neighboring one around Mt. Albert, are either above timberline or only very sparsely timbered. The sides of the plateaus are precipitously steep with cliffs, couloirs, and alpine cirques heading down toward the ocean. Though the peak altitudes are not very high, the actual vertical is considerable since the mountains and the snow run right down to the water's edge.

The flora and fauna of the Chic-Chocs are different, as well, from that of the New England mountains. The forest is an isolated sample of the boreal forest found farther to the north; it is a conifer forest rather than a hardwood forest. The reason usually given for its existence is that the great ice sheets of the Ice Age did not go over the plateau tops, and thus a remnant of the original forest survived on the island plateaus. There are also remnants of Ice Age fauna. The Chic-Chocs are home to the only remaining herd of mountain caribou in the East.

The peninsula has historically been isolated from the population centers of Quebec and Montreal. On the north coast only French is spoken, and it's a dialect very different from the French you might have learned at school. The population is concentrated in small towns strung out along the coast. Fishing has long been the principal industry. Agriculture has been limited because the mountains come right down to the ocean. Hardly anyone lives in the interior, and the 60-mile drive across the mountains from New Richmond on the south to Ste. Anne des Monts on the north is unique in the East for the lack of habitations or towns along the way.

The road around the north coast is one of the most spectacular in the East—cut into the side of the mountain massif that drops straight into the sea. It's from the North Shore Road that you'll find access to most of the exciting skiing. From the town of Ste. Anne des Monts, Quebec 299 heads south across the peninsula to the town of New Richmond. About 20 miles from Ste. Anne des Monts is a resort called La Gîte, closed in winter. The massive plateau on which Mt. Jacques Cartier is located sits to the east of the resort. On the other side of the road is the plateau of Mt. Albert.

The most accessible alpine skiing in the Chic-Chocs is on Mt. Albert. A marked trail heads up a creek on its southeast side, called the Ruisseau du Diable. At the head of this creek, 3 miles from the road, is a very large bowl with several subsidiary fingers providing excellent treeless runs with north, east, and south exposures. The summit of Mt. Albert is a nearly flat, treeless expanse 5 miles long by 2 miles wide. The highest point is 3,755 feet high.

The McGarrigles Plateau is about 7 miles away, across the road from Mt. Albert. Whether or not access is easy depends on the price of copper. There is a road to a mine that is close to the top of the plateau, and when I visited the Gaspé this mine was open. We were able to ski the large bowl next to the mine and then camp in comfort, courtesy of the very friendly miners who also gave us a midnight guided tour of the mine. Now the price of copper has dropped and the mine, I am told, is closed. Access to the plateau and Mt. Jacques Cartier is now more difficult.

The plateau is very large, roughly 10 by 6 miles. Think of it as a rectangle. The east side is a scarp that runs north and south from Mt. Jacques Cartier. Its southern anchor is Mt. McWharter and the northern anchor is Mt. Ste. Anne. On the west side the southern corner is Mt. Richardson and the northern corner is Mt. de la Table.

These mountains are little more than bumps of 1,000 feet or so off the plateau. Unlike Mt. Albert, this tableland is thinly forested but there is no trouble traveling wherever you want. In terms of camping, the forest is advantageous because you can find shelter from the wind in groves of trees. The peaks all rise above timberline. Off the edges of the plateau are good downhill runs with as much as 2,500 feet of vertical drop.

The other peak in the Chic-Chocs that is commonly skied is Mt. Logan, which has very steep runs down its north side. There is a road to its summit from Cap-Chat on the north coast, but it does not get there very directly. It's probably easier to get to the top directly by cutting cross-country from a road out of Cap-Chat that runs under the northern scarp, but it will be a steep 4-mile-long climb.

The Chic-Chocs are constructed almost like one of the Western fault-block ranges, though they run east to west rather than north to south. There is a continuous scarp on the northern side from Rivière Matane in the west to Mt. Jacques Cartier, a distance of more than 65 miles. Typically it drops steeply for 1,500 feet and then tapers down another 500 feet or so. Behind the scarp is a rolling highlands about 7 to 10 miles wide. It's a natural idea for the wilderness ski tourer to attempt a traverse along the length of these highlands. Indeed, French–Canadian skiers have skied for as long as 17 days through the Chic-Chocs. Many variants are possible. The section from Mt. Logan to Mt. Albert should be a good one for a traverse. The whole trip is 25 to 30 miles long and never drops lower than 3,000 feet, which is high in these mountains.

As in the Olympic Mountains in Washington, a heavy snowfall brings penalties along with the reward of a long ski season. The weather in the Gaspé is often atrocious during the winter. Above timberline, areas situated so close to the ocean are naturally susceptible to high winds and dense fog. Most of the locals do their Gaspé skiing during the spring. I have heard rumors, passed along with guilty grins, of deep-powder skiing in early April. Sometimes a midwinter trip makes good sense. In most of the years that were snowless disasters for New England skiers, the Gaspé had a normal snowpack. It's a long trip (600 miles from Boston), but if you really want to go ski touring on natural snow you are likely to find it there even if there's not a flake within hundreds of miles of your home. It's not that Gaspé is a last resort for diehards, either. A spring trip there even in a good New England year is worth it for its alpine skiing, its proximity to salt water, and its wealth of wilderness.

Vermont

Teardrop Trail

TOUR The Teardrop Trail on the south side of Mt. Mansfield, Vermont.

IN A NUTSHELL This old down-mountain trail, cut in the 1930s, may have powder skiing in the trees and can be used as part of a loop tour by heading back over Devil's Dishpan Pass (shown on the map as the Needle's Eye) to join the cross-country trails of the Mt. Mansfield Touring Center.

WHAT MAKES THE TOUR SPECIAL While alpine skiers are skiing ice down the north side, tourers can ski powder in solitude on the south. It combines thrilling downhill and cross-country trail skiing through beautiful forests.

LEVEL OF DIFFICULTY It can be difficult with a steep, narrow trail at the top and changing snow conditions along the way. However, if the snow is good it's worth the trip for intermediates (downhill). You must be in shape for a full day of skiing.

BEST TIME TO GO January to March.

HOW TO GET THERE Take a single ride up the Mt. Mansfield ski lift to the Octagon. Climb around and up from the lift, circling the Nose (the rocky peak above the ski lift), then ski down the south side. It can be hard to find the starting point.

SPECIAL EQUIPMENT In winter be prepared for extreme cold and wind at the top. Metal-edged skis are good for icy conditions at the top.

MAPS USGS, Mt. Mansfield, Vermont.

LODGING AND SUPPLIES Stowe, Vermont.

R ead a story about colonial New England—a history of the French and Indian Wars, for example, or Hawthorne's *The Scarlet Letter*—and you'll find that the forest is as powerful a character as any human. The forest obstructs travel, hides surprises both pleasant and unpleasant, and has a powerful atmosphere that flavors all else. Modern-day ski tourers will find the New England forest to be just such a presence in their ski trips. It obstructs them when it is thick, surprises them when it opens up enough to be skied, and gives them pleasure when it protects the powder snow from the assaults of wind, sun, and other skiers. At the summits it takes the shapes of snow-encrusted "ghost" trees, while lower down there are beautiful glades of birch gleaming white in the sun. The strange thing is that many Eastern skiers don't believe there is any skiing in their forests; they think the trees are always too tight to be skied. This is wrong. There are tours that, if conditions are favorable, are as beautiful and interesting as any in the country.

One of the very best is the tour that circumnavigates Mt. Mansfield, Vermont, by linking up the abandoned Teardrop downhill trail on its back side with the modern touring trails on its front (north) side. This trip takes a full day and includes a tremendous variety of skiing, ranging from powder skiing to tree slaloms, from bushwacking to cross country on set trails. It also has a few trick moves through steep rocks (avoidable, if you wish). To me it's a symbol of the potential of Eastern touring, a potential that I think is still largely undeveloped.

Mt. Mansfield is the highest peak in Vermont. Even so, its altitude is only 4,393 feet, which is not very high by most mountain standards. New England, however, has weather that is much harsher than the weather at the same latitude and altitude in the West, and 4,000 feet is, in fact, very close to the tree line. The north side of Mt. Mansfield has been developed into one of the best downhill areas in the East. It's famous for its steep and narrow trails. It's also famous, as are all eastern areas, for its icy snow conditions. The weather is exceedingly variable. It can be 50° F. and raining one day and −20° F. the next. This variability, when combined with the heavy skier traffic on the narrow trails, compacts the snow and makes it icy.

The prevalence of hard snow in the Eastern downhill areas is yet another factor that discourages skiers from trying backcountry touring. Experience shows, however, that without heavy skier traffic the snow in the backcountry forest is rarely normal Eastern boilerplate (hard, icy, gray snow). Instead it is usually some sort of soft snow (though there may be crusty layers in it). In fact it's not at all rare to find good powder lying under the backcountry trees. One of the nicer features of the Teardrop is that at the same time that downhill skiers on one side of the mountain are scratching their way down icy slopes, tourers on the other side can be having a great time skiing powder.

To start the Teardrop tour you must first get to the mountain's south summit, called the Nose. I've done this in the past by climbing up the Toll Road ski trail from the Toll House area where the administrative offices of the ski area are located. This is an easy road with a climb of about 2,200

Skiing Teardrop Trail, Vermont. Photo by Steve Barnett.

vertical feet. At the time the ski area wouldn't permit Nordic-equipped skiers to use their lifts, so there was no alternative. In the last few years the ski company has allowed Nordic skiers to ride up the lifts and has banned uphill traffic on the road. Since there is downhill-skier traffic on it and since they are mostly beginners, this is understandable. Unfortunately they haven't yet made up for it by issuing a single-ride ticket to the top of the chairlift. It is nice to start the tour with a good climb, but you can make up for it by reclimbing the better parts of the skiing on the other side. Once at the top of the lift you must climb up just a little way and follow the road that goes around the Nose to the right. You cross the summit ridge to the north of the Nose, and then you have to find the start of the down-mountain trail. This may not be easy. The local skiers are not interested in encouraging the masses to go down their favorite trail, and the start is obscure. I know for a fact that if you really want to find it you will be able to do so. Local sentiment seems to be that the Teardrop, though straightforward to a good skier, is out of the reach of most Eastern tourers. The whole trip is too long for the unfit.

The top of the trail is narrow and runs between dense, snow-encrusted trees. This may be the most difficult part of the tour. The snow there is likely to be windblown. Glare ice is also common on any New England summit in midwinter. Bear with it and the skiing rapidly gets easier. The trail widens and the snow gets much better just a little way down. This is now a classic Eastern ski trail cut by CCC labor in the 1930s. It's fast and rolls beautifully with the terrain. To ski it well you have to be able to turn fast and keep your composure in a confined area.

Lower down you enter a more open forest and no longer have to stick strictly to the trail. For the most part the forest is composed of deciduous trees. It is open enough to ski but not wide open, making for what is best described as "feasible" tree skiing. There's a lot of area in this skiable forest. You have to be fast on your feet and ready to dodge branches and tree trunks. It provides an experience that most local skiers don't think exists in the East.

If you just kept going down through this forest, you'll eventually end up in the town of Underhill Center. This is what those downhillers who ski the Teardrop do. This is a much shorter trip than the around-the-mountain tour, and it does leave you on the other side of the mountain from Stowe. Tourers, however, will do better to stop their descent at the junction with the 5-K Trail and start a climbing traverse toward the left (south) on this trail through the forest. The junction can be tricky to find— look for red rectangular trail markers. Follow these for 5 kilometers to a junction with the Underhill Trail. Go left for 1.5 kilometers to the pass called the Devil's Dishpan, which is on the ridge heading south from Mt. Mansfield (this pass is called the Needle's Eye on the map). Just before the pass there is a beautiful stand of birch trees that, when I skied it, glowed bright white in the afternoon sun.

At the Devil's Dishpan you have a choice. If you continue on the trail it will circle the obstacles directly in front of you to the right. Go straight ahead and you'll face a problem—there are no simple slopes heading down. Instead there's a narrow chute running down through rock cliffs. It's very narrow, but not very long, so the correct procedure is just to point your skis straight down and go. You then have to work your way down small bands of cliffs. The forest is a bit tight here and some trick maneuvering is in order. The best route is to the right side of the cliffs. That's where you'll meet the trail that went right and then left coming down from the Dishpan. The skiing opens up below these cliffs, and very quickly you'll reach the top of the Mt. Mansfield Touring Center trail system. You should follow these set tracks back to the Touring Center. The quickest route back is Overland Trail to Bruce Trail to Burt Trail to the touring center. It's a great cross-country finish to the day. It's hard to think of a tour anywhere that has such an excellent and harmonious mix of different types of skiing, that offers such challenges and unexpected pleasures, and does all this on such mellow hills as Vermont's Green Mountains.

The Teardrop is the best of these New England trails that I know of, but it is far from being the only one. Many down-mountain ski trails were built in the 1920s and 1930s in the first flush of enthusiasm for downhill skiing, before there were lifts. The builders of these trails weren't building them in order to attract masses of condo buyers or to sell lots of lift tickets to beginners. They were building them for their own skiing pleasure, and many of them are master examples of how to use the terrain to get the most exciting ski ride possible with the least amount of cutting and bulldozing. Some of these, such as the Taft Trail on Cannon Mountain and the Nose Dive at Stowe became the nuclei of future major downhill areas. Others fell into disuse until the revival of ski touring in the 1970s. Examples of those that you can use for fine days of touring are the Johansen Trail near Mt. Tremblant, Quebec, and the Bruce Trail at Stowe. Other good trails are the hiking trails on the Camel's Hump in Vermont, Mt. Marcy in the Adirondacks (which has its own chapter in this book), and the newly cut Wildcat Trail on the backside of Wildcat Mountain, New Hampshire. Another highly recommended tour in the Stowe area that is more mellow than the Teardrop is the route from Bolton Valley Ski Touring Center to Nebraska Valley Road.

The character of the skiing in these Eastern forests is completely different from that of ski touring in the West. You don't go into them to find deep powder or wide-open spaces. The most avid practitioners, best described as skiers of the absurd, delight in narrow trails with thick, forested sides, patches of ice with the tips of branches protruding and windy arctic summits covered with blue ice. This may sound horrid, but it's really great skiing. You have to go into it with a different frame of mind than you might use out West. You have to look upon it as a mental challenge. "Can this be skied?" "One way or the other, I'll do it." It's also frequently an engineering problem—"How can a pair of 6-foot-long skis be maneuvered down this 5-foot-wide slot with a branch sticking up right in the middle?"

The narrow Eastern trails and the tight Eastern forest are not places for those interested in beauty or grace in skiing. Their "zen" is of quite a different nature. Quick reflexes, cunning route finding, and a general willingness to bail out at a microsecond's notice are the mind-sets that are applicable. Some of these descents are like a linked series of one-liners—each situation is unique and takes a quick and witty response. Hop over or duck that branch while telemarking around that rock, lurch through that patch of breakable crust, but get an edge ready for the icy patch just beyond, plant both poles to jump over that downed branch, and turn on a dime right beyond it to hit that hole in the trees. Believe me, it's exciting.

One of the best parts of going to New England to go touring off-trail is that there are like-minded skiers there who are about the most fun to ski with of all the skiers I know. Maybe it's their conscious attitude of being seekers of the ridiculous in skiing and their increasing delight as the skiing gets more and more unlikely that attracts me. "Better dead than mellow!" is one slogan I've heard them use. They are the type of skiers who, given a snow-covered, boulder-filled stream bed running through a forest thicket "where a rabbit couldn't go," would still smile as though it was a glacier full of powder in the Bugaboos.

New York

Mt. Marcy

TOUR   Ski descent of Mt. Marcy in the Adirondack Mountains of New York State.

IN A NUTSHELL   From Adirondacks Loj (named by a nineteenth-century spelling reformer), climb and descend the ski trail to the summit. The trip takes about 7 hours round-trip and gives a fine descent of 3,500 vertical feet.

WHAT MAKES THE TOUR SPECIAL   The Adirondack Mountains are a unique near-wilderness area of peaks and river valleys. Mt. Marcy is the highest point in the range, and its ascent is an excellent introduction to this area. Furthermore, the trail up makes it the most easily skiable of all the high peaks. The run is long by Eastern standards and moderate by the rather high standard of Eastern down-mountain trails.

LEVEL OF DIFFICULTY   If snow conditions are at all difficult, this could be pleasurable only for the advanced skier, although there is enough room on the trail for intermediates to pick their way down. It demands the ability to link many turns in a relatively narrow space. Snow conditions really determine how difficult it will be. The whole range from powder pleasure to desperately difficult is possible.

BEST TIME TO GO   January to March.

HOW TO GET THERE   From Lake Placid, New York, take NY 73 to the turnoff to Adirondack Loj. The trail starts from the lodge.

SPECIAL EQUIPMENT   Skins are useful. Extreme weather is possible and not completely predictable beforehand, so be well prepared for cold and wind. Carry a map and compass, too.

MAPS   Trails of the Adirondack High Peak Region. Available from the Adirondack Mountain Club, 172 Ridge Street, Glens Falls, NY 12801.

GUIDEBOOK   *Northern Adirondack Ski Tours* by Tony Goodwin is published by the Adirondack Mountain Club (address above).

LODGING AND SUPPLIES   Lake Placid, New York.

Through some quirk of history, New York State, one of the nation's oldest and most populous, has been able to set aside the largest state park in the nation. This is the Adirondack Forest Preserve, 290 miles north of New York City and just south of the Canadian border. A large portion of the park is roadless and offers a solitude that is rare in the thickly populated Northeast. For skiers the most interesting parts of the preserve are the high Adirondack peaks at its core, which rise above timberline at Mt. Marcy 5,344 feet, the highest point in New York State. The concentration of high peaks and their lonely nature are what give Adirondack skiing its special feeling. The descent of Mt. Marcy is a classic Eastern-mountain ski tour. Marcy, though, is just part of a larger group of wilderness peaks, many of which can also be skied. There are also easy and highly rewarding ski tours in the valleys underneath the peaks.

The Adirondack wilderness is not contiguous but is divided into several packets whose protection is guaranteed by the state's Constitution. There is not much development in them either, with the glaring exception of Lake Placid. The contrast with Vermont is startling. There, virtually every high peak in the Green Mountains has a ski lift on it (only the Camel's Hump is an exception). There are 23 peaks in the Adirondacks higher than the highest peak in Vermont, and only one of them has a ski lift, Whiteface Mountain, site of the 1980 Olympics alpine events. Winter is a very quiet time in the Adirondacks.

The wilderness feel of the Adirondacks has been appreciated for a long time. Verplank Colvin, who surveyed the mountains for the state, was one of the first to articulate the necessity of preserving areas of untouched wilderness for future generations. Bob Marshall, avid proponent of the National Wilderness system, spent his youth roaming about in every corner of the preserve.

The Adirondacks may not be heavily used compared to neighboring New England, but they have a long and honorable history of skiing. The founder-hero of modern skiing, Fridtjof Nansen, visited the range in 1912 and may have been the first to ski one of the high peaks (he and his daughter skied Whiteface Mountain). Shortly afterward Erling Strom, a telemark skier famous for his skill, taught skiing in Lake Placid. In 1915 Hermann "Jackrabbit" Johannsen made his first visit to the area. Jackrabbit, an inexhaustible natural source of energy, pioneered the ski descents of peak after peak. Neither bad snow nor long distances fazed him. Supposedly he got his nickname from his technique of bouncing from tree to tree on downhills. Just deceased at this writing (at the age of 111 years), he is one of the true heroes of American skiing.

Of all the high Adirondack peaks, Marcy is the easiest to ski from the summit. There is a hiking trail leading to the top that is wide enough for comfortable skiing and that is never dangerously steep. It must be one of the most pleasant down-mountain trails in the East, yet it is still a considerable downhill achievement and is not for beginners or timid skiers. You can get down with less than great technique but not without touches of courage, cunning, and fast reflexes. Good snow is the biggest help of all. You also have to be in good shape for the trip. Worse than the skiing difficulties are the possible mountaineering difficulties. Even though the altitude (5,344 feet) is negligible by Western standards, it is high enough in the Northeast to be above timberline by about 300 feet. The winter weather on the high Eastern peaks is ferocious by any standard. Arctic cold, high winds, and blinding fog or blizzard are always possible—even well into the spring. Marcy is a semiwilderness peak and help may be far away. In other words, you must be prepared for foul conditions by carrying suitable clothing and by carrying a map and compass that you know how to use.

Getting up and down will take most of a day. Seven hours is a good estimate. The trail is 7.6 miles from the parking lot at Adirondack Loj to the summit. It climbs 3,500 feet in that distance. The first 2 miles are relatively flat, rolling along until you get to Marcy Dam. The trail crosses the dam and then starts climbing steadily on the other side. You don't see any sign of Mt. Marcy itself for quite a while. Finally at around 4,300 feet altitude you attain the spine of a long, curving ridge that will lead you to the summit. From there you get a clear view of the peak. If your eyes have become accustomed to the New England standard of mountains rather than the Alaskan one, Marcy will seem impressive. It has a massive white top rising above the trees. It still seems a long way away, but it's not. Many of the other Adirondack high peaks will be in view. To the west are Mts. Wright and Algonquin. To the east are the Gothics, the two Wolfjaw Mountains, and Mt. Haystack. Further east are Mt. Dix and Giant Mountain. All alone in the north is Whiteface Mountain.

The high peaks look well eroded. There are a few steep rock slides

Mt. Marcy, New York. Photo by Steve Barnett.

and cliffs on the very tops. The rest is relatively gentle. There's good reason why these peaks look eroded—they are among the oldest surviving mountains in the world. The peaks are cut out of the Laurentian Shield, the huge granite plate that covers much of eastern Canada. The basic rock of the shield is 2-billion-years old.

The topography is different from that of the neighboring Green Mountains in Vermont. Those are basically high bumps on a long, narrow ridgeline. The Adirondacks are like an uplifted plateau that eroded to form a more random scatter of bumps spread over a large area. The peaks generally are on lines running southwest to northeast with such rivers as the Hudson and Ausable draining the areas between them. From the Adirondack peaks, the rivers drain both to the north and to the south. The uplift is large enough that it actually extends into Canada where it forms the Laurentian Mountains north of Montreal. Those, too, have some excellent touring on old down-mountain trails. Even as far west as northern Minnesota the range of hills (up to 2,200 feet high) that run through the Boundary Waters Canoe Area are called the Laurentian Divide and are part of the same uplift.

Looking out from Marcy's summit, it's striking how few signs of humanity you see from the summit. It is many miles in any direction to any road. The standard route up from Adirondack Loj is the shortest of all routes, and it is still 7.6 miles long. This means that skiing up from any other direction requires a long overnight trip. Other routes have been skied, but they have longer approaches and require much tougher skiing—the kind that attracts the hardest-core Adirondack skiers, the charter members of the "Ski-to-Die Club" who can ski beyond the abilities and determination of most skiers.

The very top of Marcy has some small cirque-like bowls and small blocky cliffs. The top few hundred feet, above timberline or through open shrub-like trees, is all of the wide-open skiing to be found on the route. If time and snow conditions allow, it is fun to spend extra time up there exploring the possibilities. More often than not, the wind will have worked its will on the snow and the skiing above the trees will not be very good. Once in the trees the snow will improve. You will have to stick more or less to the trail. The surrounding forest is in many places not too thick and it is possible to do some open-forest powder skiing, given good snow conditions. The trail is not a steep, narrow challenge suitable only for the best and bravest, as are many other Eastern-mountain ski routes. It is wide enough to permit rapid telemark or parallel turns and gentle enough that even a snowplow can get you down most of it—given good snow conditions. The lower 2 miles make an excellent cross-country finish to top off the 3,500-foot descent.

The Adirondacks do not normally get as heavy a snowfall as the Green Mountains. This presumably is because of a "lake effect" in which moisture from Lake Champlain gets added to storm clouds on their way eastward into Vermont. Marcy, however, is high enough for there to be reliable skiing on its higher elevations. From what I can gather from local skiers you have about a 50–50 chance of finding good skiing on it in midwinter, and an even better chance in the spring. Like most Eastern summits in midwinter, you can expect frequently to find Arctic temperatures and conditions, including blue ice. When I was there in mid-March, however, the snow was fine spring snow all the way down from the top.

The ski ascent of Marcy hardly exhausts the possibilities of Adirondack skiing. Its height singles it out from the other peaks, and its ski trail makes it the most straightforward one to ski on. But for adventure and skiing excitement, the less straightforward peaks may top it. There is one other ski trail, also cut in the 1930s, on Wright Peak. It has not been maintained much since then but can still be followed. Beyond that the paths up and down the peaks are based on hiking trails, stream beds, rock slides, or burned-out forest clearings. These can provide exciting, difficult skiing, calling on those standard Eastern virtues of indifference to rocks, stumps, or snow conditions, and joy of skiing no matter what you are skiing on or through.

It was written about Jackrabbit Johannsen in 1922, "Mr. Johannsen is a believer in his skis. . . . When there is snow, he skis in that, but he has no unreasonable prejudice against rocks, stumps, or roots, provided they are white in parts at least." This type of skiing is basically for the best skiers, but the idea of being able to ski such challenges and have fun should be an inspiration for any ambitious skier. It's fun for an outsider to hear the local "Ski-to-Die Club" members boast about forging routes on nearly impossible peaks by skiing down stream beds or rock slides.

The Adirondacks are more than a preserve of peaks. They comprise a great area of near-wild woods, lakes, hills, and rivers. There are good, long, cross-country ski tours that cross this wild terrain. The ultimate of such trips is the 124-mile-long Northville to Lake Placid trail. Almost all of it is through wilderness. This is probably too much for all but the most dedicated skiers, but there are fine shorter trips as well, which are better than Marcy for the beginning or intermediate ski tourer. One tour that is on its way to becoming a classic goes from Adirondack Loj over Avalanche Pass to Lake Colden and back. Tony Goodwin, author of *Northern Adirondack Ski Tours*, says that it is "undoubtedly the singularly most spectacular and beautiful ski tour in the Adirondacks." Basically, it goes along a deep cleft in the range defined by Avalanche and Colden lakes. Skiing out in the middle of these lakes you get views of the high peaks rising around you. If car shuttles can be arranged, it's possible to extend this trip another 5 miles or so past the Flowed Lands and down Calamity Brook to the Upper Works parking lot. This makes a perfect one-day trip through the heart of the high peaks.

West Virginia

Dolly Sods Wilderness

TOUR   Tours in the Dolly Sods Wilderness Area in West Virginia.

IN A NUTSHELL   A 4,000-foot-high plateau offers an arctic landscape only 4 hours from Washington, D.C. Many tours can be done in and around the plateau.

WHAT MAKES THE TOUR SPECIAL   The northern flora and the desolate, snowy landscape give the Dolly Sods a sense of place totally alien to the Southeast. Snowfall is reasonably reliable, and the wilderness is big enough for adventurous backcountry trips. There is a touring center nearby in Canaan Valley where rental equipment and lessons can be found.

LEVEL OF DIFFICULTY   There are many easy tours here, including some on set tracks at the White Grass Ski Touring Center. There is also more difficult skiing across untracked areas, and some downmountain skiing as well. The weather can be very cold and windy, and it is easy to get lost on the plateau.

BEST TIME TO GO   December to March.

HOW TO GET THERE   From US 50 east of Grafton take US 219 south to Davis. A road leads from there to Canaan Valley.

SPECIAL EQUIPMENT   Be prepared for cold weather. Carry a map of the area and a compass.

MAPS   USGS Laneville, Blackbird Knob, Blackwater, all in West Virginia.

INFORMATION   Write or call White Grass Ski Touring, Rt. 1, Box 299, Davis, WV 26260, (304) 866-4114.

LODGING AND SUPPLIES   Davis, West Virginia.

To residents of Washington, D.C., there is a mystical land only 150 miles away where a large chunk of arctic tundra sits incongruously in the midst of the Middle Atlantic states. Legend populates it with wolves and bears and covers it with 40-foot-high snow drifts in the middle of winter. This piece of Hudson's Bay transported to the south exists in reality as well as myth and is known as the Dolly Sods. It's a wilderness area in the mountains of West Virginia. There, a plateau over 20 miles long and more than 3 miles wide is lifted to an altitude of 4,000 feet. In northeastern West Virginia that is high—high enough to have a ferocious winter climate and a boreal forest interspersed with tundralike openings of meadow and bog.

Skiers use old roads and trails to gain access to this region. Once high up they can to a large extent set out on their own, depending on the weather and snow conditions. Their rewards are gorgeous views, a complete change of scene and atmosphere from almost all other aspects of life in the region, and not least the thrill of skiing. There are long cross-country trips to be made on the snow-covered roads, as well as downhill on the grass-covered balds on the sides of the mountains.

The Dolly Sods is an unusual wilderness area in that it is not primeval at all but a regenerated landscape. One-hundred-fifty years ago it was the site of perhaps the most magnificent stand of red spruce in the eastern United States. Until the railroad came by it had been too high and cold for farming and too remote for resource exploitation. Then when a railroad was built it was logged almost to the point of baldness. To add insult to injury, huge fires, some started purposely in the mistaken belief that they would convert the area into pasture, burned the peat soil off enormous areas of the highlands. What has grown back is not another forest of giant trees but a desolate land of bog, heath barrens, and sedge with occasional forest groves, which seems very similar to arctic tundra country far to the north. This very desolation is what has kept the Sods wild, de facto, until now. It is a small miracle that an area that has been so abused still inspires the feelings one gets in natural wilderness and is still so interesting for its natural history.

The Dolly Sods is part of a long north-south ridge system. It is framed

WEST VIRGINIA

on the west by the long, 900-foot-high scarp of Cabin Mountain. On the east there is another steep scarp, the Allegheny Front, which drops down 2,500 feet to the Potomac River. Between the two parallel scarps is the plateau of the Dolly Sods. Much of the wilderness area is drained to the south by Red Creek.

There is access to the Dolly Sods from both east and west. Forest Service Road 19 crosses the plateau at the southern end of the wilderness area. To the west it becomes Country Road 45 and goes through the town of Laneville. Forest Service Road 75 branches off from Road 19 at the crest of the Allegheny Front and proceeds north for 7.5 miles before dropping down to the Potomac Valley. More than 9 miles of these two roads are at the 4,000-feet contour line, but if there is a lot of snow low down there will be a long approach to get to the more interesting high country. Still the roads make a good, easy, cross-country route for day trips.

There is also easy access from Canaan Valley on the west. The valley itself is high enough to frequently have snow in it. Indeed there is a touring center there, the Whitegrass Ski Touring Center. A road climbs up from there to the plateau, as do two trails maintained by the touring center. The touring center is the place to go for lessons, equipment rentals, guided trips, information, and an extensive network of trails that reach up from the valley to the plateau.

Most tourers go no farther than the edge of the wilderness, or a little way along the main road across the plateau. One reason is the general inexperience of the mass of Southern ski tourers. It's a new sport there, and there is no tradition to encourage people into deep explorations of the high country. A related reason is that conditions for travel on the open areas of the plateau are often difficult. Everyone I know who has experience with the climate up there has stressed how fierce the conditions can be. High wind is normal; in fact, it is the principal factor in determining where skiing is possible and where it is not. Frequently snow will be completely cleared from one side of a meadow or frozen bog and deposited deeply on the other side. Thus finding your route may mean finding paths from one long drift of snow to another. In midwinter the cold may be completely the equal of the famously bitter New England cold, a mix of high humidity, wind, and sub-zero temperatures.

Of course, such conditions don't stop New Englanders, and they needn't stop skiers in the Dolly Sods, either. It's only that New Englanders grow up knowing how to face the winter weather with an aplomb that is hard for the Southern-born to match. Good equipment, route selection that seeks protection from the wind in the forest, and touring when the weather eases or in the spring are all parts of successful touring in the Dolly Sods. There are also those times when on top of a good, solid base, 8 inches of good snow falls undisturbed by the wind. Then the skiing is heavenly.

The most unique skiing out of Canaan Valley is actually found just to the north of the actual boundaries of the Dolly Sods Wilderness, on private land owned by a railroad company. This area is the headwaters of Red Creek. An old railroad grade climbs up from the Red Creek Campground. The country this grade goes through is a wind-blasted, barren heath, but the snow on the grade itself is usually protected from the wind. Once you are up high you can climb Cabin Mountain to the north, which has open forest suitable for easy downhilling back toward Canaan Valley. Another favorite ski route in the Red Creek headwaters is to descend the hill heading north from Blackbird Knob, where a slope drops between the forks of Red Creek. It is forested with big, spacious trees of sugar maple and spruce, and because it is somewhat wind sheltered it collects snow. Yet another interesting tour in the Red Creek area is a visit to Dobbins Slashing, a huge, empty bog that was once the richest forest of red spruce in the east. It was logged long ago, and now visitors sometimes use snowshoes, in summer, to cross it. In winter it is, of course, frozen and easy to travel on with skis. It's possible to combine some of these excursions into day-long loop trips from the ski-touring center in Canaan Valley.

There are also extensive skiing possibilities south of the Dolly Sods. It is possible, in fact, to construct a long, high-altitude tour from the Dolly Sods south for 60 miles. It could go something like this: south along the Red Creek Plains to the Roaring Plains to Mt. Porte Crayon to Job Knob to Middle Mountain to Sinks of Gandy to Gaudinier Scenic Area to Gaudinier Knob to Cheat Mountain to Snowshoe-Silver Creek. From there, it could continue on into the Cranberry Wilderness (the biggest wilderness in the East). If these trips interest you, one thing to keep in mind is that the Dolly Sods and adjoining terrain is a trackless area in winter and is easy to get lost in. You have to be proficient with map and compass to go far from the popular trails.

The Dolly Sods probably has the most reliable snow and the largest wild area of the southeastern mountains, but it is far from being the only place where ski touring is developing. Farther to the south on the top of Roan Mountain, North Carolina, there is another ski-touring center, situated in the midst of mountains higher and more spectacular in some ways than those of New England. Given a good snow year, there are backcountry possibilities there and on the surrounding ridges and peaks. The touring center, with its equipment rentals and instruction, makes this a good place for Southerners (who have been turning to downhill skiing in large and increasing numbers in the last ten years) to experience cross-country skiing. Another accessible area in North Carolina with very good ski touring is near Blowing Rock, a bit east of Roan Mountain. Where the Blue Ridge Parkway goes through Moses Cone State Park there is access to a variety of interesting trails winding through forests of virgin white pine. These are easy trails that can be enjoyed by almost anyone.

There is still a lot of pioneering left for ski tourers in the southeastern mountains. It should be an exciting time for them. Just as in the desert Southwest, this seemingly unlikely zone for skiing hides wonderful experiences on skis for those who have faith and are willing to wait for the snow.

Minnesota

North Shore Trails System

TOUR Skiing the North Shore Trail System along the North Shore of Lake Superior, Minnesota.

IN A NUTSHELL There is a unified system of set track some 120 miles long, winding in and out of the hills along the lake. It's possible to ski from lodge to lodge. There is also off-trail skiing on the frozen rivers running down to the lake.

WHAT MAKES THE TOUR SPECIAL The terrain is perfect for cross-country trails, rolling up and down with many scenic views down to Lake Superior. There is a lot of trail, but it can all be reached from any one lodge of the system. Or it can be done, just as sensibly, as part of a lodge-to-lodge trip. The off-trail skiing down the frozen rivers is unique, interesting, and fun skiing. There is a lot of solitude and feeling of wild country here.

LEVEL OF DIFFICULTY Everything from very easy to difficult track skiing can be found here. The river trips are mostly easy, but there are some tricky moments skiing down frozen cascades.

BEST TIME TO GO February. Usually there is good skiing from November to March.

HOW TO GET THERE US 61 runs north from Duluth along the shore of the lake. The lodges of the trail system run from Tofte up almost to Grand Marais.

SPECIAL EQUIPMENT Racing skis or fast, light, touring skis will be best for the tracks. For the river tours and for skiing off track in the trees, light touring skis will be best.

MAPS Issued by Lutsen Tofte Tourism Association, Box 115, Lutsen, Minnesota 55612. Buy also the Superior National Forest Map, issued by Superior National Forest, Duluth, Minnesota 55801.

LODGING AND SUPPLIES Lutsen, Minnesota.

W hat is good for cross-country skiing is not necessarily the same as what is good for downhill skiing. Downhill skiing in the Midwest is tinged with absurdity, marked by scenes where the lift lines are longer than the lifts and where the hills are so small that it's easy to miss them while driving by. Yet the Midwest has excellent and unique ski touring that compares well with that found anywhere else. It's true that most

NORTHERN MINNESOTA

of the land is extraordinarily flat, that the weather is variable with sudden thaws and hard freezes, and that most of the wilderness was obliterated long ago. There are places in the northern Midwest, however, where these rules are broken, where you can find an ideal combination of wilderness, hilly terrain, grand scenery, and reliable snow. You must go north to the country bordering Lake Superior.

As you leave Duluth and travel north along the shore of the lake, the land becomes less populated and more rugged. West of the lake the hills of the ancient Sawtooth Mountains rise over 1,000 feet from the water's edge. The shore of the lake itself is rugged and cliffbound. Snowfall this far north is relatively reliable, and thaws are rare. It has the ingredients to be a perfect area for Nordic skiers.

The North Shore has long been a popular area for summer vacationers, and there are a number of good lodges and resorts strung out along US 61, which borders the lake. Just a few years ago, the lodge and resort owners banded together with the National Forest Service and with several state parks to form an association that would build and maintain a large trail system for cross-country skiers. Now the North Shore has one of the longest trail systems in the nation.

One aim of the trail system was to make it possible to ski lodge to lodge along the shore of the lake. From each lodge there would be a network of trails radiating back into the hills. The lodge-to-lodge network now covers a distance of 25 miles. The lodges are always joined by beginner or intermediate trails, and the distance is never more than 5 to 6 miles. The steeper trails go into the hills. The total system length is about 120 miles. It features quiet, lonely skiing through forests of pine, birch, and maple. Not far away, to the north, are other extensive trail systems, the Gunflint Trail, the Grand Marais trails, and the Grand Portage trails. Long wilderness trips are possible in the nearby Boundary Waters Canoe Area. There is no trail fee for use of the trails, though donations are always welcome in the form of both money and labor.

Given the geographical spread and the variety of the resorts, it was a natural idea to create a "ski-through" program. A group of skiers can ski from resort to resort day by day, and their luggage will be transported by the resorts. A special package price is offered for the whole vacation and includes a well-prepared map set covering the whole trail system. It's an idea with good potential for many other touring centers as well—a step on the way to creating European-type amenities for American cross-country skiing.

In the center of the system is the Lutsen Ski Area, one of the few Midwest downhill resorts that has enough vertical to be taken seriously. The manager of Lutsen has cut cross-country trails running down from the

The Lake Superior Shore. Photo by Steve Barnett.

lift-served tops of the hills. You can use the lifts and then ski for miles along the high ridges before dropping back to the base. The longest such trail descends from the summit of Moose Mountain and was cut specifically to provide guests with the experience of wild-woods running, otherwise absent from Midwestern downhill skiing. The forest at the top is old maple and relatively clear of underbrush. Sometimes in the spring or after a thaw, a hard-enough crust forms on the snow so that you can travel freely through the forest. With even more luck there will be a layer of powder on top of that. Then you can ski downhill for hundreds of vertical feet through the trees, rejoin the trail, climb up again, and do another downhill segment.

A particularly scenic part of the North Shore Trails is in Cascade Falls State Park, anchoring the northern end of the system. Some of its trails run alongside the banks of the Cascade River, which flows over numerous small waterfalls on its way to the lake. Others climb up some 550 feet to yet another Moose Mountain (a popular name), from which there is a great panoramic view of the lake. Cascade Park has the only pieces of trail in the system that are right on the lakeshore. While short and easy, these are exceptionally scenic.

There is another set of trails in the highlands above Cascade Park. This area is called the Bally Creek Region. A long trail connects the Bally Creek system to the Cascade Park trails. It is 15 miles long and descends almost all the way. This is a pleasant trail to ski due to its length and occasional downhill thrills. You can spend hours descending it, through forest and open, logged-out patches dotted with a few remaining snags. These are probably ugly in the full light of day but were rather ghostly and atmospheric when I skied through them in the fog. The trail ends with a fast or even too fast (depends on your route) finish through Cascade Park.

My favorite trail in the North Shore System is the Picnic Loop in the southern sector of the system, the part called the Sugarbush Trails by local skiers. It is 18 miles long and climbs high above the lake into the maple forest. This forest was never cut, and it is clear enough of underbrush that you can take off at random through the beautiful trees. The trail climbs to a high ridge running parallel to the lake. There are repeated climbs followed by fast drops with sweeping turns. Your total climb while running the loop will be more than 1,200 feet. On a fast pair of racing skis, the repetition of the sweat of climbing followed by the adrenaline of the downhill is truly exhilarating. It's the essence of cross-country skiing. It is not often that you can find such a long trail with such skiing interest, even in major cross-country areas. The mountains are larger in the West, but there is a definite shortage of the kind of rolling terrain that is found here on the North Shore and allows such enjoyable cross-country skiing.

Wildlife is common in the trail system. Deer, wolf, and fox are all present. Wolves sometimes are seen out on the ice of the lake. They try to drive deer out of the forest and onto the ice. Once there, the deer with their slippery hooves are at a fatal disadvantage compared to the wolves. Pileated woodpeckers aren't uncommon.

The season is relatively long and reliable. This far from any ocean there are fewer thaws and snow droughts than in New England. Usually there is skiing from late November into mid-April. The lake is large enough to moderate the climate along its shore. There is a lot more, longer-lasting snow and colder temperatures just a few miles inland (and hundreds of feet higher) from the lake. Even when the lakeside trail system is in marginal condition, the higher trails will be excellent.

The lake's moderating effect on temperatures is sometimes welcome.

There are many days in the Midwest, especially in the north, where just stepping outdoors is like being on an arctic expedition. International Falls, Minnesota, up on the Canadian border, is often the coldest spot in the nation. But it is warmer on the Lake Superior shore. Just because it drops to −45°F. in International Falls at night—a common occurrence—doesn't mean that it won't be a decent day on the lakeshore. As long as there is no wind you're likely to find conditions (say −20°F. at night and up to −5°F. in the day) that are just warm enough to allow you a comfortable day. There are many other times when the sun shines, the temperature hovers at a perfect 15° to 25°F., the air is still, and the day is glorious. Then the kind of skiing you have on the North Shore is pure pleasure, drifting or running along the set trails through the forest, climbing up to a viewpoint, roaring back down toward the lake.

Is there off-track skiing to be found in these Midwest hills? Yes, there is, and it follows routes unique to this section of the Midwest. The greatest obstacle to free travel through the hills above the lake are the forests, which

Skiing the Minnesota North Shore. Photo by Steve Barnett.

are filled with dense underbrush since they were logged in recent times. There are several lines of weakness through these forests. First is the system of maintained ski trails. Second are the natural lines of weakness used since ancient times in the area—the rivers and lakes. It seems that any route used by canoes can be skied, given good snow conditions. That is saying a lot since Minnesota is famous for its canoe touring. Third, some old forest that is open enough to offer good skiing still remains.

It's one of the strong points of Nordic skiing that it can take advantage of small verticals. Ridge systems with 500 feet of relief can provide endless downhill-skiing thrills. You climb up on a trail and then ski down every slot in the trees you can find. In many of these areas there are trails running at the bottom of the hills, and you can run back up them to the ridge and find another shot. You will be making several short runs instead of one long shot, with the pleasures of doing a variety of types of skiing, downhill turns, and miles on the track. Such skiing is limited here by the denseness of much of the forest. The best tree skiing is up on the high ridgetops where the maples grow. These are generally down in the southern end of the system, around Lutsen Mountain and around the Picnic Loop. Locals say that the best time for such skiing is in the early spring when a good crust forms on the snow. Then you can go up to the top of one of the ridges and ski through the forest wherever you like.

The most interesting off-track skiing, though, isn't up on the hills but down on the rivers. Several streams penetrate the barrier of hills and drop down to the lake in series of cascades. In winter these freeze over, are covered with snow, and are natural routes through the woods from the high country to the north down to the lake. With luck, the snow-covered ice will be a fast and fun surface on which you can skate and double pole down the river, enjoying the thrill of effortless mile-eating motion. The frozen cascades provide natural downhill thrills. There are a few spots of open water, but these can easily be seen and avoided. Just use common sense about how close to the edges of the open water it is safe to go. To find out about conditions, routes, and possibly a guided trip, contact Steve Asch at the cross-country shop at Lutsen Resort.

One excellent short river tour is Onion River. Take the road labeled Lake Superior Hiking Trails, just north of the Best Western Motel. Drive up it a few miles to a sign that says, "Point of Interest 1000 feet ahead." Go a bit farther, and on the left there will be a road and a sign that says, "Access to Private Driveway." Ski down the road to the river, and get on the ice just below the bridge. Then ski down the river. It goes into a narrow gorge and falls down several cascades. Scout these out before you go down them, but they are usually skiable. Just before you get to US 61, take a side trail out to the left and ski down to the pullout on the highway just north of the river. The tour is only an hour or two long, but it's a scenic and skiing treat.

The easiest and most popular of the river tours is Poplar River, which runs down to Lutsen Mountain Ski Area. To get to it, drive up the Caribou Trail Road. Ski off to the left and across Lake Agnes. You have to climb the hill above it, and there is a trail that goes up to the summit and then down to the river. The river is wide and flat and is easy skiing, a natural highway through the hills toward the lake. When you get to a washed-out bridge, there is a trail off to the left that is part of the Lutsen cross-country system and takes you quickly to the ski area.

The Manitou River offers a longer and wilder river tour and is located south of the North Shore Trail System. There are two major cascades on it. The first is skiable, but the second is not—it can be admired but not descended. Enter the river from Crosby-Manitou State Park, an excellent skiing area by itself, or from a bridge above the park. Crosby-Manitou Park is a hilly area, more rugged than most of the North Shore mountains. It contains remnants of old-growth forest. Foot trails wind through the hills, some of which are easily skiable and some are steep enough to require some skill. The park is quiet and little used in winter, and I found it one of the most enjoyable touring areas I visited in Minnesota.

To get to the river, we had to ski down some steep and difficult trails that deposited us just below the first cascades. After several hours of pleasant but uneventful skiing down the river, we came to the second falls. They would have been eventful if we'd tried them, but they were so big and steep with an open pool yawning below that we exited instead to the right, and joined a hiking trail to an overlook of the falls. Then we skied out to the North Shore Road (US 61).

While the North Shore is a major center of cross-country skiing, it is not a resort in the same way that Sun Valley or Stowe is. Mostly it's a lonely, rural, nearly wild region with a string of supporting lodges spread out along US 61. There's a magic to being able to move silently through the limitless North Woods forests, a magic that in summer draws canoeists from all over the U.S. and that is equally attractive to skiers in winter.

Minnesota

Boundary Waters Canoe Area

TOUR   Skiing in the Boundary Waters Canoe Area in northeastern Minnesota.

IN A NUTSHELL   The BWCA is a forested flatland with 30 or 40 percent of its area covered by lakes. The lakes are interconnected by streams and by portage trails. The ski routes follow the summertime canoe routes.

WHAT MAKES THE TOUR SPECIAL   The varied lakes of the BWCA and the portage trails that connect them have identities as individual as mountains. The area provides midwesterners and others a chance to take trips ranging in length from a day to several weeks in a pristine and lonely wilderness environment. With the right snow conditions, travel across the lakes can be fast and exciting cross-country skiing.

LEVEL OF DIFFICULTY   The skiing is usually easy. The major difficulties are the sometimes harsh weather and inconsistent snow conditions.

BEST TIME TO GO   From late February through March.

HOW TO GET THERE   Ely is on MN 169 in the northeast corner of the state. Sawbill Lodge may be reached via the Sawbill Trail from Tofte on the North Shore of Lake Superior. The Gunflint Trail begins at Grand Marais on the North Shore.

SPECIAL EQUIPMENT   Skiers should be prepared for both extreme cold and for wet thawing weather. Carry warm sleeping bags, jackets, and boots, goggles and face masks, rain jackets, and a small hatchet. Group equipment should include rainflies for the tents, as well as maps and compasses.

MAPS   The best are the McKenzie Maps, which have good route and topographic information. They are available from McKenzie Maps Creative Consultants, 37 Providence Bldg., 32 W. Superior St., Duluth, MN 55802.

Another good map to have is the Superior National Forest Map (the BWCA is in the Superior National Forest). It is available from the Forest Supervisor, Superior National Forest, Box 338, Duluth, MN 55801.

LODGING AND SUPPLIES   Duluth and Ely, Minnesota.

The Boundary Waters Canoe Area (BWCA) in northern Minnesota is the historic center for wilderness canoe trips in the United States. A map of it shows a land peppered with hundreds of lakes interconnected by streams and portages. It's a land where moose and wolves still make their homes. In winter the frozen lakes and rivers and the snow-covered portage trails form natural ski routes through the forested wilderness. This is the place for wilderness skiing in the Midwest. Conveniently, it's very close to both the North Shore Trail System described in the previous chapter and the similar Gunflint Trail System, and it is natural to combine trips to these areas, mixing semi-civilized skiing on prepared tracks with wilderness trail-breaking out of sight of the works of man.

There is a strong sense of place skiing in the BWCA, and there is more to it than just the nostalgia of those who have spent weeks canoeing there in the summer. It's composed of traveling through seemingly endless forests and of visiting the countless lakes, each in its own way as distinctive as mountain peaks are. Given the right snow conditions, the lakes are as natural an arena for cross-country skiing as the mountains are for telemark downhills. Part of the charm of the area is the nearly infinite combination of lakes, trails, and portages, which can be put together to form different routes.

There are good day trips possible here, based from lodges on the BWCA boundary, such as the one on Sawbill Lake, or from the lodges on the Gunflint Trail, or even from the resorts on the North Shore of Lake Superior. But the real spirit of skiing in the BWCA is best found in multiday ski camping trips. Basically most any good summer canoe trip will be a good one to ski in the winter. Since skiing skills aren't really needed to tour in the BWCA, it's a good place for beginners to learn about winter camping and to gain confidence that they know how to survive and be comfortable in the winter wilderness environment.

Skiing across a Minnesota Lake. Photo by Steve Barnett.

Winter is a sure thing in northern Minnesota. The cold and the snow are both exceptionally reliable. Up in the BWCA, at least a thousand feet higher in altitude than Lake Superior, even in a bad snow year there will probably be sufficient snow for good touring. Only rarely will a thaw in the lowlands be strong enough to do much damage up in the wilderness lakes country. Too much cold is more likely to be a problem than a sudden thaw. This area is home to the arctic high in the United States, bringing temperatures of 30° or 40° below F. Should you stop reading right now and go to another chapter, perhaps the one about skiing in Baja California? No, not yet. There are great rewards to skiing here and there are countermeasures to take against the cold.

The simplest countermeasure is to travel late enough in the season to have a reasonable chance of avoiding extreme cold and still be early enough to miss the spring thaw. Wait at least until the last half of February. By then the days are getting long enough so that the nights spent camping out are not as oppressive as they were a month earlier. March may be even better. Ideal conditions occur when a cold-weather crust forms after an earlier thaw or rain and is topped with a couple of inches of fresh snow.

The next countermeasure is to be well-equipped. A heavy jacket of down or synthetic fibers and a very warm sleeping bag are essential. If you don't feel like spending hundreds of dollars for the best in winter-weight down sleeping bags covered with Gore-Tex (which will be too warm to use in summer), a very effective solution is to use two medium-weight down or synthetic bags, one inside the other. That way you have sleeping bags that are useful summer or winter. An important ingredient for warmth while sleeping is a thick foam pad or pads under your sleeping bag. I'd recommend using two pads. Use ethafoam or blue foam rather than ensolite because it's lighter and stays flexible in extreme cold. Thermarest inflatable pads are very comfortable and they are warm, but since they occasionally develop leaks always back them up with a foam pad. For crossing lakes on windy days you'll need goggles and a face mask. Keeping the wind out of your insulating layers is one place where a Gore-Tex outer layer really excels. The new generation of lightweight double boots, such as the excellent Asolo Glissade 400, are made to order for keeping your feet warm during a day of skiing through very cold snow, and they are exceedingly comfortable as well. For further foot protection an insulated overboot, such as those that Ramer, Yeti, Chouinard, or Outdoor Research manufacture, should be used over the boots. Two pairs of socks and an insulating insole are effective insulation with single boots. Some people go even further and use vapor-barrier protection for their socks, sandwiching them between two sealed, impermeable layers. Thick plastic bags are one possibility, and commercially made vapor-barrier socks such as the ones made by Chouinard are another, more durable one. In any case carry extra socks and keep them dry in plastic bags. For camp take along an extra pair of down or fiber-fill booties, après-ski moon boots, or even the heavier but very functional Sorels. Then you can be assured of warm feet while your activity level is low after skiing and you can dry out your boots and socks.

Careful siting of campsites so that they are protected from the wind adds a lot of comfort to a camp. Small lakes are generally better than large ones. If wind is a problem a snow wall can be built around the tent. Wood is plentiful, so building campfires is reasonable, and there is little that cheers up a winter camp so much or that makes the night hours go peaceably by so fast as a good campfire. Since the snow here is not as deep as in the western mountains, you don't usually have the problem of your fire melting its way down into a ten-foot pit.

In summer camping is restricted to certain specified campsites that contain fire pits with grates and primitive outdoor toilets. Winter campers are not required to use these sites, but when possible it is a good idea. By using them, winter campers won't leave piles of charcoal and ashes or piles of human waste for the summer campers to find. Always try to be careful about contaminating the lakes and streams. This is a pristine area where you can still drink water right out of the lakes in summer. One tool that is particularly useful in BWCA camping is a small hatchet for chopping through lake ice to get to unfrozen water.

As in the mountains, your main problem traveling in the BWCA is likely to be wildly varying snow conditions as you cross from one side of a lake to another. Sometimes there will be deep powder, other times hard windpack. Frequently there will be both at different places on the same lake. Worst of all is slush, where water from a lake seeps up into the absorbent snow. It will freeze to your skis and leave you standing stupidly with two absolutely useless clubs of ice tightly attached to your feet. Again, the best time for good conditions is a little later in the season when occasional warm days may have consolidated the snow and put a layer of crust on it. In any case, you will get good at reading snow conditions by the appearance of the surface from a distance, and you will choose your route accordingly.

Along with protection from the cold you should carry protection from wetness. Sometimes it rains in the BWCA in the middle of winter. There can be fast and extreme temperature changes. That means that you should carry a rainfly for your tent and a waterproof jacket. You should also carry at least a partial change of dry clothes, including underwear and socks, which is important whether you get wet from sweating on a cold day or from rain on a warm day. When you are done skiing, brace yourself, quickly change into the dry clothes, and you'll be much more comfortable from then on. When the sun comes out, as it frequently does in the BWCA winter, you should quickly take advantage of it and dry everything that's damp. Even on sub-zero days the sun's radiation is strong enough to dry sleeping bags and clothes.

How heavy are the backpacks of people doing week-long winter trips in the BWCA? With all the gear for camping comfortably they may weigh as much as 55 to 75 pounds. Having the lightest but most expensive gear is one way around this. Another very good solution is to use a sled to carry the camp, and BWCA terrain is ideal for this. There are very good sleds commercially available from such manufacturers as Mountainsmith. Or you can build your own by bolting and gluing together two children's plastic sleds and making a rigid harness with conduit or water pipe. In any case it's not always necessary to be skiing with a heavy load on your back or trailing behind you. You can also set up a comfortable base camp and spend several days exploring on day trips, eventually moving the camp to another good base, and so on.

Every winter large groups of inexperienced campers are guided through the BWCA by such organizations as the American Lung Association and Outward Bound. Despite the harshness of the climate the participants on these trips, people who often have no winter-camping experience, almost universally stay reasonably comfortable and enjoy themselves immensely. That's because their leaders teach them the basics of keeping warm in the wilderness and guide them into following the procedures that prevent uncomfortable events from happening.

How do you plan routes in the BWCA? First of all don't expect to match summertime canoeing speeds. With large groups, progress is only about 5 miles a day. Smaller, more experienced groups will go much faster, but days are still short, time must be allotted for breaking and setting up camp, and snow conditions may keep skiers from moving fast. Falling through the ice has proven to be a very rare occurrence, but you should still take precautions. Try to skirt areas near stream outlets and inlets or anywhere else that there is moving water. Beaver ponds often have thin ice since the water underneath them is moving. Since the skis spread out the skier's weight, they make travel on the frozen lakes far safer than it would be on foot. The snow is usually shallow enough that you can take off your skis to walk across troublesome terrain, such as a very steep section of a portage trail. The long trails in the BWCA, such as the Kekekabic, are not usually as good as the lake and portage routes.

Even though it's in the Midwest the terrain of the BWCA is not absolutely flat. In fact there's at least one lake on the Sawbill Loop that gives a glimpse of mountains rising out of the water. These aren't high mountains—their vertical is measured in hundreds rather than thousands of feet—but they add a lot of drama to the scene and on some trips will add a lot of excitement to the skiing. These "mountains," the highest hills in Minnesota, are part of the Laurentian Divide, which comes around Lake Superior from the Canadian Shield. Even away from these hills there will be hilly sections on the portages between lakes on some tours.

Start with day trips. It's good to try a couple of these before winter camping so you can get a good idea how your equipment functions, how to navigate, and how to read the snow on the lakes. Sawbill Lake is a good starting point for day trips because the resort there can give you some support. The other trailheads are rides of a half-hour to an hour beyond the last habitations. If it's cold and your car won't start on your return from skiing, you have a problem. It's also good to have someone who can raise an alarm if you have a problem and don't get back by nightfall.

Midwestern ski touring at Porcupine Mountains, Michigan.
Photo by Steve Barnett.

A good simple trip from the resort is a loop from Sawbill to Kelso to Alton lakes and back to Sawbill Lake. The views are especially nice on Alton Lake. You can easily extend this to longer trips because strings of lakes reach out from all three lakes.

Another good day trip is the Angleworm Lake Loop, reached from the Echo Trail (County Road 116) near Ely on the western side of the BWCA. This trip is longer than the Sawbill Loop described above and is more difficult than most other BWCA day trips due to the hilly trail. Another very good day trip in the Ely area starts from the North Arm Road, which branches off the Echo Trail. It is a route that was specifically designed as a ski trail, and it runs through the finest stands of virgin forest left in the BWCA. The trail makes about a 10-mile loop through Coxey Pond, Cummings Lake, and Ole Lake. The trail is 10 miles long and likely to be a packed track, making for fast skiing.

The Gunflint Trail is another good starting point for day trips. Along with ski tours into the wilderness area there are many groomed cross-country trails reaching out from the resorts on that road. For a particularly good day trip, park at Bearskin Lake and ski into Duncan Lake. Then take the spectacular Stairway Portage, which goes by several waterfalls, to Rose Lake. Some turn back at the portage because of the more difficult skiing on the trail. Others continue on to complete a circle to Bearskin Lake via Daniels Lake.

With the incredible number of permutations of lakes and trails, it is hard to single out particular multiday trips. The starting points for these trips are the same as for the day trips; they just go farther. Any trip deep into the BWCA will reward ski tourers with the solitude of real wilderness.

Porcupine State Park in Michigan's Upper Peninsula is another Midwest area with good potential for wilderness ski touring. The Porcupine Mountains, rising about a thousand feet above the south shore of Lake Superior, get a much larger snowfall than any other Midwestern area—one comparable to that in the mountains of the West. Roads into the state park are plowed only a short distance to a small downhill area. Beyond that skiers will be all alone. There is good skiing on trails running through the hills, along the lake shore, and down the forested hillsides.

Rockies

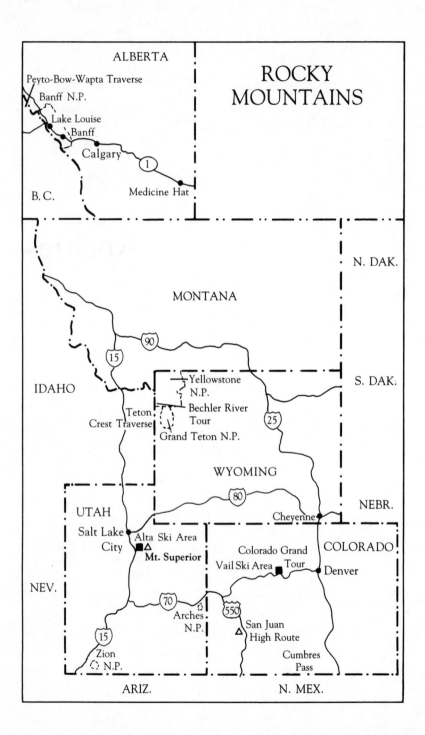

Alberta

Peyto-Bow-Wapta Traverse

TOUR   Peyto-Bow-Wapta Traverse in the Canadian Rockies of
Alberta and British Columbia.

IN A NUTSHELL   The route starts at Peyto Lake on the Icefields
Highway and moves from Peyto Glacier to the Wapta Icefield to the
Waputik Icefield, past Mt. Balfour, over the Niles-Daly Col, and down
to Wapta Lake on the Trans-Canada Highway. It is a trip of three or
four days.

WHAT MAKES THE TOUR SPECIAL   This is an easily accessible glacier
traverse that has the unique combination of easy skiing, well-spaced
huts for every night out, and the wonderful mountain scenery of the
Canadian Rockies.

LEVEL OF DIFFICULTY   This traverse is relatively easy for a high-
mountain traverse. Most of the skiing is easy touring on gentle
glaciers.

BEST TIME TO GO   April and May. Much of it will be possible well
into July.

HOW TO GET THERE   Bow Summit and Bow Lake are reached from
Alberta 93, the Icefields Highway.

SPECIAL EQUIPMENT   Since huts will be used, loads can be relatively
light. Take a rope and crevasse rescue gear. An altimeter is useful for
navigation in flat light. Also carry maps and compass.

MAPS   Hector Lake, Lake Louise, Blaeberry River.

LODGING AND SUPPLIES   Banff, Alberta.

The Peyto-Bow-Wapta Icefield Traverse on the crest of the Canadian Rockies is probably the most popular high-level traverse in Canada. It's certainly the most popular one in the Rockies. It follows gentle icefields from hut to hut for over 25 miles through the distinctive and spectacular glacial mountain terrain of the Rockies.

The Canadian Rockies look nothing like the principal chains of the Rockies to the south, in Colorado or Wyoming. The former are a long plateau of sedimentary rock, mostly limestone, that has been lifted straight up and then cut away by glaciers and streams. The plateau is sliced again and again into vertical walls that are universally decorated with the horizontal stripes of the rock strata. The strata aren't bent, or twisted, as in so many other ranges; they just lie horizontally. This gives the range its unique appearance. Compounding the stratification is the nature of its glaciation. The plateau-like surfaces raised to high altitude are perfect for the creation of large icefields. When the glaciers reach the sharp edges of the plateaus they simply break off. Thus the walls of the Rockies as seen from below have a peculiar appearance. The final strata on many of them is a white layer that is a clean-cut cross-section through the glacier.

In Canada the Rockies are the third major range inland from the Pacific, after the Coast Range and the Interior Ranges. Thus one would expect them to be dry and have little glaciation. But there are such relatively cool summers and such an extensive high-altitude area that large glaciers can form. The firn line, or line of permanent snow, is at 8,500 to 9,000 feet on the main crest.

A series of increasingly large plateau-icefields starts at Lake Louise and heads north along the crest of the Rockies. Paralleling the crest along its east side is the Icefields Highway (Alberta 93), which runs between the towns of Banff and Jasper. The whole area is administratively enclosed in the Banff and Jasper national parks.

The largest and highest of the icefields is the Columbia Icefield, which is easily reached from the highway. It is a huge dome of ice more than 10,000 feet high and surrounded by peaks such as Mt. Columbia (12,294 feet). Most of these peaks are skiable from the icefield, though some of North America's largest mountain walls are found on their other, northern faces. The Columbia Icefield is well-suited as a basecamp for serious ski mountaineering, with a season that extends into the summer. Farther to the north is the Clemenceau Icefield, which is beautiful but difficult to get to and not ideal for skiing. South of the Columbia Icefield is the Freshfield Icefield, which is said to have excellent skiing. A small hut is there, erected by the Alpine Club of Canada.

Southernmost of the icefields is the continuous ice of the Peyto, Wapta, and Waputik glaciers. The route from Peyto Lake in the north,

Crossing a Canadian Rockies icefield. Photo by Steve Barnett.

along the glaciers and down to Sherbrooke Lake at the southern end of the uplift, is one of Canada's classic ski trips. The access is easy from plowed roads on both ends. The skiing is relatively easy, too. It's a ski-touring rather than a ski-mountaineering adventure. The scenery is fantastic. And not least, there are huts placed along the way that make camping secure in an otherwise exposed, above-timberline landscape.

The traverse can be started from either Peyto Lake or Bow Lake. Both are on the Icefields Highway. The Bow Lake start gives a shorter trip by cutting out Peyto Glacier. The directions given here are for the longer Peyto Lake start. Peyto Lake is just north of Bow Summit on the highway. You can start from the summit and ski down to the south end of the lake. Then circle around to the west and head up the valley to the glacier moraine, which will take you up to Peyto Glacier. Sometimes the snow will be blown off the moraine and it will be easiest to climb up it without skis. The Peter and Catherine Whyte Hut is situated on the left side of the headwall above the glacier. To get to it easily go up the middle of the glacier to the col and then head left. Too early a turn to the left will lead you into crevasses.

The hut is a new one, well insulated and designed so that the sun heats it. There is no stove, since there is no wood nearby, but cooking stoves and lanterns are there. There are several high peaks rimming the glacier. Mt. Baker to the north is 10,407 feet high. Mt. Rhondda, which is a good side trip on skis from the traverse, is 9,900 feet high.

The next hut, the Bow Hut, is only two to three hours south of the Whyte Hut. This would be your first destination if you were coming up from Bow Lake. Most parties go directly from the Whyte Hut to the Balfour Hut, which is more directly on the route and a reasonable day's ski away. To get there climb up past Mt. Rhondda. Keep high and go past Mt. St. Nicholas on its west side. You will arrive at the St. Nicholas—Olive Col. A 2,000-vertical-feet run goes down to the Balfour Hut from there.

This hut is small (12 people) and cold. It is situated at an altitude of 8,200 feet. There is some excellent skiing around it, though. On the south side of the icefield, the north side of Mt. Gordon (10,500 feet) is a good ski descent. Another good ski run from the hut can be had by climbing up the Diableret Glacier, which offers an exceptional view from the col at its top.

To continue the traverse from the hut, drop 150 feet and then climb up 2,500 feet to Balfour High Col. This is a fine viewpoint and the high point of the trip at 9,800 feet. On the right as you climb is the east face of Mt. Balfour, which can be skied from the southeast. Also on the right is a beautiful icefall. To the west is the Little Yoho Valley, reachable on skis, and the site of yet another hut. To the east is Hector Lake.

From the Balfour High Col descend to the Waputik Icefield and head across its flat expanse to Niles Peak and the Niles-Daly Col. From the col ski directly down to Sherbrooke Lake, a descent with potential avalanche hazard. From Sherbrooke Lake keep heading down till you get to the highway and West Lake Louise Lodge at Wapta Lake. This final descent of the route from the Niles-Daly Col to Wapta Lake is 3,400 vertical feet. The whole last day from the Balfour Hut to Wapta Lake covers a distance of about 15 miles.

The route is straightforward for the most part. The climb up to Balfour High Col goes by a crevassed area, and you should use your glacier rope at least for that section. Other areas are not bad for crevasses but caution is always in order. The Rockies do not get the heavy snowfalls and mild winter temperatures of the Coast Ranges, and snow bridges on Rockies glaciers are correspondingly thinner and weaker.

Since the route is entirely above timberline, and since a lot of it is flat and well above any defining drainages, navigation can become desperate if there is a fog or a snowstorm. Skiers should always keep map, compass, and altimeter handy and should be constantly keeping track of their altitude and the directions to important landmarks and to their destination.

The best time to do the trip is in April or May. By then the weather, which can be ferociously cold in midwinter, will have moderated and the snow will be stabilized. Individual parts of the traverse can be skied with enjoyment in most years as late as mid-July.

The Peyto-Bow-Wapta Traverse is just a small part of a much longer traverse that ambitious skiers can consider doing from the Columbia Icefields to Lake Louise. This harder trip is done a few times every year. In the mid-1970s a group of adventurous Canadian ski mountaineers successfully completed a traverse of all the major icefields from Yellowhead Pass at the northern end to Lake Louise in the south, a trip with major mountaineering difficulties.

Most skiers opt for the shorter and easier Peyto-Bow-Wapta trip. It's a classic trip of medium length, following a natural route without serious obstacles, in a pristine mountain environment of flat white glaciers, striated peaks, and deep cliff-hung valleys.

Wyoming

Yellowstone National Park

TOUR From Old Faithful to the Bechler River Ranger Station in Yellowstone National Park, Wyoming.

IN A NUTSHELL The route starts at Old Faithful, heads to Shoshone Lake, and then to 3 River Junction at the head of the canyon of the Bechler River. Then it goes down the canyon, out through Bechler Meadows, and ends at the Bechler Ranger Station for a trip of 30 miles. Likely there will be 12 more miles of skiing down the road to Ashton, Idaho, until you get to where it is plowed.

WHAT MAKES THE TOUR SPECIAL Geysers, wildlife, waterfalls, meadows, and, especially, many hot springs. Some of these are swimmable, an indescribable pleasure on a winter camping trip.

LEVEL OF DIFFICULTY The skiing is all easy. The trip is a long one, though, so endurance and camping skills are important. Also bad weather, including extreme cold, is always possible in Yellowstone.

BEST TIME TO GO Late March or early April when the snow has consolidated and the temperatures are more moderate.

HOW TO GET THERE During the winter season take the snow coach from the east, north, or south entrances of the park to Old Faithful to get to the trailhead. If you go in April the road may be plowed from the west entrance to Old Faithful. Check ahead to see what travel status in the park is at the time you will be there. There could be a problem if you go just after the park finishes its winter season in mid or late March. But there is always a way to overcome such obstacles, such as catching a ride with a park employee or skiing in from Ashton, Idaho.

SPECIAL EQUIPMENT   You will need two cars to do the trip as outlined here. If you just do a loop from either side to 3 River Junction in the middle (site of the best hot springs) then you can do without the extra car.

MAPS   Trails Illustrated topo map of Yellowstone National Park, available from Trails Illustrated, Box 2374, Littleton, CO 80161.

OUTFITTERS   TW Services runs snow coaches and runs Old Faithful Snow Lodge, Yellowstone National Park, WY 82190, (307) 344-7311, and Yellowstone Alpen Tours, (406) 646-9591.

LODGING AND SUPPLIES   West Yellowstone, Montana.

F latlands, river bottoms, high mountains, deep canyons. Camping by hot springs, swimming in hot rivers, waking up to a 30°-below morning. Skiing by herds of bison and elk while geysers spout in the background. All this is part of the mystique of ski touring in Yellowstone.

Yellowstone is so big and has such a multiplicity of attractions that it is a hopeless task to pick out any one tour as the classic one in the park. As I started this book, I talked with as many people as I could who had experience skiing there. They all agreed that the park should be included in any collection of North America's classic ski tours, but they each seemed to have their own candidate for a tour that best exemplified the attractions of the park. This basically means that you can't lose on a ski trip to Yellowstone. Whether you are trying day jaunts on set tracks around the geysers or multiday wilderness treks through deep untracked snow, your trip will be a special one. One trip was mentioned more frequently and more vehemently than any other, the route from Old Faithful through the Bechler River Canyon to the Bechler Ranger Station in the southwest corner of the park. I'll describe it in some detail along with shorter descriptions of some of the other good tours in the park.

What are the attractions of Yellowstone for the ski tourer? They are pretty much the same as they are for the summer visitor, with the addition of much greater solitude. It is the best accessible place in North America to see wildlife while skiing. You can ski through an unmatchable set of geothermal features—geysers, hot pools, and steam vents—and on the Bechler tour you can enjoy soaking in hot pools after a hard day's skiing.

The greater part of the park is a high plateau that is the remnant of a collapsed volcanic caldera. It is a new landscape by the standards of geology, and the volcanic fires that built it are still active. There are thousands of hot springs, steam vents, and geysers scattered throughout almost every portion of the park. The altitude of the plateau is quite high for this northern latitude, around 8,000 ft, so snow is reliable and deep. The dominant tree covering most of the park is lodgepole pine, not a tree that is usually ideal for skiing since its forests are often uncomfortably tight. Compensating for that there is a good network of trails going to most of the points of interest in the park, and the forest is frequently broken by meadows. These trails and meadows make excellent ski routes. The caldera is bordered by high mountains on its northwest corner (Gallatin Range) and on its eastern edge (Absaroka Range). There are also some scattered peaks within the central portion of the park, such as Mt. Washburn and Mt. Sheridan. In terms of alpine grandeur these mountains are overshadowed by the spires and glaciers of the nearby Tetons, but they still have good terrain for ski mountaineering, and you can get a fine view of park features from many of their summits.

Yellowstone is one national park that encourages winter travelers. The road that runs across the northern boundary of the park is kept open all winter. Other roads are snow-covered but kept open to snowmobiles. There is regular commercial service via "snowcoach" to many points in the park, and these coaches are a good way to get to and from trailheads for ski trips. Cross-country track is set near Old Faithful and also in the north near Mammoth. Finally, the Snow Lodge at Old Faithful is open from December to March.

Despite all this activity, it should be made clear that all is not clear sailing for Yellowstone-bound skiers. If you are staying at the Snow Lodge at Old Faithful and skiing on the set trails, then there will be little problem whatever the weather or snow conditions. But if you want to camp out you must know that in midwinter Yellowstone is frequently the coldest place in the United States. Temperatures of 30° or even 40° below zero are not at all uncommon. Thirty degrees below in Yellowstone is not as gruesome as 30° below in Maine (it is invariably clear, calm, and dry in Yellowstone when it is extremely cold), but it is still cold. Skis act as though you were skiing on sand rather than snow, and no wax seems able to make them go really fast. Even if they move well on a packed trail, in midwinter you'll come to a halt as soon as you leave the trail. The constant cold keeps the snow from consolidating, and you are likely to end up wallowing, expending lots of energy without getting back any of the pleasure of skiing.

Thus for midwinter skiing it's best to stick to the short trips and set trails. These are still unusually rewarding ski tours. They'll take you to herds of bison and elk and around geysers and steam vents. There is also a commercial service that offers three-day trips with nights spent in heated tents.

If you want to try a longer trip like the one to Bechler Canyon, then it's best to wait till spring. One group tried it in midwinter in 1985 and had to be rescued after a storm left them floundering in deep powder snow. They simply could not make any progress. The best time for the trip is usually late March or early April. By then the snow will be much better consolidated and travel will be easy.

All of the people I know who have done the Bechler trip rave about its quality. But what makes it special? By the yardsticks used for most of the tours in this book, it is unexceptional. It does not climb any mountain and has little downhill skiing. There are no spectacular vistas of nearby peaks and glaciers. But there are other yardsticks that don't even apply to most other tours. What other tour offers hot baths and even hot showers? The route passes by some of the finest hot pots in the park. It also has unusual wilderness value. It is a long trip through country far from any road. The route fully samples the gentle beauty typical of Yellowstone—first through several thermal areas and then following the Bechler River down through its canyon, passing many frozen waterfalls along the way. The thermal features, the waterfalls, the open meadows, and the wildlife you will see along this route are its answer to the crags and slopes of the high mountain tours. One of my informants for this route called it "one of the world's best ski trips." I can't comment on that; after all it's a big enough job to find the best tours in North America, let alone the world, but such vehement praise indicates that this one should be on the list.

The trailhead is at Old Faithful. From there it heads to Lone Star Geyser, 3.8 miles away. The only problem you are likely to find along the way (and in Shoshone Geyser Basin further along the route) is getting your ski bottoms wet skiing over thermal areas and then having them freeze when you get back onto cold snow. Beyond Lone Star Geyser 1.5 miles, the trail leaves the Firehole River and starts climbing toward Grants Pass. The climb is minuscule by mountain standards, only a few hundred feet. Just below the pass the trail forks. The right branch goes to Bechler Canyon. The left branch goes to Shoshone Geyser Basin. Many groups travel the extra 2 miles to visit Shoshone Geyser Basin. It's a good place to camp, some 9.5 miles from the start and well worth a visit since it is one of the most scenic geyser basins in the park. Shoshone Creek is swimmable where hot springs mix with its cold water. You are likely to see such wildlife as elk in the thermal basin where the heat keeps the ground clear of snow. Birds and maybe even otters are found at Shoshone Lake, just a mile away and described by another one of my informants with these words: "Shoshone Lake has got to be one of the most beautiful places on earth."

Yellowstone in winter. Photo by Gary Halsey.

The Bechler Trail from the junction below Grants Pass runs through rolling forested country, going back and forth across the Continental Divide on its way to the headwaters of the Bechler. Finally the trail starts dropping toward the Bechler. On the way to 3 River Junction, where the Littles, Gregg, and Ferris forks join to form the Bechler, the route passes Twister Falls and Ragged Falls, which are just a taste of what's to come. The Bechler region of Yellowstone, the southwest corner of the park, has more waterfalls than any other section of the park, and quite a few of them are along or near the ski route.

The best swimmable hot pots in the park are located just a short way up Ferris Fork from 3 River Junction. In fact there are places where the whole stream runs warm enough to swim in. Where it runs over small falls you can take a hot shower! The usual policy of the Park Service vis à vis bathing in hot springs is to discourage it, but they make an exception for the Ferris Fork Hot Springs. There is a short trail leading to them. There are also many waterfalls up Ferris Fork.

For those seeking downhill thrills and a higher viewpoint, it is possible to climb up to the Pitchstone Plateau from 3 River Junction, a climb of about 1,400 vertical feet. The top of Pitchstone is a remarkable place to be on a good winter day. It's a congealed lobe of lava, almost 9,000 feet high, nearly flat on top, and forested with only very scattered trees. To the south you'll have an excellent view of the Tetons. It's also a remarkable place to be on a bad winter day, remarkable for the ease with which you can get lost, as well as for how little shelter there is from wind and cold.

From Old Faithful to 3 River Junction is 16.5 miles or two days steady traveling (not counting the side trips to Shoshone Geyser Basin or Pitchstone Plateau). From 3 River Junction the route starts dropping through the canyon of the Bechler River. This 7-mile-long canyon is notable for such large waterfalls as Colonnade Falls and Iris Falls. It also contains a chain of hot springs and a hot waterfall.

From the canyon the trail leads out into several miles of meadows. Here you may see bison or elk. People who have seen them here early in the spring say that often they appear to be just barely hanging on. If they moved down to the meadows to escape the deep snows of higher elevations, they made a serious mistake. Despite relatively low elevation of only 6,400 feet, the Bechler Meadows area receives the heaviest snowfall in the park. This is due to its position on the southwest side of the plateau. It's the first uplift that storms coming from the Pacific reach after hundreds of miles of southern Idaho desert. The west side of the Tetons, just a few miles to the south, get fully as much powder snow in the winter as the much better known Wasatch Range in Utah, that is, as much as anywhere in North America. Some groups have made side trips from Bechler Meadows to visit Silver Falls and Dunanda Falls to the west.

The final 3.5 miles of trail to the Bechler River Ranger Station run through dense woods. You've traveled 30 miles from Old Faithful. The trip isn't quite over yet since the road is not plowed in winter all the way to the ranger station. Most years you'll still have 12 boring miles left, skiing down the road. Since it is groomed for snowmobiles, it should at least be fast skiing. The road goes to Ashton, Idaho, where it joins the road from West Yellowstone, Montana. The entire 30-mile trip should take at least six days.

The whole trip is quite a long and involved venture. It requires two cars and a fair amount of time. Only one or two groups a year complete the whole trip. Many more do smaller portions of it. The trip from Old Faithful to Shoshone is quite popular and so is the trip from Old Faithful to 3 River Junction. To do the latter and return is just as long in distance as continuing down through the canyon, but it does relieve skiers of the hassle of shuttling cars. It's also not unusual for groups coming from Ashton to ski up to Bechler Meadows and the waterfalls bordering it.

Orville E. Bach, author of *Hiking the Yellowstone Backcountry*, writes, "The Bechler area or Cascade Corner of Yellowstone National Park is truly magnificent; no other region in the park better exemplifies Yellowstone's more gentle and serene wilderness." This is as true in winter as in summer—

maybe more so, since in winter the hot pots take so much of the sting out of winter camping.

Another good overnight ski trip in Yellowstone is to go to Heart Lake and climb and ski Mt. Sheridan. This is a shorter trip than the Bechler trip and has a different character. The trailhead is on the south-entrance road. The trail takes 8 level or descending miles to get to Heart Lake and Heart Lake Geyser Basin. It then continues south for 1.5 miles where it joins the Mt. Sheridan Trail, which climbs 2,700 feet in 3 miles to the summit at 10,308 feet. You probably won't actually follow the summer trail but generally climb up the north ridge. From the top you can see many of the special features of the Yellowstone region. Yellowstone Lake is to the north and the Tetons are to the south. Pitchstone Plateau is to the west and the Absaroka Mountains are to the east. The ski route down need not be the same as your ascent route. If conditions are very stable it is possible to ski down a large avalanche chute, the "Tube," almost all the way to the lake. It's an excellent run in an extraordinary region, but you must be very careful with evaluating the stability of the snow. The Heart Lake–Mt. Sheridan trip should take three days.

There are many even shorter popular trips in the park. I've already mentioned the set trails in the Old Faithful and Mammoth areas. The road along the northern edge of the park between Gardiner and Cooke City is kept open all winter, and there are several good tours from there. The Lamar Valley is an excellent place to see wildlife while skiing. The Slough Creek Valley is also reputedly an excellent trip.

Wyoming

Teton Crest

TOUR   A traverse of the crest of Wyoming's Teton Mountains.

IN A NUTSHELL   The route starts at Teton Pass and heads north via gentle bowls and providentially placed horizontal shelves. The short version ends by descending Cascade Canyon on the north side of the Grand Teton. It is possible to continue on and traverse the entire range.

WHAT MAKES THE TOUR SPECIAL   The scenery is some of the finest and most rugged in the west. The route, however, is surprisingly mild—a perfect ski highway through a land of jagged peaks. Access is easy. A perfect 3- to 4-day trip.

LEVEL OF DIFFICULTY   The skiing is, for the most part, not difficult. There is some avalanche danger. Escape is relatively easy in case of problems.

BEST TIME TO GO   Spring is the best time, but due to the easy access it should be possible to do it earlier given favorable snow conditions.

HOW TO GET THERE   Teton Pass is on WY 22, which connects Jackson, Wyoming, with Victor, Idaho.

SPECIAL EQUIPMENT   Carry avalanche beacons and shovels.

MAPS   Grand Teton National Park by Trails Illustrated, Box 2374, Littleton, Colorado 80161.

LODGING AND SUPPLIES   Jackson, Wyoming.

The sudden view of the Teton Mountains as you cross Togwotee Pass from the east is one of the most stunning sights in all of North America. The mountains seem to rise straight up out of the lakes at their base—a single swoop, with no foothills, of 7,000 vertical feet to the snowcapped summits.

Spectacular as the view is, none of it looks very favorable for finding moderate skiing. There are some very steep runs, maybe, down those jagged peaks but not any obviously gentle slopes, and certainly no routes going from peak to peak.

But the Tetons are a false-fronted range, and behind the wall of great peaks is a gentle above-timberline region of perfect ski terrain. The view of this region from the west (for instance, from the summit of the Grand Targhee ski area) is, to a ski tourer's eyes, just as spectacular as the more famous view from the east. A combination of shelves and glacier-cut bowls forms a traversing route that can be run for the entire length of the range from Teton Pass in the south to Berry Creek in the north.

The recommended route is a shorter version of the long traverse, comprising just the southern half. The long version is an excellent trip, but it takes a week to do and the chances of getting good weather for that long are slim. Furthermore, the northern half has more complex terrain with harder skiing and route finding, and greater avalanche danger. The short trip is less adventurous but has all the features it needs to be a classic on its own. You are much more likely to get good weather for the length of the short traverse. The terrain allows mostly easy skiing and relatively small slide danger, both of which are almost miraculous in a range with such jagged peaks. It goes through some of the most beautiful mountain terrain to be found anywhere. You can escape from the route at almost any point in case of problems. Access is easy in winter as well as in spring. Put it all together and it's hard to think of a more perfect mid-length trip of 3 to 4 days.

The Tetons are a small range, but one of great character. They are a fault block range running north to south with a precipitous east side and a gentle west side. As with the Sierra Nevada or Steens Mountain, this architecture is ideal for ski traverses. Skiers can stay high while sneaking around the peaks on the gentler west side. The range is only 40 miles long and 15 to 20 miles wide. Some numbers will show just how precipitous these mountains are: the highest point, the summit of the Grand Teton, is 13,770 feet and is only 3 miles horizontally from the plain at the base of the mountains, 7,000 feet lower.

Deep, narrow canyons separate the high peaks from each other. Erosion has cut the heads of these canyons well behind the line of the peaks. Thus the hydrographic crest of the range does not lie along that line but is to the west of it. That is where the ski route goes. The west side of the range is like a huge table that's been tilted upward and then cut by streams and glaciers. Many of the mountains on this side are perfect, easy ski descents. Table Mountain and Housetop Mountain are two examples of mountains that offer long runs on wide open slopes with nearly constant grades.

There are trails up most of the west-side canyons and a road penetrates deep into the largest of them, Teton Canyon. These are good escape routes in case of trouble on the traverse.

Just like the Sierra, the Tetons get their heaviest precipitation on the western slope. Unlike the Sierra, the inland location and northern latitude of the Tetons mean that wet snow is unusual. Instead, the west side is one of the prime powder snow areas in North America, and there is a ski area on that side, Grand Targhee, that gets fully as much powder as the more famous Utah ski area of Alta.

This powder is great for downhill skiers and also for car-served skiers skiing Teton Pass, but it is not so good for those attempting the traverse. Sometimes conditions will permit the trip early in the season, although I don't know of anyone trying it then. Otherwise spring is the best time after warm days have settled and consolidated the snow. This is one trip, however, where both access and escape are easy, and if unusually stable midwinter conditions prevailed, it would be practical to try it.

The Teton Traverse starts at Teton Pass, on WY 22, which joins Jackson, Wyoming, with Victor, Idaho. The route is kept open all winter. It starts with a climb up Mt. Glory, directly north of the Pass, then it traverses the west side of the crest until it drops to Phillips Pass. This stretch is all mellow skiing. From Phillips Pass, one follows the Teton Crest Trail as it traverses behind Rendezvous Peak, whose east side is the home of the great Jackson Hole ski area. This is where you first start seeing the architecture of north-to-south-running shelves that offer easy skiing in the middle of otherwise steep terrain. These shelves are the magic that makes the Teton traverse work. The skiing is far easier and more continuous than it should be in such a rugged, high-altitude, mountain environment.

At the head of Moose Creek is a climb of some 500 feet to a pass into Granite Creek. This is a good place for a first camp. From the pass the traverse drops a short way down the Middle Fork of Granite Creek and then climbs back up to Marion Lake. Up to this point, the route has been mostly in the trees. Avalanche danger has been relatively low. From Marion Lake skiers climb up to Fox Creek Pass. This is where the route gets really spectacular. Just a few minutes out of Marion Lake, skiers will find they have climbed above timberline to a view of the great peaks of the range.

At Fox Creek Pass the route crosses back onto the east side of the Tetons. Then it follows one of the unique terrain features of this route, the Death Canyon Shelf. The Shelf is like a four-lane highway, nearly level, with cliffs above it to the left and below it to the right. Without it skiers would have a hard time with lots of climbing and descending on steep slopes. With it, they can cruise for miles at an altitude of 9,500 feet with little work and much reward from the glorious scenery all around. The Shelf allows access to this classic route to less-skilled skiers as well as experts.

The Shelf ends at Mt. Meeks Pass. From there the route leads across the flat summit slope of Mt. Meeks and then topples off the side down a steep slope (the Sheep Steps) into Alaska Basin, a huge glacier-cut bowl. This slope is a potential point of avalanche danger. Alaska Basin is a good place for the next campsite. Within the basin is a short climb upward to Sunset Lake and further on to Hurricane Pass. The skiing possibilities in Alaska Basin alone are enough to fill several days. Whether skiing there or just lazing about at the campsite, the tone of life will be uplifted by the constant view of the snow-encrusted tower of the Grand Teton. The terrain is easy but interesting, climbing in gentle rolls up to Hurricane Pass. It's a fantastic place, made for skiers, whether they are mainly interested in downhill thrills or just standing mesmerized by the views.

From Hurricane Pass there is a good run down into the South Fork of Cascade Creek. Running right underneath the Grand Teton, this is also the scenic summit of the traverse. About 3 miles down the South Fork is Cascade Junction. On the short version of the Traverse, skiers will continue traveling down Cascade Creek all the way to Jenny Lake. A few miles of skiing around the lake will bring them to a plowed road.

It is prudent to keep an eye on the slopes above while going down Cascade Canyon. There is considerable avalanche danger there due to the steep walls overhead. In the spring special care should be taken on hot days.

The short version of the Teton Crest Traverse is such a perfect and unique trip that it should become a popular classic. The complete traverse is a much harder trip. For the long version of the traverse, skiers head back up the North Fork of Cascade Creek to Lake Solitude. A col above the lake permits access to the base of Littles Peak. There is a plateau-shelf system running for 5 miles north from Littles Peak. This gives a fantastic cruising run if the snow is right. The shelf is long, flat, and continually slopes gently downhill. It ends at a bowl heading down into Badger Creek. This is a fine place for multiple downhill runs. From here on the route gets more difficult. The magic shelves that helped so much previously disappear.

The problems start at the appropriately named Bitch Creek. After a climb to the top of Dry Ridge Mountain, the traverse follows the ridgecrest to the South Fork of Snowshoe Creek. This section is the crux of avalanche danger on the traverse. It is wide open, long, steep, and hard to avoid. The traverse goes around the head of the creek, then follows a ledge that sneaks

Alaska Basin and the Grand Teton. Photo by Steve Barnett.

its way above cliff bands over Talus Lake. A very steep couloir goes down to the lake, which is a good camp spot.

The route then goes up and over the ridge into Moose Basin. It circles around the west side of the basin to the Moose Basin Divide. Staying on the crest leads to Red Mountain and then to Forellen Peak. The terrain is easier here and drops back into the trees. The route from Forellen Peak leads into Berry Creek and out to the Snake River. It's a swampy 4-mile hike north along the river to the Reclamation Road that is the trip's end. When one group finished the trip, this section was so swampy that they kept their skis on to walk across the snowless swamp.

The Jackson Hole–Yellowstone area is one of the richest in ski-touring possibilities—as well as in scenery and wildlife—in the whole country. Besides the tours discussed at length in this chapter and the chapter on Yellowstone, there are many other meritorious ski tours here. Teton Pass, for example, is probably the best place in the country for the semi-decadent sport of car-assisted ski touring. A short drive up the pass opens up runs as long as 3,000 vertical feet. These can get crowded after a good fall of powder snow. There are good runs both to the east and west of the pass and on both the north and south sides of the road. Some of the better runs have considerable avalanche potential and should be evaluated carefully before being tried. On any good day some of the locals will be there and can probably provide valuable information about avalanches.

The Wind River Range, south of Jackson Hole, also has good terrain for long ski traverses. It is a much larger and wilder range than the Tetons, and trips into it are correspondingly more involved.

For those more interested in ski mountaineering epics on single peaks rather than relatively easy traverses, it is possible to ski the main Teton peaks. They have some of the longest and steepest down-mountain runs you can find in North America. The descent of Grand Teton is a famous example—and it has been done on 3-pin equipment. This is extreme skiing and requires special mental composure as well as a high level of skiing skills. Other runs, such as Mt. Moran, are easier but still steep enough and long enough to keep adrenaline junkies satisfied.

Utah

Mt. Superior

TOUR   Ski descent of the north side of Mt. Superior via Lake Blanche in the Wasatch Range of Utah.

IN A NUTSHELL   Climb up from Alta along the powerline on the south-facing slope opposite the ski area. Climb the east ridge up to Mt. Superior, ski down into Mill Creek, then up and over Cardiac Pass on the west side of the bowl to the ridge above Lake Blanche. Ski down to Lake Blanche and out to the S-curves on the Big Cottonwood Canyon Road.

WHAT MAKES THE TOUR SPECIAL   The whole western front of the Wasatch Mountains has what is probably the finest powder skiing in the world. The trip off Mt. Superior combines a long vertical drop with perfect powder-skiing terrain and great scenic beauty.

LEVEL OF DIFFICULTY   This is a steep descent, so a high level of skiing skill is required. More importantly there is a very high potential for avalanche here, so a high level of mountaineering sense is required. There are many tours nearby that are nearly as rewarding with less danger and difficulty.

BEST TIME TO GO   Any time from late November until May.

HOW TO GET THERE   From Salt Lake City, drive or take a bus up the Little Cottonwood Canyon road to Alta, only 30 minutes away.

SPECIAL EQUIPMENT   Avalanche rescue gear is essential. Carry a shovel, as well as an electronic locator or an avalanche cord. Wide, uniformly soft skis are best for skiing powder snow.

MAPS   USGS Dromedary Peak, Utah, and Mount Aire, Utah.

GUIDEBOOK   *Wasatch Tours* by Alexis Kelner and David Hanscom.

LODGING AND SUPPLIES   Salt Lake City, Utah.

To many skiers, downhillers and tourers alike, deep powder skiing is as close to heaven as they will get on this earth. They fly in the snow, banking and swooping with a rooster tail of powder spraying over their heads. It's totally exhilarating and not difficult to learn.

In all the world of skiing the Wasatch Mountains just east of Salt Lake City, Utah, probably provide the finest and most consistent deep powder skiing. Not only is there regularly new snow of just the right consistency for skiing perfection, but the terrain is just right for taking advantage of that snow.

The Wasatch Range is the easternmost of the Basin and Range fault-block mountains and is as special to skiers in its way as the first of these ranges, the Sierra Nevada of California. It rises 7,000 vertical feet in a spectacular north-south wall just east of the Great Salt Lake. Tucked between the mountains and the lake is Salt Lake City. Storms coming from the Pacific coast cross the long flat area of intermountain desert and pick up extra moisture over the lake. Then, when they hit the mountain wall they drop snow in house-burying depths. The snowfall drops off rapidly as the crest of the range is crossed. Thus Park City on the east slope of the Wasatch gets only half as much snow as Brighton, only a few miles away.

Much of the Wasatch ski activity centers on the big canyons that cut deep into the scarp of the range from the city limits of Salt Lake City, namely Big Cottonwood and Little Cottonwood canyons. Big Cottonwood Canyon is the northern one and contains the ski areas of Brighton and Solitude. Little Cottonwood Canyon is the more dramatic one. Alta and Snowbird are the ski areas in its upper end.

For many years powder skiing in the Wasatch meant skiing Alta. This was (and is) one of America's finest ski areas, and it had a powder-skiing mystique that attracted serious skiers from all over the United States. But there were many fewer powder skiers then and Alta powder could still be found in nooks and crannies many days after a storm. Skiing Alta is somewhat like touring—you have to make long traverses to reach many of the better slopes—and few powder skiers were serious enough in days gone by to ski out to the farther reaches of the area.

Nowadays, however, there are two first-class ski areas in the canyon, Alta and Snowbird. Utah has become a major destination resort for skiers despite its stringent liquor laws. There are often crowds and the lift-served powder is skied out fast. To get good powder skiing at the resorts, it's best to ski right in the middle of the storm. After the storm is over the best powder skiing is found ski touring.

Mt. Superior, Utah. Photo by Steve Barnett.

Lift-served skiing and ski touring complement each other in a natural way. When the big storms are raging it's not safe to tour because of the deadly avalanche hazard. The ski areas are carefully controlled and are the only places where it's safe to ski during or just after a large storm. By the time the storm is over and the snow stabilizes, the ski area's powder is going or gone and the touring powder is waiting. The Wasatch area is not extremely large, and the number of users makes it crowded by the standards of most western ranges. But there is enough room left for touring skiers to find some of the most enjoyable skiing imaginable anywhere in the world.

In some mountain ranges, such as the North Cascades, mountain touring is usually a matter of getting somewhere, of achieving a goal like a specific peak, a certain traverse, or some particularly high and beautiful ski run. It is rare that skiers there would consider the downhill run alone as the principal aim and thus repeat it again and again on any given day's tour. After all, only fanatics would boast, even to themselves, of skiing 6,000 vertical feet of breakable crust on their own power. At Alta the style of mountain touring is quite different.

Powder snow skiing at Alta is so reliable, the slopes so excellent, and the mountain runs so accessible that the downhill thrill is the focal point of tourers, just as much as it is for the helicopter skiers who share the Wasatch Range with them. In fact, day touring in the Big Cottonwood and Little Cottonwood canyons has as much in common, in spirit, with helicopter skiing as with wilderness touring. No wonder the style of touring here is to ski a shot of fresh powder and then climb, traversing to yet another one, and so on until you absolutely have to go home. It's common to climb 4,000 or 5,000 vertical feet in a day, getting in as many shots as possible. The willingness of the local skiers to work all day for their skiing is what keeps the touring from being completely decadent. They may get only 5,000 vertical feet of skiing instead of 15,000 feet, but they will get equal thrills and satisfaction. Like the heli-skiers, they count their runs. But while heli-skiers use vertical feet skied as a measure of the day's achievement, tourers are always figuring out how many turns there are in a given shot, as in, "That's a 100-turn shot there." If you hear someone talking that way, whether you're in Alaska or North Carolina, chances are they've been part of the Wasatch touring scene.

If you're skiing good powder with the telemark, you'll find it easy skiing once you learn to keep your weight from going forward as you finish your turns. The general rule is to keep an even weight distribution between both skis, to stay in the fall line, to ski faster than you dare, and to ski steeper than you dare. If you are parallel skiing, the same rules apply.

Wasatch powder is fun to ski with any skis, even ones as stiff as 2×4s. Even when it's deep it's usually forgiving. Still, some touring skis work better than others. Currently popular are wide skis like the Atomic Telemark O-T, or the Karhu Tele-Extreme. My experience with them is that they ski considerably faster, smoother, and easier than normal touring skis. Using them may be right in line with the oft-maligned process of "reinventing the alpine ski," but if the shoe fits why not wear it? They work better for this type of skiing.

Of course this skiing paradise cannot be without flaws—that would violate some universal cosmic rule of compensation. The flaw here is called avalanche—insidious, deadly, and common. Just when the skiing seems the most irresistible—with wide open, steep slopes and head-high fresh snow—is when the monster is hungriest. Practically everyone here has had some experience with avalanche activity. Even the most careful can tell about a slope that went when it really should have been stable. Avalanche danger is always a presence in Wasatch skiing. Perhaps its presence keeps the experience just a bit wilder and more intense.

The situation is lightened considerably by the ease with which information is available from the local ski patrols and from the heli-guides. They keep close tabs on the state of the snowpack at all altitudes and all exposures, and they are liable to know of any serious instabilities before you get going on your tour. Check. Whatever their assessment of the stability, you must carry avalanche rescue gear, such as electronic locators and shovels. You always must be aware of the condition of the snowpack—if it settles or cracks or if there are pockets of potentially dangerous snow blown in by the wind.

There are hundreds of good touring routes in the Wasatch canyons. Fortunately there's an exceptionally good guidebook available. It's *Wasatch Tours* by Kelner and Hanscom. One of its typical touring routes will start from one of the ski areas, climb up a neighboring slope, cross the ridgeline, and go down the basin on the other side. The routes are not at all difficult in terms of routefinding or complexity. The skiers make the tours last all day by repeatedly climbing up and skiing down the best parts of the downhill runs.

There are so many great touring routes in the Wasatch that it's hard to pick one out as the classic Wasatch tour. The run down from Mt. Superior to Big Cottonwood Canyon via Lake Blanche is typical of the best ski trips. It is a steep and frequently dangerous tour.

The trip starts with a climb from Alta to Cardiff Pass. It goes up a south-facing slope with few trees that climbs about 2,000 feet. The slope is steep enough to present an avalanche hazard, and your route should be carefully considered. There is a powerline running up to the pass, and it is wise to follow it as much as possible since its route was laid out to avoid slides. At the pass you traverse westward along the ridge (toward Salt Lake City). Then with skis off you climb up the rock and snow of the east ridge of Mt. Superior to its summit. Mt. Superior is a beautiful peak and a dominating presence over Alta. It is 11,132 feet high. From the east summit there are two chutes heading north down into the bowl at the top of Mill D South Fork Creek. They are both steep and dangerous. Much of the time the slide danger will be too high to ski them, but if conditions are right they are exciting skiing. You ski down these chutes (about a 250-foot drop) and continue down into the steep and treeless bowl below them. When I skied them the snow in the chutes itself was thick and difficult, perhaps because the heli-guides had used explosives to blow out any latent avalanches. Just as likely it was the natural effect of the wind loading snow over the summit into the chutes. Below them the terrain was protected from the wind and the powder was superb.

It's quite possible to continue on down Mill D South Fork, and it's a great tour on its own. But there's an alternative that will give you a bit more vertical drop and a wider variety of terrain. Climb up on the west side of the bowl to Cardiac Pass and on to the next glacial bowl, Mill Creek B South Fork. It is also possible to reach it without skiing from the summit of Superior by traversing under the peak. By any route the trip to the pass crosses slopes that are avalanche dangerous. Use extreme care on this tour and only try it when the snow is exceptionally stable. From Cardiac Pass you ski down to Lake Blanche at 9,926 feet. Along with Lake Blanche, there are Lake Lillian and Lake Florence in the wide upper drainage of the creek. The route below the lake drops steadily to 7,600 feet where it gets narrower and more forested. There is a summer hiking trail that you can follow on skis. It eventually drops you onto Big Cottonwood Road just above the S-turns at an altitude of 6,300 feet. That means the route has a vertical drop of 4,800 feet. This ski tour is described in some detail in the guidebook *Wasatch Tours*, which says on one hand, "Lake Blanche is considered by many to be among the finest ski tours in the Wasatch Range," and on the other hand, "The bowl under Mt. Superior is one of the most hazardous avalanche areas in the Wasatch."

I could go on about the touring pleasures of the Wasatch, but no description I give can really do it justice. I've been going there for 20 years, and I have yet to have a trip where the skiing was less than great. I know that sometimes they have bad years, but it can't be very often. There are a few other spots in the intermountain region that also stand out for their reliable deep powder, though no others have the same perfect combination of snow, terrain, and access. The best that I know of are the west side of the Tetons, the Bridger Mountain area near Bozeman, Montana, and the area around the Whitewater Ski Resort near Nelson, British Columbia.

Colorado

Colorado Grand Tour

TOUR   Colorado Grand Tour.

IN A NUTSHELL   This is a seven-day, high-altitude traverse from ski area to ski area, going from St. Mary's Glacier to Vail, via Winter Park, Loveland Basin, Arapahoe, Breckinridge, and Copper Mountain.

WHAT MAKES THE TOUR SPECIAL   Every night is spent in a resort along the way so that heavy camping gear need not be carried. Much of the climbing is circumvented by using the ski-area lifts. The skiing is often above timberline, and some of it is very good. This route was designed to be an American analogue of the famous Haute Route in the Alps.

LEVEL OF DIFFICULTY   Expert skiing is not required. Solid maneuvers that can get you down in poor snow are what you need. Good sense about avalanches and mountain difficulties are required, at least of the leader.

BEST TIME TO GO   April and May.

HOW TO GET THERE   The route repeatedly intersects I-70 or US 40 west of Denver.

SPECIAL EQUIPMENT   Maps, compass, altimeter, avalanche locator beacon, shovel. In winter, double boots, face mask, and goggles should be carried, but it's better to do this trip in the spring and be able to enjoy the sun.

MAPS   USGS Empire, Berthoud Pass, Byers Peak, Loveland Pass, Grays Peak, Montezuma, Keystone, Boreas Pass, Breckinridge, Copper Mountain, Vail Pass, Red Cliff, and Vail East.

LODGING AND SUPPLIES   Winter Park and Vail, Colorado.

In Europe, wherever there is a concentration of resorts there is also a network of established ski-touring routes connecting them. Mountain touring there is an established sport practiced occasionally by a large percentage of the downhill skiers. In the United States, the sport has just a tiny fraction of the popularity it does in Europe, and high-level traverses connecting ski resorts have not for the most part even been explored. Paul Ramer, a Colorado manufacturer of ski-mountaineering equipment, asked himself why. One reason, he decided, is that high-mountain ski touring is far more convenient in Europe than it is here. Huts are spaced along the popular routes so that instead of camping in the snow—and, incidentally, having to carry on their backs tents, stoves, sleeping bags, and such—ski tourers can sleep in comfort each night, eat a hot meal prepared by the hut staff, and carry light packs. Furthermore, access is easy almost everywhere in the Alps since virtually every mountain valley has a town or ski resort in it.

Ramer decided to find a route in Colorado that would be comparable to the famous High Route in France and Switzerland. Since Colorado is presently the home of the greatest concentration of downhill-skiing resorts in North America, it is the one place where such a traverse might be possible. The route he created, called the Colorado Grand Tour, connects most of the important northern Colorado resorts. It covers 90 miles in 7 days. You never have to camp out since you spend each night in a resort along the way. As much as possible, it uses resort lifts to gain altitude. The Grand Tour is thus much more European than the usual North American wilderness trip. It does reflect American realities in that it goes from road to road rather than from hut to hut. It's best to have two cars in the group to shuttle to and from the various trailheads.

The route goes from St. Mary's Glacier on the east side of the Continental Divide to Vail on the west side. You will climb a total of 20,000 vertical feet and will be rewarded with 27,000 feet of downhill skiing. There is no need to do the whole route all at once. It is likely, in fact, that as it becomes popular, it will be skied piece by piece over the course of several trips until the tourer has completed the whole tour.

Each day's skiing has a flavor distinct from that of any other day's tour. All have at least 3,000 feet of downhill running and range in length from 3 to 10 hours. Any segment makes a good day tour. Overall, the Grand Tour is unique in North America for its combination of length, high-altitude skiing, and civilized camping.

There are some serious problems with ski touring in Colorado. Those same meteorological facts that make the state so desirable as a destination for downhill skiers do not work in favor of mountain ski tourers. Colorado has a continental climate: the mountains are very high; the snowpack stays cold from late fall until early in the spring; a thorough thaw, as is common in the Sierra or the Cascades, is very rare in Colorado; and the total snowfall is lighter than it is in the coastal ranges. All this means that it is normal for a thick layer of depth hoar to form at the base of the snowpack early in the season and to stay there until spring. High winds are frequent over the Continental Divide, where much of the Grand Tour route wanders.

Thus the avalanche danger for ski tourers in Colorado is potentially higher than in any other popularly skied area in the United States. The problem is that weak layers remain dangerous for a long time due to the constantly cold snowpack. Avalanches in such conditions are unpredictable. Added to the problem of safety is one of difficult travel. The light powdery snow, beloved of downhill skiers, is not very good for tourers if it is deep. It gets even less dense if there are continuously cold nights and the snow metamorphosizes to TG snow. In midwinter in Colorado skiers commonly wallow in deep snow on the flatter parts of a tour. When it gets steep enough for skiers to move under the power of gravity, then the danger of avalanches increases and those slopes may need to be avoided entirely.

In some years some parts of the Grand Tour shouldn't be done until spring. Other legs can be done safely almost any time. For the most part the route follows as safe a line as can be found, and there are alternates, which I'll describe, for some of the more dangerous segments. In general, spring is the best time for mountain touring in Colorado. In the mornings the snow will have a good hard surface, excellent for fast travel. If your timing is right you can get to the top of each slope just in time to catch perfect corn snow for the trip down. By using the contours of the slope either toward or away from the sun, you can try to keep skiing just the right level of thawing snow as far down as you can. As long as the slope is frozen or just thawing, avalanche danger is likely to be minimal. You'll know when the danger is high by the unpleasant and soupy snow you'll be on, and you can take measures to avoid the danger. In some years there is no good spring skiing, due to continuous storms followed sometime in late May or early June by instant summer. April is statistically one of the stormiest months in the Colorado Rockies. But usually there will be a period of excellent spring skiing late in April or early in May. Even in late March or early April the snow will have consolidated tremendously from its midwinter level, and high-altitude touring will be easier, more pleasant, and safer.

There are some segments that are fine for midwinter. These are generally the lower-altitude and more popular ones, where skier traffic puts in a good track, where the forest protects you and the snow from the cold wind, and where the slopes are angled low enough to avoid most avalanche danger. The two best runs of that kind are the Commando Run from Vail Pass to Vail and the Day 5 Route from Montezuma to Breckinridge.

Now for the detailed route description, which follows closely that provided by Paul Ramer in *Alpine/Nordic 2* magazine.

On the Colorado Grand Tour. Photo by Steve Barnett.

Day 1: St. Mary's Glacier to Winter Park
Distance: 9 miles
Time Required: 7 to 9 hours
Maps Required: USGS Empire, Berthoud Pass

This leg crosses the Front Range over a 12,800-foot-high ridge. The Front Range is a notoriously windy place. Winds of 50 to 100 mph are not unusual along the crest of the Divide. At least this particular route gets you over the top quickly. Another possible first-day route, from Lake Eldora to Winter Park via Corona Pass, is not recommended because you spend a great deal of time slogging away while exposed to the elements above timberline and because the downhill skiing is not nearly as good as it is on the recommended route.

The tour starts near the old townsite of Alice. The nearest major town is Idaho Springs on I-70. Getting to the right starting point involves some careful map reading since there is a confusing maze of roads in the vicinity. Follow the Loch Lomond Road a short way from the Glory Hole, then drop down to a series of lower roads that lead to a level valley at 10,225 feet. If there is too much mud or snow on these roads, start the tour from the paved highway. The starting point is a sharp hairpin curve at the 9,600-foot elevation, right below the word "Fall" on the Empire topo map. Follow the nearly level jeep trail up to the large reservoir at 10,800 feet. Follow the left bank of the reservoir and take the road to Chinns Lake. The road starts just before a set of steel gate posts marked with "Private Property" signs. From Chinns Lake climb west-northwest to Slater Lake. You can also climb straight up from the reservoir to Slater Lake via a steep open gulch that goes up due west.

From Slater Lake follow the low ridge south of the lake up a broad valley to the high bowl south of Mt. Eva. Find a way through the cornices to gain the ridgetop. Descend the ridge to the south to reach the saddle below Mt. Flora. Ski down the huge bowl to the west. This will probably be windblown at the top but may hold good powder skiing down lower. We found good powder there in May. Keep out of the potential avalanche traps formed by steep, wind-loaded gullies. End the day by skiing along Eva Creek until it meets US 40 at the last hairpin just above the entrance to the Mary Jane Ski Area. Surprisingly, even though this creek follows a narrow path through thick forest, there was always a clear way down. The resort of Winter Park is just below you on US 40, and that's a good place to spend the next two nights.

Day 2: Berthoud Pass to Henderson Mine
Distance: 12 miles
Time Required: 5 to 6 hours
Map: USGS Berthoud Pass

The Berthoud Pass Ski Resort is on US 40 above Winter Park. Take the lift up its south side. Then an easy tour west followed by some scrambling up steep rocks gets you onto the flat ridgetop. You are on the Continental Divide. Since 7 miles of this day is on the Divide, it can be hellish if there's a high wind and fantastically scenic if it's a nice day. You can adjust your exact route accordingly. A long, gentle downhill traverse takes you to Vasquez Pass. If the weather is bad, drop down to the west side of the Divide and traverse southwest at the 11,800-foot contour until you get to the pass. There are several variants to the route from Vasquez Pass, and which one is best depends primarily on the weather. In the worst case you can ski down from Vasquez Pass and traverse at 11,200 feet to get to the jeep trail that goes down to the Henderson Mine. Go any lower and you will do as we did—spend hours fighting the way through thick brush. It is much better to continue along the Divide from Vasquez Pass. Either climb straight up the steep knife-edge ridge from the pass or traverse to the right of the ridge. You will get to a large, gentle bowl west of the Vasquez Tunnel. An easy climb will take you back up to the Divide. From here you can ski south down a gentle bowl. Some tree skiing at the bottom of the bowl will lead you to an obvious jeep trail. Follow it all the way down to the Henderson Mine. If the weather and the snow are both good, the best choice is to continue along the Divide and climb 500 feet up to the shoulder of Vasquez Peak. A number of bowls and gullies can be skied down from the ridge south of Vasquez Peak. This is excellent open terrain and generally not likely to avalanche because of its western exposure. The 2,000-foot downhill run is one of the best on the Grand Tour. Once in the valley, follow the Jones Pass jeep road back to the Henderson Mine.

Day 3: Henderson Mine to Loveland Ski Area
Distance: 12 miles
Time Required: 9 to 10 hours
Maps: Berthoud Pass, Byers Peak, Loveland Pass, Grays Peak

This is the toughest day of the tour. In compensation it has the greatest wilderness feeling of any stretch of the Grand Tour and it's exceptionally scenic.

From the Henderson Mine trailhead, take the main trail west for a short distance until you reach the Butler Gulch jeep road that heads sharply to the left. Follow the road or the drainage for 2 miles up to a huge level valley below the Divide. The remains of a few old mine buildings are still visible. Pick a safe route directly west and gain the ridge via a gap through the cornices. The best route down to the hanging valley below is a wide, steep bowl reached by traversing south along the ridge for about ½ mile. The bowl makes a fine downhill run. If there is avalanche danger, try the huge snow roll descending a shoulder to the north instead of skiing the bowl. You can reach this by walking west over the Divide. You can't see it until you are almost there.

Once into the hanging valley you can traverse south toward Bobtail Creek. Climb up Bobtail Creek and up the headwall below Hagar Mountain. This is a potentially dangerous spot. A mile's traverse (we did it on foot as the snow was mostly blown away here) will take you to a low spot on the Continental Divide just south of Hagar Mountain. Descend a few hundred feet, being very careful of danger from hard-slab avalanches, and make a long descending traverse south toward Mt. Trelease. From there you can ski straight down to the east portal of the Eisenhower Tunnel or traverse south to the packed runs of the Loveland Ski Area. The best bet for lodging for the next several nights is in the Keystone resort area on the western side of Loveland Pass. I'd like to particularly recommend the Inn Montezuma in the old mining town of Montezuma, where the food and the atmosphere are extraordinary, and where the owner is a mountain guide who knows every inch of the Grand Tour route.

Day 4: Loveland Basin Ski Area to Montezuma
Distance: 10 miles
Time Required: 6 to 8 hours
Maps: Loveland Pass, Grays Peak, Montezuma

This is an easy day since most of your climbing is done via ski lift. You start at the Loveland Basin Ski Area's #1 lift. Check in with the ski patrol before you go, and ski up to the low peak above the lift. Head for the divide and traverse southeast toward Loveland Pass. If the snow is good you can follow the west ridge and ski directly down the Little Professor avalanche path to Arapahoe Basin Ski Area. If you are unfamiliar with the area you should drive to Arapahoe Basin ahead of time, have the Little Professor pointed out to you, and memorize its location so that you can find it from above. This run absolutely should be avoided if avalanche warnings are out. A safer alternative is to traverse down to Loveland Pass, cross the road, and ski down the gentle valley to Arapahoe Basin. The Little

Professor faces south, so it can be soupy, miserable skiing—as well as dangerous—if you hit it too late in the day in the spring.

The next leg for this day is to use the Arapahoe Basin lifts and then climb up and cross the ridge above the ski area. You will have to make arrangements with Arapahoe Basin to be allowed by them to do this. From the top of the Lenawee lift, it's a short climb to the saddle above the bowl of Thurman Gulch. The top of the gulch is steep, and there are large cornices there. It's a potentially very dangerous spot. Under some conditions you shouldn't try it at all. Other times it can be snuck around and you can work your way to safer ground on the rockier edges of the gulch. And sometimes, particularly in the spring, it will be okay to just go ahead and ski it down the middle. Then it's an excellent, exciting run. Near the bottom of the bowl is a flat, forested area. Stay high on the left side of the valley and enter the trees no lower than 11,600 feet. A route through the trees is flagged and will lead you to the Argentine North Fork pack trail. (If you miss the trail you will be in for a really awful bushwhack.) You will intersect the Peru Creek Road near the old site of Chihuahua. From there follow the road west. At 10,174 feet take the old Montezuma Toll Road to the left and follow it for 1½ miles to Montezuma.

Day 5: Montezuma to Breckinridge
Distance: 16 miles
Time Required: 7 to 9 hours (a shorter version can be done)
Maps: Montezuma, Keystone, Boreas Pass, Breckinridge

This is the longest leg of the tour, but it is also the least difficult. Ski up the jeep trail directly across from the Inn Montezuma to the ghost town of Saints John. Follow the gently climbing valley to the broad pass west of Glacier Mountain. Go through the pass and ski the wide bowl that leads to the North Fork of the Swan River. You should pick up the jeep trail that follows the North Fork just beyond the two obvious avalanche paths you must cross. A fast four-mile schuss brings you to the valley floor a mile south of the old townsite of Tiger. You can exit at Tiger if you don't want to go via the long route. Otherwise, follow the snow-covered road south to Parkville and ski up the Georgia Gulch jeep trail to Humbug Hill. A screamingly fast run down the jeep road on the other side brings you to the end of the plowed road at Lincoln, just 3 miles from the resort town of Breckinridge.

Day 6: Breckinridge to Copper Mountain
Distance: 5 miles
Time Required: 4 to 6 hours
Maps: USGS Breckinridge, Copper Mountain

This is the shortest day on the route, but it does have an excellent downhill run. Take the lifts at Breckinridge as far up Peak 8 as you can go (if you do this in May the lifts will be closed and you'll have an extra 1,500 feet to climb). From the top of the T-bar, traverse to the north (left looking down) and then ski down a large bowl to the trees. Keep heading left and climb up to the saddle north of Peak 7. On reaching the saddle keep climbing to the top of Peak 6½ (12,438). There was a major avalanche accident in this area in 1987 (4 skiers killed). Be careful. Now ski down a huge bowl to the west and reach the top of a very steep avalanche chute. This offers a beautiful downhill run—if you catch it when snow conditions are good. In the spring travel the chute early in the morning. Soon you will come to a snow-covered road running parallel to Tenmile Creek. Ski down this road about a mile and you will see a trail heading left. There is a post marking it as the way to Copper Mountain. Ski on the trail over a bridge over the creek and out to the highway next to Copper Mountain Resort. If there is avalanche danger you can ski southwest from the pass below Peak 7 and follow the Wheeler Pack Trail. Stay to the right side of the steep gully in the trees. Use your compass and altimeter to ensure hitting the trail as it turns northwest out of the gully. Otherwise you will be in for bad bushwhacking.

Day 7: Vail Pass to Vail via the "Commando Run"
Distance: 18 miles
Time Required: 9 to 12 hours
Maps: Vail Pass, Red Cliff, Vail East

A Day 6½ from Copper Mountain to Vail Pass is missing here but is optional. There is a ski trail running for 5 miles along the I-70 freeway, but that trail is not aesthetically satisfying. You can also cross the ridge separating Copper Mountain from Vail Pass, and that is a decent but short tour with more uphill on it than downhill. It is scenic and at least it's not on the highway.

The leg from Vail Pass is a popular day tour called the Commando Run. It is one of the most scenic legs of the Grand Tour and has interesting skiing as well. It is highly recommended as a day tour in its own right. Follow the Shrine Pass Road north from Vail Pass and cross Shrine Pass. Keep following the road and Turkey Creek until you descend to about the

10,800-foot contour on the Red Cliff map. Contour northwest to a saddle at the head of Timber Creek. At this point start climbing west toward an indistinct rise that is actually 1,000 feet above you. The climbing is not very steep, but it is easy to get disoriented in the dense forest. Once on the ridge, follow it west, rising and falling, to Point 11,696, and then north over Point 11,618. Don't stray off the ridge or you will be in trouble. There are trail markers most of the way. A fine downhill run through the trees takes you to Two Elk Pass. From here there is a 1,000-foot climb up the treeless south-facing slopes of Siberia Peak. From Siberia Peak you can either go west along the ridge to the top of the Vail Ski Area or north down the gentle slopes of Mushroom Bowl. A road along Mill Creek at the bottom of the bowl will take you to the lower slopes of the ski area.

This is the official end of the Colorado Grand Tour. It is possible to extend it to the Beaver Creek Ski Area and then to Aspen. A low-level route, the 10th Mountain Trail, is already partially in place between the two resorts. A high-level route running past the impressive peak, Mount of the Holy Cross, should also be possible. From Aspen it would be natural to continue on to Crested Butte, making a very grand tour indeed, lasting at least two weeks.

It seems only right while on such an extensive tour of the central Colorado high country to climb at least one of Colorado's 54 14,000-foot-high peaks. One of them, Quandary Peak, is skiable to the summit and can be climbed in an easy day trip from several of the resorts on the Grand Tour. The peak has steady, moderate slopes with a vertical descent of 4,000 feet. To get there take CO 9 past Breckinridge toward Hoosier Pass. Quandary Peak will be prominent to the right just a few miles below the pass.

Colorado

Aspen to Crested Butte

TOUR   A ski route from Aspen to Crested Butte, Colorado.

IN A NUTSHELL   This 20-mile route follows a primitive jeep road from the townsite of Ashcroft to Pearl Pass. The Tagert Hut is situated just north of the pass. The route then heads down the East Fork of Brush Creek into Crested Butte. There is another hut, the Friends Hut, on the south side of the pass. Between the huts skiing is above timberline.

WHAT MAKES THE TOUR SPECIAL   Aspen and Crested Butte are both popular ski resorts. This is a moderate route with relatively low avalanche hazard. Because of the huts it can be an unusually comfortable high-mountain tour. The huts make good bases for exciting above-timberline skiing, including ski ascents of Castle Peak and Star Peak.

LEVEL OF DIFFICULTY   Moderate.

BEST TIME TO GO   March and April are best, but anytime from December to May is reasonable.

HOW TO GET THERE   From Aspen, take Castle Creek Road to Ashcroft, where the trailhead to Pearl Pass is located.

SPECIAL EQUIPMENT   Carry goggles and a face mask.

MAPS   USGS Pearl Pass, Crested Butte, Hayden Peak.

GUIDEBOOK   *Colorado High Routes* by Louis Dawson, The Mountaineers, Seattle, 1986.

HUT INFORMATION AND RENTALS   For the Tagert and Wilson huts write to Fred Braun, Hut Committee Chairman, 302 Main Street, Aspen, CO 81612.

For the Friends Hut write to Friends Hut, Inc., Box 3055, Aspen, CO 81611.

LODGING AND SUPPLIES   Aspen and Crested Butte, Colorado.

There's only one resort in the United States that is developing an extensive surrounding network of mountain huts. That resort is Aspen. The network opens up the nearby backcountry to vacationing skiers as well as to the local ski tourers. It's possible that the huts and the convenience and comfort they imply for winter camping will introduce the sport of skiing wild snow in wild mountains to many more downhill skiers than are now interested in it. So far the hut network has been highly successful. It doesn't hurt that the huts are in one of Colorado's most scenic ranges, the Elk Mountains. The most famous mountain scene in Colorado, that of the Maroon Bells from Maroon Lake, is in the Elks.

The Elk Mountains run generally from east to west. Aspen is to the north of the crest, and Crested Butte lies to the south. The resorts are not far apart as the crow flies, but there is no easy way to get from one to the other in the winter. The trip by car is nearly 300 miles long. It shouldn't be surprising then that the ski route between them, only 20 miles long, has become a favorite of skiers in both towns. It is a classic trip both in the sense that it is already one of the most popular above-timberline ski tours in the country and that there is some very exciting skiing possible along it.

There are several routes between the resorts, and each has its good points. The route that goes over Conundrum Pass has the enormous advantage of passing by Conundrum Hot Springs, which fact alone should place it in the rank of classic tours. It's also very scenic. The trouble with it is that there is a lot of danger from avalanches along the way and there are also potential route-finding difficulties. Basically it's a route that should only be done in the touring season of March, April, and May.

The route over Pearl Pass (12,800 feet) isn't as spectacular as the Conundrum route, but it has two huts to take the place of the hot springs, is much safer, and can be done any time in the winter. It is a good trip in either direction, and I'll describe it starting from the Aspen side. The route to Pearl Pass is 8 miles long from its start and climbs 3,200 feet. The starting point is the townsite of Ashcroft, which is reached from Aspen by the Castle Creek Road. Two miles up the snow-covered Castle Creek Road there is a turnoff to the right to the Pearl Pass Road. About 4 miles out of Ashcroft there is a series of steep switchbacks. Right above them there is another turnoff to the right. This goes to Montezuma Basin and is the route for a ski attempt on 14,265-foot Castle Peak. If you continue on the Pearl Pass Road for ¼ mile beyond the turnoff, you will see the Tagert and Wilson huts on the hillside just to the east of the creek. The huts are just a little below timberline, and as you approach them the road may get lost under the windblown snow. Because of the popularity of the huts the trail is almost always packed out by previous skiers, and thus you can avoid the dreadful midwinter Colorado problem of wallowing in the cold, deep, powdery snow.

The huts are rustic A-frames that each can hold about twelve people. They have wood stoves for both heat and cooking and Coleman lanterns for lighting. You must reserve space in order to be able to use the huts. The appropriate addresses are given in this chapter's sidebox.

The huts are on the direct route to Crested Butte, but they are also conveniently located as a base for a good range of high-altitude skiing in the Pearl Pass area. It makes sense, if possible, to take an extra day and explore some of the skiing possibilities.

Three large peaks are accessible in day trips from the hut, Castle, Cathedral, and Conundrum peaks. Castle Peak, in particular, can be a great ski-mountaineering ascent and descent. To get there just go back down to the Montezuma Basin road, climb up to its end, and climb up the bowls above. With good conditions you can ski off the summit itself, down the ridge to the northeast, and then down a gully to the snowfields below. This is a tour that should only be done in the spring, when the snow is stable. In fact it is one of the few Colorado tours that can be done in the summer— for a few years one entrepreneur even ran a portable ski lift in Montezuma Basin throughout the summer months.

Montezuma Glacier is not a real glacier—there are no crevasses or other signs of slowly flowing ice—but it is a large permanent snowfield. In most places in the world outside of the Tropics, peaks as high as the Colorado Rockies would be glaciated, but they actually have almost no real glaciation. The snowfall, while modestly deep and quite reliable, is not so deep and especially not so heavy as it is in the coastal ranges. Also, the summers are hot. The first sizeable glaciers you will encounter in the Rockies are in the Wind River Range of Wyoming, and even these are small by Cascade standards. The Canadian Rockies do not have much, if any, greater snowfall than the Colorado Rockies, but the summers are cooler and great glaciers can grow at much lower altitudes than you would need at the latitude of Colorado. You can judge the relative climates by the timberline. In the

Canadian Rockies it is at around 7,000 feet. In central Colorado it is at 11,500 feet. Even in the tropical mountains of Peru the treeline is no higher than 12,500 feet, which shows just how arid and how hot in summer Colorado is.

Earlier in the season when Castle Peak and its neighbor, Conundrum Peak, are still inaccessible because of avalanche danger, it is possible to ski in the gentle bowls above the hut, in Pearl Basin under Pearl Pass. These are all above timberline and are often wind scoured. This tends to make them safer from avalanches (except for lee pockets in the steeper walls above the bowls, which can be the site of small but dangerous slides even when conditions seem safe), but it creates difficult snow for skiing. Wind-scoured snow mixed with pockets of powder and patches of ice is typical when skiing above timberline in the Colorado Rockies or in almost any other range. You will have to learn to live with it and enjoy it if you want to enjoy the splendor of skiing in the vast white spaces above the trees. On the Aspen to Crested Butte tour, you do have some choice in the matter since one side of the pass is north facing and the other, the Crested Butte side, is south facing. Thus in March you might have good soft-snow conditions on the south side while it's still a windblown, icy mess on the north. In April it might be good on the northern exposure while it's too soft on the south.

Above timberline the wind may also eradicate the trail left by other skiers. You will have to navigate carefully to be sure of going over Pearl Pass and not getting sidetracked over one of the pseudopasses on the ridge west of the route. Keep heading to the southeast. There are steeper slopes just below the pass that might be wind loaded and dangerous. You have to keep track of the snow conditions and vary your route accordingly. When going above timberline in the mountains, it's a good idea to keep a compass handy and have a clear idea where your landmarks and your destination are. Whiteouts caused by fog or windblown snow can develop with remarkable speed, and once you are in one you can't see anything. Also, the terrain above timberline in Colorado is often much more confusing than that below, where you are usually following one drainage or another. In this case it's important to keep from skiing down into Cooper Creek, which is the natural drainage for Pearl Pass.

The absence of trees above timberline lets the wind blow at you unimpeded. It's a good idea to have goggles and a face mask so that you can function comfortably above the timberline. Sometimes in midwinter at those high altitudes there will be very cold temperatures. Fortunately it's rare to have both high wind and intense cold together. The Colorado sun is intense and the air dry so that cold temperatures there needn't stop you.

Once over the pass, you want to descend on the east side of the basin. There is another hut there, the Friends Hut, which sits on a knoll at 11,400 feet in the last stand of trees before timberline. It is about 4.5 miles from the Tagert and Lindley huts.

The Friends Hut is newer than the other huts and is more spacious, lighter, and better furnished. Particularly interesting is its photovoltaic lighting system. It also has a propane cooking stove. There is several days' worth of good skiing around the hut. The best mountain descent within reach is that of the south side of Star Peak, 13,521 feet high. The skiing there ranges from advanced to extreme. The bowl below Pearl Pass has good intermediate skiing. All of these slopes are south facing and thus will have very different snow conditions, sometimes much better and sometimes much worse than the slopes on the other side of the pass.

To get to Crested Butte from the Friends Hut, continue traversing, dropping slowly for 1.5 miles until you get to the valley of East Brush Creek. Just below, at 10,800 feet, you will meet a pack trail that comes up the creek. You follow it down, diverting yourself only to avoid several large avalanche runouts. The trail will become a snow-covered road and then join other such roads coming down the Middle and then the West forks of Brush Creek. Finally, about 11 miles from Pearl Pass you will get to the end of the plowed road, just a few miles away from Crested Butte.

How do these huts compare to the Durrand Glacier Hut described in the Durrand Glacier tour in this book? First of all they are meant for a somewhat different purpose. The Tagert, Wilson, and Friends huts are all meant to be way stations on the route between Aspen and Crested Butte. The fact that there is good skiing easily reached from them is something of a coincidence. The Durrand Hut was carefully sited for maximum access to the great skiing around it and was meant to be a base for ski explorations in every direction. The Colorado huts don't have good tree skiing below them; but you aren't likely to face being trapped by a storm in them. You can just about always ski out easily. The Durrand Hut has good tree skiing, but it needs it since it's easy to be pinned there by a storm that doesn't allow the helicopter to fly.

The Aspen to Crested Butte tour is a simple, classic trip that, thanks to the huts, you can do with light packs and still enjoy spectacular high-altitude skiing. It's probably the forerunner of a type of skiing experience that will someday be common around the ski resorts of the mountain West.

There are many other ski tours of rare quality in the Aspen area, including several good mountain descents. An exceptionally useful guide to them is Lou Dawson's *Colorado High Routes*, published by the Mountaineers of Seattle.

Colorado

San Juan High Route

TOUR   San Juan High Route.

IN A NUTSHELL   A three-day trip connecting four old mining towns on the western side of the very rugged and high San Juan Mountains of Colorado. Each day leads from one old mining town to another by crossing an above-timberline ridge or pass.

WHAT MAKES THE TOUR SPECIAL   These are Colorado's most rugged mountains. The route gives you a chance to travel through them while spending each night in a different town. The skiing is spectacular and exciting. Each town has great character. The range as a whole is the most beautiful in Colorado. The weather in the spring is likely to be hot and sunny in the day and cold at night, perfect for good corn-snow skiing.

LEVEL OF DIFFICULTY   This trip demands the ability to ski steep slopes. It also demands knowledge about avalanches. There is very high potential avalanche danger, though it can be minimized by traveling in the mornings in the spring.

BEST TIME TO GO   Late April to June.

HOW TO GET THERE   Silverton, the first town on the route, and Ouray, the last one, are both on US 550 in southwestern Colorado.

SPECIAL EQUIPMENT   Skis should be good for serious downhill runs, either heavy, metal-edged Nordic skis or alpine touring gear. Avalanche beepers and shovels should be carried, as well as maps and compass. Sun protection is also necessary.

MAPS   USGS Telluride, Ophir, Silverton, and Ironton; all are Colorado quadrangles.

LODGING AND SUPPLIES   Telluride, Colorado.

Colorado is the downhill skier's Mecca in the United States. It has the glitziest, best-known resorts, easy access through a major metropolis in Denver, and reliable snow and sunshine. It also has most of the highest mountains in the United States. After all this it must be said that many of the same factors that are good for downhill skiing are bad for touring. There's little deep wilderness like you find in the Cascades or the Sierra; too many old mining towns and old mining roads penetrate even the highest areas. The avalanche danger in winter is relatively high; the constant cold allows instabilities to linger long after storms are over. Below timberline, the midwinter snow is often too dry and unconsolidated for easy traveling; good powder skiing on the downhill means wallowing on the way up. The summer skiing is not as good as it is in the Cascades; the sun is too reliable and the snow too dry to last long. The scenery for the most part is not up to the standards of the Tetons, the Wasatch, or the Sierra; the mountains, while high, start high and are for the most part big, rolling, above-timberline lumps.

One major exception to the last problem, scenery that is majestic rather than spectacular, is the subrange of the Rockies in southwestern Colorado called the San Juan Mountains. These mountains rise to 14,000-foot heights in a series of horns and spires. They're the most alpine of all the Colorado mountains, and they get some of the state's heaviest snowfalls. Not surprisingly they contain some of the best ski touring in the state as well.

There are two big problems with San Juan touring. One is that the avalanche danger is very high in midwinter, because of just those factors that make them attractive, steep mountains and heavy snowfall. Second, access is difficult. These mountains are a long way from either Denver or any other major urban center. This is a problem you can't avoid; you just have to assume that the trip is worth it. At least they are on a natural route from Denver to the wonders of the southwestern desert.

The problem with avalanches is circumvented by going there in the spring when the morning skiing will be safe. As it warms up and the snow gets soft, try to stay on northern exposures. When they get too soft, well into the afternoon, retire for the day. This is one place where you have a good chance of having real Bikini weather on a ski tour—hot sun, good corn snow, and beautiful mountains all around you.

There is a great multiday ski traverse in the San Juans that is really a linked series of day trips between old mining towns. You can carry light loads and enjoy civilized comforts overnight while still enjoying magnificent big-mountain skiing during the day. It's the type of trip that's common in Europe but very rare in the American West. The only other one that is close is the other long Colorado tour in this book, the Grand Tour.

The trip goes through four old mining towns—Silverton, Ophir, Telluride, and Ouray—and crosses three 13,000-foot passes between them. Only one of the towns, Telluride, is a regular ski resort, and it has managed

On the San Juan High Traverse. Photo by Peter Shelton.

to retain a great deal of its old-time charm. Start at Silverton and climb up to the Ice Lake Basin. The drainage is gentle, with scattered trees and frozen lakelets along the way. As you pass timberline the ground gets steeper, and at the headwall over the basin you're on really precipitous ground. Over that barrier you enter the Upper Ice Lake Basin, a treeless, alpine bowl, and also a giant reflector oven in the hot afternoon sun. If the snow is getting too soft you may have to camp there. From the basin climb up to a high pass (between the unnamed peaks 13,333 and 13,400). From there you have a choice among three steep couloirs that lead down to Waterfall Canyon, which in turn takes you to Ophir. Just which couloir you take depends on how courageous you feel that morning. After braving the couloirs, open bowls below them offer delightful and easy skiing before narrowing down into the canyon. Ophir is very small and undeveloped; to stay there it's best to cultivate a friendship with a local.

The next step after Ophir is Telluride, a day away. Start up Chapman Gulch, on the east side of Ophir, and work your way up its huge pile of avalanche debris. It leads onto open slopes that you follow straight up for thousands of vertical feet. It's a long climb. The point you're aiming for is marked 13,432 on the map, a small peak that stands above three drainages: Ophir Valley (you just came up Ophir Creek), Bridalveil Creek, and Bear Creek (the one that goes down to Telluride). It's a beautiful piece of skiing real estate and one of the favorite high tours for the skiers of Telluride. Like so many of the other parts of the trip it starts out steep, continues with easy alpine skiing in a vast setting, and finishes with a steep but short couloir. Telluride, a ski resort of more than usual charm, offers all the amenities you could want for a day or two of recuperation.

From Telluride take one of the old mining roads that criss-cross the area and climb up Tomboy Road to Tomboy Mine. Above it is Savage Basin and Imogene Pass, 13,114 feet high. Down its other side to Ouray is one of the finest ski runs in Colorado, a vast alpine basin with open-glade tree skiing lower down (often missing in Colorado skiing where the forests tend to be thick with lodgepole pine). Pick up the remains of the mining road that comes up from the Camp Bird Mine and follow it down till you run out of snow or reach Ouray, whichever comes first.

The best time for this trip is in the spring, April or May. Most winters any piece of it would be too dangerous to contemplate. In unusual years when the midwinter snow is stable it could be possible, and you might compensate for the harder going, slogging uphill, by deep powder runs on the downside. You also don't have to do it all at once. Any one piece of it will make an excellent short tour and will give you an exposure to the San Juans.

High levels of skiing skill and mountain sense are required for this trip. There is more mandatory steep skiing on this route than on any other in the book. The potential avalanche danger is also at least as high as on any other tour described in this guide. Both are caused by the double-cirque architecture of this part of the San Juans. There are steep slopes at the bottoms of the mountains, gentler areas in their middles, and steep, glacier-cut cirques at the tops. This is exceedingly rugged country. Of course that's also its appeal—to be able to forge a great ski route through the cliff bands and cirques and underneath the spires and summits of the San Juans. The San Juans extend south into New Mexico. The gentle area around Cumbres Pass, Colorado, just north of the border, is a favorite of New Mexico tourers. It's a perfect area for cross-country skiing mixed with short mountain downhills.

Desert Southwest

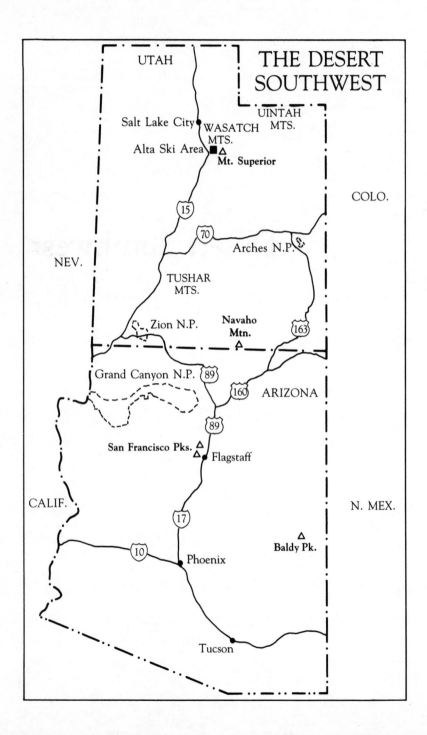

Utah

Arches National Park

TOUR   Skiing in Arches National Park, Utah.

IN A NUTSHELL   Even a thin layer of snow on the sandy trails or smooth sandstone formations lets Arches National Park become a fantastic skier's playground. Most of the ski tours are short trips, but overnight ones are also possible.

WHAT MAKES THE TOUR SPECIAL   The tour is on, through, and around some of the world's most beautiful and unusual desert scenery.

LEVEL OF DIFFICULTY   These are easy tours.

BEST TIME TO GO   The skiing is good whenever there's a sufficient snowfall, usually by some time in December or January. It's best to call ahead to the park headquarters, (801) 259-8161, for information about snow conditions.

HOW TO GET THERE   Arches National Park is only a few miles north of Moab, Utah, on US 191.

MAPS   The park maps available at the Visitor Center will suffice.

LODGING AND SUPPLIES   Moab, Utah.

A rches National Park in Utah has some of the strangest, most astonishing, and most fun ski touring in the entire world. Its desert environment is what makes it so special.

137

Arches National Park. Photo by Steve Barnett.

To many people, the deserts of the Southwest seem almost as alien as Mars. Bare rock rises in impossible shapes and with colors of unreal intensity. The sun is intense, too, as is the cold at night when the day's heat radiates away into a clear sky. But while strange, the desert parks are seen by many people not as wastelands but as natural treasures with a sense of place unique in all the world. Their strangeness has such geometric order, such a wealth of exquisite detail, and so well fits our aesthetic sense of color and form that for some people the inhospitable desert exerts a fascination greater than any other place. The writings of Edward Abbey exemplify this desert obsession and have hit a responsive chord with many other people.

I too have felt the fascination of the Southwest and have made several trips to Zion, Arches, Bryce, and Canyonlands national parks. Even though my favorite mode of wilderness travel is skiing, it took a long time for me to realize what an exceptional experience skiing in these desert parks can be. After all, as a downhill skier I've been conditioned to think of skiing as something you do in areas of consistently heavy snowfall. But one of the beauties of cross-country skiing is that it allows you to take advantage of the year's only snowstorm, one that coats a normally most unwintry scene and totally transforms its character. Gliding on skis through such formerly familiar surroundings—now quite exotic—feels magical. In the snow-covered desert this pleasurable feeling of transformation and unreality becomes even more intense because the surroundings are so exotic and because the contrast of red rock, white snow, and blue sky is aesthetically perfect.

In January 1978, a friend and I stopped in Arches National Park for a day of hiking. We were en route from Alta, Utah, to Telluride, Colorado, on a long ski vacation, and we had no intention of skiing at the park. There wasn't even any snow at the park entrance. But at the road's end, 1,500 feet higher, there were about six inches of sun-hardened snow with two inches of fresh powder on top of it. That doesn't sound like much, but it was enough to keep us from hitting rocks and soft enough on the surface to be really enjoyable. We skied through a natural gateway in a wall of sandstone fins, a narrow slot, and then continued on toward Landscape Arch, the park's biggest. We were stunned by the beauty of the snow-covered forms. The storm that had deposited the powder was still lingering, so distant spires moved mysteriously in and out of view as the fog shifted.

This part of the park consists of a long ridge, the top of which is covered with systems of parallel sandstone fins, some of which have eroded into towers and arches. These fins are mostly wide and smooth enough to ski on top of so it's possible to go along the ridge on top of the fins, occasionally making a tricky move to get from one to the other and sometimes skiing in the slots between them. The terrain is so complicated with hidden cul-de-sacs, arches, and side valleys leading off the ridge that there's always a sense of discovery, of wondering what will be around the next corner.

Landscape Arch is 300 feet long and positioned so that you tend to miss it at first since it's difficult to pick it out from the background. Then, all of a sudden, it snaps into view. It's so thin, delicate, and big, you can barely believe it can exist. We climbed up to it and telemark turned under it before returning to the car and continuing on our way to Telluride.

Skiing Arches for half a day was probably the high point of a trip full of high points of skiing mountains in deep powder. It seemed necessary to come back again and spend a longer time exploring the park in winter. Luckily the winter of 1978 to 1979 was the coldest and snowiest in the Southwest that anyone could remember. There was snow everywhere: Monument Valley, Zion, Escalante, and Canyonlands. What was really unusual was that it stayed on the ground for months instead of melting off in days. I returned to Arches around February 1 with Mark Hutson, an adventurous Washington ski mountaineer who had never previously visited Utah. A group of friends from Alta joined us. All were overwhelmed by the skiing and the scenery.

I had thought of Arches as a small national park. It has only one road and few long trails. However, it turned out to be more varied than I had supposed. Every region had a unique sense. One day we'd ski in open desert up to isolated arches or towers, another day through red walls like a medieval town. One of the nicest ski tours was along Courthouse Wash, the bed of a highly intermittent stream. This was nearly flat and covered with several inches of ice topped by half a foot of snow. It was a perfect surface for fast cross-country running. The wash runs for miles past the Courthouse Towers and into a canyon that gradually closes. Frequent side can-

Delicate Arch, Arches National Park.
Photo by Steve Barnett.

yons with their own washes and sandstone monuments demanded explora-tion. Sometimes we'd go up a side canyon, take off our skis, and climb as high as we could up the horizontal ledge systems in the canyon walls. Once the ledges were so interconnected that we actually could climb the wall on skis, leading to some truly bizarre downhill between ledges later on.

Another unusual ski trip was up to Delicate Arch, one of the most beautiful in the park. One part of the trail leads up a wide, tilted, abso-lutely smooth sheet of sandstone. Later it threads along a steep wall with vistas of snow-covered sandstone peaks that reminded me, unbelievably, of the Canadian Rockies. Delicate Arch itself stands alone on the rim of a smooth sculptured stone bowl. The whole effect was like being above the timberline in an alpine mountain range.

Of course there were also constant reminders that we weren't in high mountains, adding to the unreal feeling of the scene. Mountains express strength—irresistible forces bending rock miles high, avalanches cleaning out miles of forest, glaciers carving thousands of feet deep into the rock. The sculptured Southwest deserts have a different sense—that just as age weathers a human face and gives it character, time has eroded the plateau and millennium by millennium has given it a surface that has enough nooks and crannies, canyons, slots, arches, and fins to reflect every year of its history. There's a constant excitement and feeling of discovery to gliding on skis through the visual splendor of this terrain, even though most of the tours are short and easy.

Arches is one place where a nonskier or a family can have a great experience on skis. No skiing expertise or mountaineering knowledge is necessary. Overnight trips are possible but are not at all necessary to enjoy the park. You can car camp in the park in the winter, but it's also possible to stay in the town of Moab, Utah, just a few miles away.

The real trick to skiing Arches is getting there when there is snow covering the ground. This happens sometime during December, January, or February during almost any winter, but it's impossible to say when. A winter like we experienced in 1978–79 when the snow stayed for months can't be anticipated. All you can do is keep calling the park to find out if there's snow in the upper portions. Remember though that a trip to Arches when the snow vanished just the week before you got there isn't wasted. It's a great place on foot as well as on skis. Furthermore, if there isn't snow at Arches, there certainly will be snow in the nearby La Sal Mountains, which are an excellent small range for skiing. They are a lacolithic range, like Navajo Mountain, covered in another chapter in this book, and like Navajo Mountain they stand all alone in the midst of glorious desert scenery, with the mountains of Colorado gleaming white in the distance.

Utah

Zion Traverse

TOUR   A traverse through Zion National Park, Utah.

IN A NUTSHELL   The route goes up from the main Zion Canyon, via the West Rim Trail, traverses the Kolob Plateau, and descends via the Kolob Canyons. It should take 5 days.

WHAT MAKES THE TOUR SPECIAL   This route goes through some of the most spectacular desert formations in the world. The weather is usually good, and the snow up high is reliable.

LEVEL OF DIFFICULTY   The skiing is not difficult. It is, however, a moderately strenuous trip.

BEST TIME TO GO   Late December to early February.

HOW TO GET THERE   The Kolob Canyons entrance of Zion Park is on I-15 just 17 miles south of Cedar City, Utah (Exit 42). The main canyon, Zion Canyon, is reached via Utah 9, which goes to the town of Springdale at the park entrance.

SPECIAL EQUIPMENT   No special ski equipment is needed, but full winter camping equipment is required and you should carry a map and compass. Extreme cold is not likely.

MAPS   The Zion National Park map is available from Zion Natural History Association, Zion National Park, Springdale, Utah 84767.

LODGING AND SUPPLIES   Springdale, Utah.

Zion National Park is one of America's special places—at any time of the year. Skiing there is a unique experience. There is a route through the park that is one of the most spectacularly scenic ski tours in the entire world. It is a trip of four to six days that touches most of the highlights of the park. Combine easy skiing with the usually sunny

Skiing the Kolob Canyons, Zion National Park, Utah.
Photo by Steve Barnett.

and warm weather of the Southwest and you have an ideal midwinter ski trip for intermediate skiers as well as experts. Considering how good the tours in Zion are, it's surprising that the touring possibilities there are almost unknown outside a small group of southern Utah skiers.

The main canyon, Zion Canyon, is like a sandstone Yosemite. The Virgin River runs placidly in the canyon's bottom through groves of cottonwoods, while above are red and white walls rising dead vertically for 2,500 feet. These walls have character. They are really sides of separate mountains. Although these mountains are relatively low, some of them are among the most technically difficult to climb in the whole of the United States. The aesthetic effect of this scene is overwhelming. It is unique in the world. When I talk to Europeans who are about to visit the United States, I always tell them to try to make Zion one of their stops. Europe has plenty of great cities and beautiful snow-covered mountains, but there is nothing there remotely like Zion.

The main canyon is too low in elevation to have reliable snow (4,300 feet). It was formed, however, by the Virgin River's dissection of a huge plateau, and the top of this plateau ranges in altitude from 7,000 to 8,000 feet. It is usually covered with deep snow in midwinter. Furthermore there is a separate section of the National Park called the Kolob Canyons, which are high enough at their bases (around 6,000 feet) to be skiable. They are just as beautiful as the main canyon but in a different way. The Kolob Canyons were formed by an erosive mechanism different from the one that cut the main canyon—wind erosion rather than river erosion—and have a different look. Along with sheer cliffs, there are also exotically shaped formations with curving, contoured walls, arches, caves, and narrow slots. Whereas the main canyon is closed in by big walls on both sides, the Kolob walls face open desert.

It's feasible to do day trips in the Kolob, now that the Park Service is plowing the road in winter. There is a short trail up the North Fork of Taylor Creek that is a fun ski when conditions are good, and you can probably follow it beyond the trail end into the canyons feeding the creek.

A little farther up the road is the South Fork of Taylor Creek, and the tour up its canyon is, while short, quite spectacular. The canyon is about 3 miles from the ranger station. Head up it as far as you can go. The floor of the canyon is quite flat, gaining altitude by occasional and easy steps. The walls rise straight up thousands of feet. As you go up the canyon the walls remain just as steep but the floor narrows. Finally it becomes too narrow to go any farther, while the walls still soar out of sight. You have to be careful in such a place. Occasional craters in the snow tell of ice falling from the rim, so don't travel directly under sunlit walls unless it's a very cold day.

Farther up the Kolob road is a trailhead, and a trail from there goes around the big walls, up a long canyon, and eventually makes its way to the plateau above, which is called the Kolob Plateau. The plateau is high enough, about 8,000 feet, to have reliable snow. The skiing on it is pleasant, easy touring. Much of it is open meadows with groves of aspens and pines. Most of the plateau is outside the National Park and it is crisscrossed with roads that are used in winter by snowmobilers. Across the terrace a side road leads back into the park and joins the West Rim Trail. This trail traverses a peninsula of the plateau and then drops straight down into a system of canyons leading into Zion Canyon.

The classic trip in Zion is to climb up out of the Kolob Canyons, cross the Kolob Terrace, and ski down into the main canyon, or to do the same route in the reverse direction. Either way offers a trip that combines

Down into the Kolob Canyons. Photo by Steve Barnett.

delightful skiing with some of the world's finest scenery, and also promises the finest skiing weather possible.

I'll describe the route going from the main canyon to the Kolob Canyons, because that's the way that I've done it. Navigation is relatively easy in both directions. There is a longer climb up from the main canyon, but there is also probably just as much or more good downhill skiing. If snow conditions are fast, then descending the switchbacks cut into the rock wall on the top of the West Rim Trail may be scary while going from the Kolob Canyons to the Zion Canyon.

One problem with this tour is that a car shuttle is necessary to cover the 50 miles of road between your starting and finishing points. One car must be left at the trailhead in the main canyon. The other should be left at the Lee Pass trailhead along the Kolob Road. Possibly this problem could be avoided by walking down from the trip's finish at Lee Pass to the Kolob Canyons Interpretive Center and arranging a ride to the main canyon.

We started at the Angel's Landing, West Rim Trail trailhead on Zion Canyon Road. There is rarely snow there. We climbed, carrying skis to a point just past where the Angel's Landing Trail diverges from the West Rim Trail, about 1,200 feet off the valley floor. There was enough snow there to put skis on. One good thing about touring in the park is that the sandstone underlying the trails is so smooth that very little snow is needed to make a good skiing surface. The skiing changes drastically as the exposure of the slope to the sun changes. It may be wet snow that's not too deep on one side of a ridge and deep, cold powder snow on the other side. The location of the trail is spectacular. Sheer walls of red and white sandstone climb all around it. You can see how Zion is not just a canyon but a range of sandstone peaks. The trail climbs, drops down, climbs again, and enters a shaded canyon. Here it traverses along a steep wall. This may be tricky skiing, with the trail buried by snow sliding from above, but it is not dangerous. A bit later the trail climbs the very same wall, going up switchbacks cut right into the rock. It's a spectacular and airy bit of skiing. When we did it, it was safe enough on skis, with only two very short places where you had to cross mounds of snow sloping off into empty space. Most members of the group did this traverse on foot, carrying their skis.

The switchbacks take you to the rim of the canyon, where the trail splits temporarily. One branch, the right one, is the short way to the Kolob Plateau. The left branch takes some extra time for sightseeing and is the best way to go. First it circles back along the rim, which is a wonderful place for a campsite, looking back down 2,800 feet into the main canyon and its many side branches. The trail gradually leaves the main canyon rim and climbs to the north. Soon it is heading along the rim of another great canyon—Phantom Canyon.

Phantom Canyon is much wilder than the main canyon and has a different look, with sculptured domes of sandstone accompanying the big walls. Much of it looked skiable from our high viewpoint, and it might make a good future trip, but it's often true with travel in the desert that what looks easy from a distance is not only not easy but sometimes not even possible. There can easily be vertical walls, slot canyons, or box-end canyons that you can't see from a distance, which block your presumed route.

The trail drops slightly to a saddle, called Potato Hollow, and then climbs again. Then from a peninsula of high ground surrounded by canyon walls on both sides, the Horse Pasture Plateau, it leads up to the Kolob Plateau. The terrain here is rolling and forested with aspen and pine. This area had the slowest skiing on our trip, with deep snow and warm sun forcing us to slog instead of really ski. We were aiming for Lava Point, a prominent landmark standing above the Horse Pasture Plateau atop several hundred feet of lava cliffs. Just below Lava Point you pick up a snow-covered road that takes you up, around the Point, and onto the Kolob Plateau. Most likely there will be snowmobile tracks on this road. Finding the tracks was a good thing for us because travel suddenly became much easier.

The Kolob Plateau is covered with forests of aspen, summer vacation homes, snowmobile tracks, and frozen reservoirs. Your map will show you which roads to follow to get to the frozen Kolob Reservoir, which you must then cross to get to the trail that drops into the Kolob Canyons. Because of the snowmobile-packed roads and the generally colder temperatures at this altitude (around 8,000 feet), the traverse atop the plateau should go rapidly with good cross-country skiing. Along the way we were able to do something I've never dreamed of doing on a multiday backcountry ski tour: We ate cheeseburgers and ice cream at the Kolob Steak House, which was open on weekends to serve snowmobilers—and they didn't discriminate against skiers.

We crossed the Kolob Reservoir to its northwest corner. There we picked up a snow-covered jeep road that first climbed for a short distance and then started dropping rapidly. Ignore the branch heading off to the right at the high point, and stay to the left at all forks. The road will eventually drop you into the canyon of Willis Creek, which will take you through the Kolob section of the park. The road also is the longest downhill section of the tour. It's a jeep road, and it descends steeply. When we skied it, the top section was delightful powder skiing. There are of course slopes above the road that you may ski as well. Since these are south-facing slopes in a sunny clime, you shouldn't expect them to keep powder snow for long, though. At lower altitudes the road turns south and the snow may get trickier. After traveling nearly 3 miles from Kolob Reservoir in a descending traverse, the road finally decides to get it over with, takes a turn to the south, and drops straight and steeply 750 vertical feet into Willis Creek. This might be exciting skiing because the road is wide enough for maneuvers. We were lucky—we had fine corn snow there, but in some years you will lose the snow before the road bottoms out on this steeply south-facing slope. Don't lose hope. The canyon floors are so shaded that they are likely to have good snow cover even if the lower road doesn't.

The road drops down until it gets to a small creek. It crosses the creek and becomes a trail, climbing slightly, contouring around a small ridge, and then dropping rapidly down the other side of the ridge. Up to this point you have been on private property, and there is a sign telling you when you cross back into the park. This trail, from Lee Pass to Kolob Reservoir, is seldom used in summer (even many rangers don't know it well) and is no longer maintained by the Park Service. This is partly because so much of it goes through private property. It's a great ski trip. Be careful to do nothing that might offend the private landowners. Also, by letting the Park Service know about your trip you help them support skier use of the park—at present there is so little ski use that the rangers have very little information about the skiing possibilities.

Once you get on the bottom of Willis Creek you are back in the land of deep snow. When we were there the creek was completely snowed over and travel was fun and easy. We spent more than a day skiing down the canyon until we got out in the open again. Since the trail is not maintained, there are fallen trees and other obstacles along it, which presented no problem as long as the creek was well covered. But 1¾ miles downstream Willis Creek joins La Verkin Creek, and from that point on there was open water. Since the trail meanders from one side to the other of the canyon this produced numerous stream crossings. There was no escaping it. Since the water level wasn't high, the crossings weren't difficult, but the necessity of taking skis off slowed our progress and was irritating. Sometimes the trail could be followed, and some of those times the part that could be followed was helpful. Other times we just created our own route. At least the sun shone in places on the canyon bottom and made pleasant oases of warmth for resting, sightseeing, and eating lunch.

About a mile from the junction with Willis Creek there is a side canyon off to the left. This is Beartrap Canyon, which is one of the park's more subtly beautiful features. It's reminiscent of the side canyons of the Grand Canyon with a smooth sandy floor, a stream with pools that wanders from one rocky sidewall to the other, and a waterfall upstream. We were able to ski partway up this canyon and then walked the remainder of the distance to the waterfall. It's a minor problem in technical climbing to get around the waterfall and continue higher. There is a route listed in a logbook at Park Headquarters that circles up Willis Creek around the canyon cliffs and comes down again through Beartrap Canyon. It should be fascinating to try it. There's also a lake hidden in a pocket of cliffs above Willis Creek, another exploration likely to be worthwhile.

The trail is maintained from Beartrap Canyon south. Soon it reaches the junction with the Hop Valley Trail, which is another access route to the Kolob Canyons from the Kolob Plateau (it might also be a good ski route). Shortly after that there are good campsites near the junction with the Kolob Arch Trail, which heads up a side stream to the right. Kolob Arch is only a short distance up this stream and is the largest free-standing arch in the world. It is tucked away, however, against a much larger wall and does not stand out the same way that the large arches in Arches National Park do.

From the Kolob Arch junction it's a relatively short distance out into the open country underneath the big walls of the Kolob Canyons. The trail descends for 1½ miles and then takes a turn to the north and starts climbing again on its way to Lee Pass. Whether there's snow or not at the lowest points depends on the particular season and time of year. I've seen it both ways. In either case the scenery is grand enough to make you forget about the hike. There's a combination here of quiet solitude, open sky, and big walls that has a strong impact on most passers-by.

Lee Pass is the end of the traverse. It's over 30 miles long, climbs 5,600 feet, and drops 4,075 feet. Scenically it's in the stratosphere the whole way.

Utah

Navajo Mountain

TOUR   A ski ascent of Navajo Mountain, Utah.

IN A NUTSHELL   From the Navajo Mountain Trading Post outside of Page, Arizona, ski up the microwave relay road to the summit and down again. Or with camping gear, stay on the top, ski the north side, and hike out past Rainbow Bridge.

WHAT MAKES THE TOUR SPECIAL   The mountain is the only high peak in the midst of a peerless desert area defined by Monument Valley, the Grand Canyon, and Lake Powell. The view and sense of place are what make this trip special. There's also a 4,000-vertical-foot descent.

LEVEL OF DIFFICULTY   That depends totally on the snow conditions. An intermediate skier should be able to enjoy this trip.

BEST TIME TO GO   December to March.

HOW TO GET THERE   Page, Arizona, is on US 89 just south of the Utah border. From Page take AZ 98 east and then turn north at the sign for Navajo Mountain Trading Post. The microwave relay road starts between the trading post and the airstrip.

SPECIAL EQUIPMENT   Metal-edged skis and boots good for the downhills will be best.

MAPS   USGS Navajo Mountain, Utah-Arizona.

LODGING AND SUPPLIES   Page, Arizona.

S tretching from Arizona's San Francisco Peaks to the San Juan Mountains of Colorado, from Utah's La Sal Mountains to the Kaibab Plateau north of the Grand Canyon, there is a huge piece of some of the most beautiful desert country on Earth with only one large mountain in it. Far from being featureless, this region contains the Grand Canyon, Lake Powell, Monument Valley, the Escalante country, and the slot canyons of Arizona, and it is the homeland of the Navajo and Hopi tribes. A ski tour to the top of that one large mountain should be a basic part of any midwinter trip to this fantastic area. Its name is Navajo Mountain.

Navajo Mountain is in the geological class of mountains called lacolithic. These are huge domes raised like bubbles by the flow of lava beneath them. The domes may be dissected into compact ranges of mountains. All of North America's lacolithic ranges are located in southern Utah. They are the La Sal Mountains, the Henry Mountains, the Abajo Mountains, and Navajo Mountain. All are spectacularly located and all have exceptional skiing potential. Navajo Mountain is the smallest and lowest of these lacolithic uplifts. It also has the least skiing. Even so, it is still massive. There are more than 4,000 feet of skiable downhill from its 10,400-foot summit. The whole uplift has a diameter of 7 or 8 miles. The summit itself is a spacious plateau-like ridge. The trip on skis up Navajo Mountain is a classic ski tour because of the way the mountain dominates its surroundings and because of its unmatched location.

Navajo Mountain is a long way from anywhere—from anywhere well populated, at least. To get there go to Page, Arizona, which is next to the Glen Canyon Dam on US 89. Take AZ 98 east toward Kaibito. Take the turnoff to the north labeled Navajo Mountain Trading Post and drive the long dirt road to the trading post. Then backtrack a short distance to the road heading off to the west between the trading post and the airstrip. That road climbs to the summit of Navajo Mountain.

The road is used by the local telephone utility to service its microwave repeaters on top of the mountain. In the winter they use a snowcat to get to the summit. This means that there will almost always be a packed track that is perfect for climbing with skis and climbing skins. That this same track will be as perfect for going downhill is less likely. The road goes up the south side of the mountain. Since you are just a hair's width beyond the Arizona border the sun will be strong even in midwinter. The snow is likely to have a crust on its surface that can be exceedingly difficult skiing, especially when you are confined in the tracks of the snowcat. When I climbed the mountain the trip up, all 4,000 vertical feet of it, went as fast and easily as bicycling around the block. Going down was a lot more exhausting. Each of the tracks from the treads of the snowcat was slightly narrower than a ski's length and the berm between them was high, sharp-edged, and made of breakable crust that loved to catch the skis and hold them.

Nevertheless we never regretted the long day or the long drive that got us there. The view is positively enchanted and only gets better and better as you climb. Like the desert ski tours in Zion and Arches, the sense of place is overwhelming. To the east you can see the San Juan Mountains of Colorado and beyond them the Sangre de Cristos in New Mexico. To the southeast you can see the pinnacles of Monument Valley. To the southwest are the San Francisco Peaks near Flagstaff and north of there the gash of the Grand Canyon. From the summit you can see north in the distance to the La Sals and the Henrys. Just under the north slope of the mountain is the blue water of Lake Powell, the huge desert lake created by the Glen Canyon Dam. The sandstone arch of Rainbow Bridge is on the northwest side of the mountain just above the encroaching waters of the lake.

The forest around you as you climb is more immediate than these faraway views, but it too is interesting. At the lowest levels, where snow is uncertain, it is desert juniper. Higher up it becomes ponderosa, well spaced, standing tall without low-hanging limbs, colored and textured so distinctively with its corrugated red bark. Higher yet the forest changes to a typical subalpine mix of Engelmann spruce, limber pine, and subalpine fir.

The forest is skiable for most of the distance; only where the road cuts up a steep cliffy area are you really confined to it. The real problem is the condition of the snow. Since the slope faces south the snow conditions are extremely variable. If you are lucky you could catch it in a cold snap following a January or December storm and get to ski powder. Or you might get there after a spell of hot weather and get to ski corn snow. Much of the time, though, you're liable to find the snow we found. If you are going up there for just a day trip, you'll have to grin and bear it, whatever the south-facing snow is like. It still is worth the trip. There is another descent that is steeper than the road but which will be free of the snowcat tracks that made skiing down so difficult for us: Follow the powerline track down from the summit until you get to the mid-mountain plateau at about 8,000 feet. Then circle back on the plateau to the road for the final descent.

If you have enough time to camp out on the summit, there is another option that gives you a chance of finding really good powder skiing. The trick is to ski down the north side. That side is likely to keep quality powder long after the last storm has passed, at least at the higher altitudes. My discussion of this option has to be a bit speculative since I don't know of anyone yet skiing it. (There are still first explorations left to do on skis, even on as small an uplift as Navajo Mountain.) Skiing the north side should be spectacularly scenic, with Lake Powell dominating the view. Study the

Navajo Mountain. Photo by Steve Barnett.

map carefully. It's not at all easy to find a good route down to the north. You don't want to get trapped by canyons at the very bottom of a long descent. Most of the north side of the mountain is steep and jagged. The best route down looks to be one that goes from the high point on the north end of the summit plateau (point 10,200) to Owl Bridge on the Rainbow Bridge trail. There are also easier looking routes down to both the east and the west. The forest at the top of the mountain is thick but it should be skiable just a little way down. A ski descent down the north side could be ended in either of two ways. One would be to climb back up and ski down to the car via the south side. The other would be to continue down and catch the primitive trail that continues around the mountain from Rainbow Bridge. Then take that trail past Rainbow Bridge back to the south side. The trip over the mountain, ending with this long and scenic desert hike, would be a ski tour with a truly classic dimension.

With a road to its top Navajo Mountain is hardly a wilderness trip. But the emptiness and spaciousness of the scene from its top give it some of the same feeling. There are some very prominent man-made features in the view. These include the smokestacks of the monstrous power-generating plant at Page, which are visible from enormous distances. The other is Lake Powell, which you might view as either a beautiful, if improbable, lake of blue in the midst of Utah's red sandstone or as an abomination that marks the grave of Glen Canyon. Both these features figure prominently in the book *The Monkey Wrench Gang,* which stands like a Bible on the bookshelves of most Utah wilderness aficionados.

If you want to find real wilderness in this region, then a good alternative trip is to another lacolithic mountain range, the Henry Mountains. These are higher than Navajo Mountain, climbing well above timberline and topped with steep, glacier-cut bowls. Snowfall in the Henrys is inconsistent because they are in the rainshadow of other large ranges. That, added to the long trip by car and the difficult access on foot, makes a ski tour there a real adventure. The highest of the lacolithic ranges, the La Sals near Moab, stands like an island nearly 13,000 feet high above a spectacular desert environment, and it is well suited to ski mountaineering, with steep drops over a long vertical distance.

Almost every trip to one of these lacolithic ranges seems to be a delightful one. It's the mixture of desert sandstone, white snow, and green forested slopes that makes it so. There always seem to be enraptured moments standing high on a mountain in brilliant sunshine with skis on your feet and infinite desert all around.

Arizona

Grand Canyon

TOUR   Skiing to the Grand Canyon's North Rim.

IN A NUTSHELL   The North Rim is the edge of a high, forested plateau that has many roads on it. These make excellent paths for cross-country skiing in a sunny and warm winter environment. Some skiers continue across the canyon on foot and exit on the South Rim.

WHAT MAKES THE TOUR SPECIAL   The edge of the canyon is a supreme scenic climax to these otherwise gentle tours. The dry air, warm sun, and frequent good weather make midwinter touring a pleasure.

LEVEL OF DIFFICULTY   Easy.

BEST TIME TO GO   January to March.

HOW TO GET THERE   From Fredonia, Arizona, take Big Springs Road, which is plowed in winter, onto the Kaibab Plateau. Unplowed side roads lead to the main park road and either the East Rim Viewpoint or Point Imperial, the North Rim viewpoint. Or you can take US Alternate 89 to Jacob Lake, and from there ski south along the park road to the North Rim.

SPECIAL EQUIPMENT   Camping equipment capable of withstanding sizable snowstorms will be needed.

MAPS   USGS Grand Canyon National Park, Arizona.

LODGING AND SUPPLIES   Fredonia, Arizona.

The Grand Canyon must be the United States' most popular tourist attraction. And deservedly so. The word grand fits it well. It's wonderful not only for sightseeing but also for many sporting activities like running the Colorado River, which runs down the canyon's bottom, or hiking the hundreds of miles of trail winding through its desert innards.

Surprisingly, skiing is also one of the sports that are natural to the canyon. Its North Rim is a plateau 9,000 feet high, which is reliably covered with deep snow every winter. This plateau is a perfect place for true long-distance cross-country skiing. There's a tremendous bonus attraction as well in that most tours there will reach the rim of the great canyon and give you a view into the chasm. The climate of northern Arizona is just right for pleasurable ski touring. You can expect to find hot, sunny days, very cold nights, and good powder snow. For the skier visiting in January or February from some more northern clime, the power of the sun will seem miraculous.

The plateau that forms the North Rim is called the Kaibab Plateau. It's really a new mountain range that's forming, a huge chunk of evenly uplifting rock. Most of it is gently undulating terrain that is as yet relatively uneroded. There's one monstrous exception, though, and that's the Grand Canyon itself. The Colorado River, existent long before the Kaibab started rising, has cut through the plateau just as fast as it has risen. Because of a tilt in the plateau the South Rim is some 2,000 feet lower than the North Rim. In the climatic zone of northern Arizona, that's just enough to make the North Rim a well watered, heavily timbered, mountain environment and the South Rim a desert one.

In summer, spring, or fall, the National Park is crawling with people and their cars, campers, backpacks, rafts, hang gliders, climbing ropes, kayaks, bicycles, etc. In winter there are far fewer visitors and almost all of them are at the South Rim. The North Rim is practically deserted. For one thing it's physically isolated from any large population concentration. To get from the North Rim to Flagstaff, the nearest large town south of the canyon, you have to drive hundreds of miles out of your way to Navajo Bridge, the nearest crossing of the Colorado River. Even when you've made that drive, you've got a long way to go. And Point Imperial, the final overlook on the North Rim, is some 45 miles south of Jacob Lake, the usual summer access point, by a road that is not plowed in winter.

That isolation hasn't kept quite a few groups, mostly of local skiers, from doing the trip from Jacob Lake to Point Imperial. They just slog their way day after day until they get to that sublime point on the rim. If they're lucky, a snowmobile driven by a park ranger will have gone ahead of them. With a packed trail to ski on, their speed will double, at the least. Once at Point Imperial, most such groups decline to ski the long distance back out and just keep going, taking the Bright Angel Trail down to the bottom of the Canyon, skiing as much of it as possible, and then crossing the river to the South Rim via the foot bridge at Phantom Ranch.

The idea of a 90-mile tour on a road didn't appeal to me very much when I went to ski the Kaibab Plateau. I was hoping that there might be a shorter way to ski to the canyon's rim. When we stopped at the local Forest Service office, we were told that it was silly to go skiing since there was very little snow up there (it was a particularly dry year). We had driven all the way from southern California and didn't really want to hear that; furthermore we had seen glimpses of white from the plateau that convinced

Skiing to the North Rim of the Grand Canyon.
Photo by Steve Barnett.

us that there would be plenty of snow at the highest altitudes. And this particular outpost of the Forest Service seemed a lot more interested in timber than in winter recreation, and it wasn't surprising that they wouldn't have much firsthand skiing information. Persisting, it turned out that there was a road in the Kaibab National Forest that was kept open for logging, ran fairly close to the canyon rim, and allowed easy access to the higher altitudes. This was the Big Springs Road, which is kept plowed every winter and is a good access route for several ski tours.

We drove up it, and for our first Grand Canyon ski tour took the shortest trail we could find on the map that led to the canyon, the trail to Parissawampitts Point. This overlooks the Tapeats Amphitheater, which is a huge cliff-rimmed basin draining into the Colorado. Perhaps the snow was less deep than normal, but to our joy it was certainly adequate (how much do you need to make a road skiable?). The sun was out, the prospect of visiting the rim of the Canyon was at hand—no wonder our spirits were rising by the minute. The skiing was often great—a surface just sun-hardened enough to bear our weight and permit skating and double poling. It was slightly downhill heading to the rim, and much of the way we could fly along. This was the essence of cross-country skiing, the super-efficient eating of miles.

At the end of the trail was the rim. There was a magnificent view down past layer after layer of cliffs to the central gash, still miles away. We took a different route back and worked our way up and down through forests of ponderosa pine and aspen, enjoying an occasional set of turns on the hillsides. It was a wonderful day trip, a good preparation for the longer trip we had in mind for the next few days.

We planned to ski east from Big Spring Road. It looked like about a 10-mile ski to reach a junction with Jacob Lake Road near Kaibab Lodge, closed for the winter. Then a further ski of only 5 more miles would take us to the East Rim Overlook. The altitude would be considerably higher than our trip to Parissawampitts Point, and the snow would be considerably deeper and more powdery.

In practice this created difficulties. The going was slow as we frequently slogged through deep snow. Despite the power of the sun, the altitude was high enough to keep the snow that was shaded by the trees from getting sun hardened. Sometimes progress was as slow as one mile per hour. Still the trip out had many compensations. The aspen forest gleaming white in the sunshine was extraordinarily beautiful. The sun was hot enough that this Pacific Northwest skier could forget about always trying to stay warm and dry and could just relax and enjoy the radiant heat. At the East Rim Viewpoint we had a pleasant surprise. While the view was spectacular, the cliffs were broken enough that there was a skiable slope heading down from the rim. What a thrill to launch ourselves off the rim and telemark turn down toward the distant slot that was the Colorado River!

Coming back we were able to ski in our own tracks. Instead of slogging, we could fly on our skis. Our speed went from 1 to 2 miles per hour to 4 to 5 miles per hour. This meant that we were having a ball on skis, skating, double poling, and striding. What had been a chore before was a delight now. The Kaibab in winter is one of the best places in the West for real cross-country skiing, which means running on skis across hill and dale for mile after mile. You're at an altitude of around 9,000 feet, skiing on roads that undulate gently through the forests. In summer this network of roads is probably an ugly mess (the road map of the Kaibab National Forest looks a lot like a Manhattan street map), but in winter all is pristine. Even snowmobiles, normally hateful scourges of the winter scene, can be helpful. Not their presence while you're there—that's still unpleasant—but their old tracks that pack down a skiable path in the powdery snow and allow fast and fun cross-country skiing. In fact if there's a snowmobile track running all the way from Jacob Lake to the North Rim Viewpoint at Point Imperial (some winters a ranger lives there), then the 45-mile trip might be quite a pleasant ski, which would go much faster than you might think. A spring crust will also make the trip go quickly. One group, in fact, used such conditions to skate the entire distance to the rim, climb into the canyon and back up to the south side in one extraordinary 65 mile day.

The Kaibab is not the only plateau of its kind in this region of the world, though it is the only one that puts you on the edge of the Grand Canyon. North of it is a string of high plateaus stretching throughout southern Utah. These all provide somewhat similar skiing experiences, though with their own individual accents. Particularly prominent are the plateaus bordering Cedar Breaks National Monument and Zion National Park. A trip through Zion Canyon and over the plateau that it cuts through is described in another chapter. Not far from the Grand Canyon there is one of the best mountain tours in the country. That's the Inner Basin of the San Francisco Peaks near Flagstaff, Arizona.

Far West

Alaska

Ruth Amphitheater

TOUR Skiing in the Ruth Amphitheater on the south side of Mt. McKinley.

IN A NUTSHELL Fly in from Talkeetna, Alaska, to the Sheldon Hut in the Ruth Amphitheater. Then from the hut do day trips, including those down the Ruth Gorge, over to Mt. Huntington, to Buffalo Pass (next to the Mooses Tooth), and up Mt. Dickey.

WHAT MAKES THE TOUR SPECIAL This is touring in one of the greatest mountain scenes in the world. The scenery is overwhelming. It is easily accessible to skiers of modest means and modest ability.

LEVEL OF DIFFICULTY The Amphitheater encompasses the entire spectrum of skiing difficulty. Some wonderful excursions can be made with no ability on skis other than how to walk. Others are extreme skiing descents.

BEST TIME TO GO May.

HOW TO GET THERE The Sheldon Hut must be reserved from Roberta Sheldon in Talkeetna. Talkeetna can be reached from Anchorage via the Alaska Railroad or by road. There are several experienced glacier pilots in Talkeetna. Reserve your flight.

SPECIAL EQUIPMENT Glacier-travel equipment (ropes, prusiks, ice axes, and crampons) are mandatory. Avalanche beacons should be carried too. Carry clothes for extreme cold though they probably won't be needed in May, the best month for travel in the Ruth.

MAPS　USGS Talkeetna D-2, Mt. McKinley A-2, both in Alaska.

LODGING AND SUPPLIES　Anchorage and Talkeetna, Alaska.

The Ruth Amphitheater in Denali (Mt. McKinley) National Park in Alaska is one of the great mountain places in the world. It is as grand, as beautiful, as awesome as mountain places get. Tremendous walls of clean granite rise a vertical mile out of the sea of white of the glacier. In other places the walls are only near vertical and are white, topped by huge cornices, covered with ice, bulging with hanging glaciers and seracs, deeply furrowed by frequent avalanches. It's a small miracle that in such a rugged and wild location one need not be a particularly competent skier to fully enjoy the experience. Furthermore, the Ruth is not only relatively accessible to the ski tourer but contains a small hut where nights can be spent in comfort.

The Ruth Glacier drains a huge area on the southeast side of Mt. McKinley. In addition to the steep sides of the peaks, it occupies a large, nearly flat basin underneath them, which is the Amphitheater. Travel to the Ruth was first encouraged by the famous bush pilot Don Sheldon who built the hut there. Don Sheldon is so closely identified with the place that on some maps the glacier basin is called the Don Sheldon Amphitheater.

I was lucky enough to go there one May as a guide for an eclectic group ranging from a Texas oilman to an eccentric southern California doctor to a professional ski-mountaineering guide from Alaska. Remarkably, everyone was able to enjoy the trip.

We started from Anchorage. Some of us drove the 90 miles to Talkeetna. Others took the Alaska railroad. From Talkeetna, we chartered a ski plane and landed on the Ruth Glacier near the Sheldon Hut. Built on a rock knoll on what is perhaps the only avalanche-safe spot possible in the whole area and surrounded on all sides by glacier, this hexagonal cabin with its airy outhouse was our base for a week of ski touring in the surrounding amphitheater.

The view from the cabin was remarkable. In fact this region must be one of the world's most spectacular mountain areas—equal to anything in the Andes or Himalayas. They certainly were the most awe-inspiring mountains I'd ever seen. They're not just bigger than any others I've seen but occupy another dimension of scenic space—they are grander, more stunning, more overwhelming. Hanging above everything is Mt. McKinley, rock and ice reaching some 15,000 vertical feet above the Ruth Glacier. In the

ALASKA, YUKON TERRITORY

ALASKA

YUKON
TERRITORY

Fairbanks

Denali
N.P.

Ruth
Amphitheater

Mt. McKinley

3

Anchorage

1

Mt.
Logan

Whitehorse

Kluane
N.P.

9

distance to the east is Mt. Silverthrone, a lovely snow cone 13,220 feet high; it looked perfect for skiing. Nearer at hand is the Mooses Tooth, a collection of fantastic granite walls rising some 4,500 feet above the glacier. Right next to the cabin is Mt. Dickey, an easy ascent (it's all skiable) from one direction but fronting a 5,000-foot vertical wall over the Ruth Gorge.

The Ruth Gorge lies between Mt. Dickey and the Mooses Tooth. The entire Ruth Glacier, draining hundreds of square miles, is forced through this one relatively small slot. The gorge is like a Yosemite Valley still in the Ice Age, except that the walls are much larger. Beside the north wall of Mt. Dickey there is the massif of the Mooses Tooth, whose granite spires and steep glaciers present some of the world's greatest climbing problems. Around the corner to the west, on another arm of the glacier, lies Mt. Huntington, a great alpine peak with faces of ice and rock on all sides. It's a beautiful peak, with a high, fluted, ice-summit ridge that glows with a blue light when the clouds are right. Typical of many of these Alaskan climbs,

its first ascent was an exercise in underestimation of the distances and difficulties involved. A very strong French team, led by Lionel Terray, the
greatest expedition climber of his day, was going to do a new route on
McKinley. Following a suggestion from Bradford Washburn they decided
to climb Mt. Huntington as a warm-up. It consumed their entire expedition. Since then it's been the objective of several "super-alpine" ascents—
stretching small parties to the limits of climbing while carrying enough supplies to live for days on the endless face of rock and ice.

Our group had much more modest objectives. We just wanted to do
day ski tours exploring as much of the Amphitheater as we could. The glacier
provides a natural highway between the great peaks. Much of the touring
is rather easy skiing on broad, low-angled rivers of ice. What makes it special
are the surroundings and the endless nature of the skiing. You can't possibly
exhaust it. Thus a skier like our Texan oilman who had never before done
a ski tour in big mountains was able to enjoy the trip just as much as any
of the hardened mountain skiers. There are also real down-mountain runs,
the closest of which is the descent of Mt. Dickey right behind the hut with
a 4,000-vertical-foot drop. But though these runs are long by normal mountain standards, they're completely dwarfed by the surroundings here. You
never feel like you've conquered anything here. If there's any dominant
component of the special sense of place you feel in the Ruth it's the scale
of everything there. It's a scale that's way beyond what's comfortable for
humans. To get up high on the peaks is not a matter of a day's climbing;
it's more likely to be a problem of expeditionary size.

An ascent of Mt. Dickey is the exception to this rule; it's 9,545 feet
high and skiable to the summit. You climb up the obvious slope south of
the cabin to Pittock Pass. There is some avalanche danger from the ice
cliff just below Pittock Pass on Mt. Dickey. You should plan your route
to avoid as much danger as possible and then move as quickly as you can
through the danger zone. We also had to cross a crevasse, belayed, just below
the pass. From the pass, climb the steep slope to the east. This might be
easier with crampons and axe than sidestepping with skis. Don't go all the
way up the ridge but traverse left above the steep section and get onto the
big slope that leads to the summit. The steep section below is skiable, but
since there are crevasses and cliffs below you might prefer to downclimb
it with axe and crampons. Two of our group skied it, the rest elected to be
conservative. It's an exciting ski descent with a vertical drop that would
be big anywhere else but in the Ruth.

There are many much easier trips as well. For example, a jaunt on
the gentle glacier highway from the cabin, around Mt. Barille, and into
the gorge past the Mooses Tooth is a fine excursion. So is going from the
cabin to the glacier's west fork and skiing up it underneath Mt. Huntington.

For telemark downhills on a smaller scale than Mt. Dickey, the small peaks across the glacier from the cabin at the base of Mt. Dan Beard offer good skiing and easy access in a phenomenal setting. For a longer excursion you can ski across the gorge, climb a pass, and ski on glaciers behind the Mooses Tooth.

If you are willing to camp out on the glacier and spend several days to reach an objective, then Mt. Silverthrone is an excellent choice. To reach it you ski up the glacier to the north about 13 miles. There's an icefall to climb up about halfway there. You can ski up to about 11,000 feet on the mountain. The rest of the way to the summit is along a ridge that is exposed but not technically difficult. The whole trip should take 3 to 4 days from the cabin.

If the sun is shining and you're out in the middle of the glacier eating lunch at noon, the Ruth seems like a pretty benign place. But there actually is plenty of danger. Avalanches will be running off of the walls so frequently that the noise is constant. Mostly these are just pieces of ice the size of a house breaking off. We never saw a really big one—where a chunk as big as a small town falls down and completely crosses the glacier—but these have happened and several climbers have lost their lives to them. Ski tourers generally hate to ski roped; it runs counter to the spirit of free travel at the heart of the sport. But these Alaskan glaciers have more than their share of hidden crevasses that have claimed their share of casualties. We compromised. We'd ski up while roped and down unroped. We'd ski unroped in the morning when the snow was well frozen, then use the rope again in the afternoon when the snow bridges were softened.

On all but one day of our week-long stay the sun was out and temperatures during the day were warm. This kind of weather isn't uncommon in the Alaska ranges in the spring. It was a lot warmer and drier there than back home in Washington State at the same time. The weather is supposed to be best in April and May. Later in the year there are more storms and it gets warm enough that the snow on the lower glaciers deteriorates seriously. Unfortunately you're particularly vulnerable to bad weather here because you have to fly out. The pilots can't land if they can't see, and it doesn't take much of a fog to make a glacier surface indistinguishable from the sky. There's a story that one party was stuck for three extra weeks in the hut.

The Ruth isn't limited to day trips around the hut. You can piece together much longer traverses. An example would be to cross Pittock Pass and ski back around through the gorge. A trip to Mt. Silverthrone would be another example. The intriguing possibility of connecting with the usual climbers' route on the Kahiltna Glacier through the pass called Ruth Gap turns out to be an exercise in technical climbing. It was part of a complete

Mooses Tooth, Ruth Glacier, Alaska. Photo by Steve Barnett.

circumnavigation of Mt. McKinley led by Ned Gillette in 1978 that was one of the more notable ski-mountaineering achievements yet done in North America.

The Ruth Amphitheater is one of the most popular glacier touring areas in the state, and you are likely to see other people while you are there. Some wilderness aficionados would even call it "crowded" though that would be just by Alaskan standards.

Alaska has, of course, nearly an infinite supply of other good ski-touring areas, many of which are completely wild. One other ski trip that deserves classic status is the run down Mt. Sanford, a 16,000-foot-high extinct volcano in the Wrangell Mountains east of Anchorage. It gives a 10,000-vertical-foot run down from the summit with reasonable slopes all the way.

Skiing in the Brooks Range in the north of the state, north of the Arctic Circle, is also an attractive idea. The trouble there, besides expensive access, is that not much snow falls in the Arctic, and because of the intense cold what snow there is turns to TG snow that is not very good for skiing. In winter the snow is too unconsolidated and the weather is, of course, very cold. In spring the wet TG can collapse totally under your skis, making travel miserable. If you get it just right you can go early in the spring when a crust of snow sufficient to support your skis has formed and then the skiing can be great. Also on the high peaks and on their small glaciers (the low snowfall means glaciers are small here despite the latitude) the wind may give the snow a usable surface.

Yukon Territory

Mt. Logan

TOUR   A climb of Mt. Logan in the St. Elias Mountains on the Yukon-Alaska border.

IN A NUTSHELL   Fly in with a ski-equipped plane to the landing spot on the Quintino Sella Glacier. Then climb up the natural glacier highway of the King Trench to Prospector Pass at 18,400 feet. Cross the summit plateau and climb the 19,580-foot summit. All in all, this is an expedition of four weeks.

WHAT MAKES THE TOUR SPECIAL   This is a primeval Ice Age environment. The scale of the mountains and glaciers is nearly incomprehensible. The peak itself, besides being Canada's highest, is for the most part an excellent ski mountain. Its climb gives the skier-climber a chance to live for a month in this extraordinary solitary environment of black rock and white glaciers.

LEVEL OF DIFFICULTY   The skiing itself is not difficult, but the work of repeatedly hauling camps up on sleds takes good stamina. The climbers have to be prepared for cold temperatures (down to −30° F.) and for spending days at a time in the tents while waiting out storms.

BEST TIME TO GO   May and June.

HOW TO GET THERE   There are two air services that fly into the St. Elias: Icefield Ranges Expeditions, Kluane Lake, Yukon Territory, and Alcan Air, Whitehorse, Yukon Territory.

SPECIAL EQUIPMENT   You'll need sleds, double boots and overboots, clothes for cold temperatures, snow saw for cutting blocks for wind-protection walls, ice axes and crampons, extra ropes and climbing gear, full glacier gear.

MAPS   Mt. St. Elias quadrangle 1:250,000. A map on a smaller scale, the Centennial Map, is also available from the Canadian government (Department of Energy, Mines and Resources) and gives a more precise picture of the mountain.

LEGAL PERMISSION   Permission for an expedition to Logan must be gotten from Kluane National Park headquarters in Haines Junction, Yukon Territory. This is usually no problem.

LODGING AND SUPPLIES   Kluane Lake and Whitehorse, Yukon Territory.

The St. Elias Mountains of the Pacific coast of southeast Alaska are the center of the third largest glaciated region in the world, after Antarctica and Greenland. They are a black-and-white world where island peaks of snow and rock rise out of seas of glacial ice. They are one of the few places left in the world that are totally primeval—without any trace of humanity.

Nowadays the only spots that have remained in that pristine condition are those places that are too alien for humans to do more than visit. It's funny how such a hostile environment holds a strong, sometimes fatal, attraction for a fringe population of homo sapiens, that most adaptable of animals. There are desert rats, there are white-water kayakers, there are undersea divers and cave divers, and there are expedition climbers. Each group lives with a fascination for a frightening, antihuman environment. Somehow making peace with such environments is the root of pleasure in those sports.

Ski touring, too, partakes a little of that spirit in that the winter world is much more hostile than the summer world. But most skiers, most of the time, stay relatively near other humans, or near such amenities as huts or trails, and also near the sheltering green forest that is an abode of life. It's only a few who commit themselves to expeditionary trips, a few who will spend a month or more living in the absolutely sterile environment of ice, snow, and rock in a great mountain range. For those few who want to taste that experience there's no better trip in North America than an attempt at climbing Mt. Logan, the highest of the St. Elias peaks.

Mt. Logan is not only the highest peak of the St. Elias, it is also Canada's largest mountain, and it may well be the largest mountain in the world in terms of bulk. The summit is 19,580 feet high, and a complete traverse can be done around it without going much over 10,500 feet. That

Mt. Logan, Yukon Territory. Photo by Steve Barnett.

circumtraverse is in fact a major wilderness expedition on its own, one that covers 120 miles and takes 10 to 20 days. There is a huge, gentle dome on the summit of the mountain, starting roughly at the 15,000-foot level. Below it, with one glaring exception, are steep walls of rock and ice. At that level the dome is 13 miles long by 5 miles wide. At the 17,000-foot level it is still 9 miles long.

The route description is simple. What is difficult is finding the endurance, the patience, and the temperament necessary to follow the route. Start with a flight by ski plane to a landing point on the Quintino Sella Glacier, which lies to the west of the peak. The altitude of the base camp will be at 8,000 to 10,000 feet. Using sleds haul your loads up the King Trench, which is a natural glacier highway bounded by steep walls on both the north and south. To the south the wall is King Peak, 16,971 feet. The King Trench is the easy route that breaks through the steep lower slopes of Logan. Climbing the trench is a trip of about 9 miles distance and 5,500 feet of vertical. The top of the trench is King Col. From there you head left on a ramp of snow up to Prospector Pass, 18,400 feet high, and then drop 1,000 feet onto the summit plateau. The ramp is a good place for camps with a view since the dropoff on one side of it is 10,000 vertical feet. It's best to camp again just on the other side of the pass and prepare for a dash to the summit. Then, in a very long day, you can make it to the summit (6 miles away from the pass) and back to camp. You contour around Logan's west peak, and then take your skis off. The final 1,000 feet up to the summit (1½ miles) is on an exposed ridge of snow. In theory it can be skied, but most groups opt for security, take their skis off, and climb it with ice axe and crampons.

One serious consideration with this route is the drop from Prospector Pass to the summit plateau. The plateau is at a high enough altitude that there is a fair possibility of some member of the party getting pulmonary or cerebral edema. If they do, they must go up over the pass to get to a lower altitude. This is an inherently dangerous situation, since going higher is absolutely the worst action for the affected climber, who might not be strong enough to climb over the pass anyway. You should be quite sure at the last camp on the other side of the pass that everyone is well acclimatized before you commit yourself and cross over to the summit plateau. This is one of the strongest arguments for taking several weeks to haul camps up the King Trench. In theory you could make a dash for it from the landing spot, but there is too strong a probability that someone will get in desperate trouble—caught by potentially fatal altitude sickness on the summit plateau.

Logan is the only trip in this book where altitude is a serious problem. You will have to deal with it on Mt. Shasta or climbing Quandary

Peak in Colorado or on the higher peaks along the Sierra Crest, but it's easy to escape from these peaks down to lower altitude and there is a big difference between 14,000 feet and 19,000 feet. What can you do to ameliorate the effects of altitude? The first and most important step is to gain altitude slowly. The general rule for acclimatization is to gain 1,000 feet a day once you are over 10,000 feet. Even very strong climbers with extensive experience at high altitudes have come down with pulmonary or cerebral edema when trying to gain altitude very quickly in attempts to set speed records on high peaks. The next step is to maintain a continuous intake of liquid well beyond what your thirst dictates. If you get headaches take aspirin. That's about all you can do. Altitude sickness is an erratic syndrome. Some people do better than others all the time, and most people do better sometimes than at others. The climb up Logan is long enough that most people are able to get well acclimatized by the time they attempt the summit.

The route is straightforward, but you should allow three to four weeks to do it. That allows for seven to eight days pinned in the tents by storm, which isn't at all unlikely. In the King Trench you may well be sheltered from the wind by the walls on either side of you, which is not so if the wind blows from the wrong direction. On the summit plateau you are also a little sheltered by surrounding ridges, but you have to expect wind. All the camps should be fortified with snow walls built around the tents.

The weather on Logan seems to be considerably better than that on such coastal St. Elias peaks as Mt. St. Elias itself. The snowfall is less, and there are a lot more sunny days. It's not California but it's not Patagonia either. The sun in May and June, the ideal climbing season, is very strong, and as long as it is out and there isn't wind you can trudge along the summit plateau in shirtsleeves, even though the air temperature might be only 0° F. Nighttime temperatures can be expected to drop to −30°F., and the summit itself might be that cold, too.

Double boots and overboots are just about mandatory for skiers. Down sleeping bags and jackets work well in this cold climate, and the sun is strong enough to keep them dried out. One other mandatory class of equipment is a set of sleds for hauling supplies. These need not be fancy; modified children's sleds will do.

What makes a trip to Logan exciting is the chance to live in an Ice Age setting with a scale beyond comprehension. In the St. Elias, individual groups of peaks rise out of the enormous open space of the icefields. Surrounding Logan are the Seward, Quintino Sella, Ogilvie, Logan, and Hubbard glaciers. Even the bulk of Mt. Logan is dwarfed by the size of some of these glaciers. The Seward is 25 miles wide. The Hubbard is 70 miles long. Some climbers have landed in the St. Elias and immediately felt deeply uncomfortable, disturbed by the sheer expanse of empty white space. For others the expanse is exhilarating. It's a return to the Ice Age, to a continent still covered by ice and snow. Some compare the experience to fasting, of being able to spend a month in a setting where the senses are deprived of sound, smell, and color.

One thing you have on an ascent of Logan that you won't have on an ascent of McKinley (by the standard route, at least) is solitude. Being the highest peak on the continent, McKinley is a magnet for climbers, and in the peak season of April and May a small town is erected on the Kahiltna Glacier. Logan is still only rarely attempted. There will be at most a half-dozen climbs a year, and there's a lot of space for each party to get lost in.

Last but not least, in the course of climbing Logan you will get to do a lot of mountain skiing of a very high order. For each load you carry up to a high camp, you get a ski run down in magnificent surroundings. The slope is just right for maximum pleasure in skiing, and the snow is often very good. By the time several weeks have gone by, the expedition members will be strong enough and well enough acclimatized to do truly incomparable ski runs. Some skiers have been able to get runs of 7,000 to 8,000 vertical feet with powder all the way. That's a long way to climb up, but in May and June it never really gets dark on Logan; it's one place where 24-hour powder skiing is a reality.

British Columbia

Spearhead Traverse

TOUR Spearhead Traverse between Blackcomb and Whistler resorts, British Columbia.

IN A NUTSHELL The route joins a series of pocket glaciers along the ridgeline joining the two ski areas. There is a hut in the middle of the route.

WHAT MAKES THE TOUR SPECIAL This is the only glacial traverse in North America that can be reached so easily (from a ski lift) and that is feasible in midwinter. It has spectacular alpine scenery, very good skiing, and a hut midway. It's an outstanding trip.

LEVEL OF DIFFICULTY This is an advanced trip, although in good late-spring conditions it probably would be fun for intermediate skiers (with some mountaineering experience) as well. You should be prepared to spend two to three days out and face the usual high-mountain mix of very good and very bad snow conditions. There are some steep slopes and some avalanche hazard. Navigation can be tricky, too, especially if the weather deteriorates.

BEST TIME TO GO March through May.

HOW TO GET THERE Start from the Blackcomb Ski Area, 75 miles north of Vancouver, British Columbia, along the Whistler Highway.

SPECIAL EQUIPMENT Besides camping equipment and a map and compass, you should have avalanche gear (beepers and shovels) and probably should carry a light rope and prusiks for glacier travel. Extreme cold is unlikely, but wet weather is possible.

MAPS   Whistler Quadrangle, 92 J/2.

LODGING AND SUPPLIES   Whistler, British Columbia.

The British Columbia Coast Range begins its rise only a few miles north of the border with Washington State and continues along the coast all the way to southeast Alaska. There is nothing in the lower 48 that can come close to it in terms of the extent of glaciation or the vistas of sharp spires rising out of seas of glacial ice. Glaciers nearly reach sea level in the vicinity of Mt. Waddington, only 140 miles north of Vancouver. Some of the icefields have areas measured in the hundreds of square miles. The interconnecting icefields are ideal for long ski trips but are mostly so remote that it takes an expedition to get into them. What is needed is a way to sample this glorious region without the use of aircraft or the need to carry 75-pound packs. The answer is the Spearhead Traverse.

The twin ski areas of Blackcomb and Whistler must have the greatest range of backcountry ski possibilities of any ski area in North America. The Coast Range around them is a vast wilderness topped with a frosting of permanent snow and glacial ice.

The Spearhead Traverse is a perfect 2- to 3-day trip going from glacier to glacier between the two ski areas. The terrain is a spectacular mix of glaciers and peaks and is excellently contoured for skiing. There is a hut midway that lets skiers enjoy a comfortable night out. And the ski area's access to the high country is simple, even in the middle of winter, with lifts that take you right to the level of the glaciers. It also is one of the very few high mountain tours in this book that is reasonable to do in mid-winter as well as late in the spring.

The Coast Range seems to be a continuation of the Olympics and Cascades just a few miles to the south, but geologically it's a separate and much larger range than either of those. It's similar to them in its maritime climate, with enormous winter snowfalls and cool summers. Since there is much more terrain above the line of permanent snow, the glaciers are much larger. It used to be that the lower parts of the Coast Range, rugged valleys filled with magnificent rain forest, were as wild as the glacial hinterlands. That is no longer true. Logging has been unrestricted, and roads penetrate most of the valleys climbing into the range from the ocean. These do not always help the wilderness traveler since after the logging is completed the roads are allowed to rapidly decay into uselessness. There is not

Monarch Icecap, British Columbia Coast Range. Photo by Steve Barnett.

even a pretense of multiple use here. Nevertheless, the high country is nearly as wild, empty, and pristine as it was in pre-Columbian times.

The Coast Range played a prominent part in the history of wilderness exploration on skis in North America. The famous couple Don and Phyllis Munday, who were the first ones to try and climb Mt. Waddington, started using skis in the early 1930s to make travel on the glaciers easier. Don Munday wrote, "Three seasons around Mt. Waddington convinced us that skis were the logical equipment to overcome the obstacles imposed by the mighty glaciers."

The Blackcomb and Whistler ski areas are spaced just a few miles apart, separated by the basin of Fitzsimmons Creek. A long horseshoe of mountains runs from one area to the other around the headwaters of the creek. The traverse follows this mountain crest. It can be enjoyed traveling in either direction. I'll describe it starting from Blackcomb, since the lifts now take you directly to the glaciers and you will get to enjoy the glacial magnificence sooner than if you start from Whistler. The proper map is the Whistler quadrangle 92 J/2. The route follows from the top of the lift to Horstman Glacier, Blackcomb Glacier, Decker Glacier, Trorey Glacier, Tremor Glacier, Platform Glacier, Ripsaw Glacier, Naden Glacier, Macbeth Glacier, and then gets into some complications we'll discuss later. Each glacier is a small pocket glacier. It can be difficult to find the right crossing places over the ridges that separate the glaciers, especially in bad weather. Sometimes the route is intricate, going from glacier to ridgeline to a short, moderately steep couloir dropping down to the next glacier. Route finding is the main reason why the trip may vary in length from 1 to 3 days. If you've never done it before, give yourself 3 days. It has been done in 10 hours by a pair of experienced Canadian ski mountaineers, Brian Finnie and Martyn Williams, who know every stone on the route, and it says something about the quality (and easy access) of the route that these two have come back again and again to try it.

Generally the best terrain is on the north side, on the opposite side of the ridgeline from Fitzsimmons Creek. There are a few places, though, where you cross over to the Fitzsimmons Creek side. One is between the Decker and Trorey glaciers, where you should cross to the Fitzsimmons side through a col and then back again to the north side through another col. Then you will traverse on the north side of the Mt. Pattison.

A major decision faces you when you get to Macbeth Glacier. The route divides, and neither alternative is trouble free. The most popular way is down Macbeth Glacier (an excellent run) and then up to and across Fitzsimmons Glacier (the source of the creek). You are now in a deep hole (the "Toilet Bowl") with only one reasonable exit. That is a steep (40°), long (1,000 vertical feet) climb up to the Overlord Glacier. If the snow is at all unstable this will be very dangerous. For example, if you were doing the traverse in late spring you wouldn't want to hit this south-facing slope late in the afternoon. Even if the snow is stable you may feel as though you are in the center of a giant solar oven. From the Overlord Glacier, climb up to the Fissile-Whirlwind Col and drop down to the cabin at Russet Lake.

The alternative route is to drop only 600 feet on Macbeth Glacier and then contour left to reach the Lago Glacier. Climb up the Lago Glacier some 900 vertical feet, and traverse around the east side of Mt. Fitzsimmons, climbing a bit to reach the Diavolo Glacier. Climb over the top of Mt. Benvolio (8,500 feet) and cross the Benvolio Glacier, holding your altitude. Then circle around Overlord Mountain and Refuse Pinnacle to get onto the Overlord Glacier. The traverse under these mountains is steep and exposed. The distance is longer with the second route, and it has about twice the vertical climb of the first one. Its advantage is that you avoid the south-facing solar cooker of the Toilet Bowl and its wet, dangerous afternoon snow.

From Russet Lake the route drops to its low point, Singing Pass. If the weather has turned bad enough to make an above-timberline traverse undesirable, you can bail out from Singing Pass down the Fitzsimmons Creek Trail. There's nothing special about this trail—it will just get you back to civilization quickly. It can be used as an alternate access to the hut as well, if you just want to ski the glaciers and slopes around Singing Pass. If the weather is still decent, the best way to go is over the top of the ridge that leads from Singing Pass to the Whistler Ski Area. This ridge is lower than the one you took to get to the hut and is not glaciated. Its peaks are rounded bumps known as the Musical Bumps, with names like Oboe, Flute, and Piccolo. Between the bumps are open bowls that offer excellent skiing. The last bump is Whistler Summit. From there a moderate drop of 1,000 feet takes you to the top of the Whistler trail system.

This trip can be done very late in the season. I've skied parts of it at the beginning of July. But because of the lifts there is no trouble getting to the alpine regions in midwinter. This is very unlike two other glacial trips in this book, Mt. Olympus and the Ptarmigan Traverse, both in Washington State, which are deep wilderness ski tours that do not have easy access in midwinter. Access is not the only advantage of the Spearhead. The Coast Range is famous for the frequency and duration of its winter storms (those glaciers have to be fed!), but there are some good reasons why it is a better place for this type of traverse in midwinter than the sunnier and better-known mountains of Colorado. The climate is maritime rather than continental, which means that the snow is wetter and the average winter temperature much warmer. Avalanches tend to occur during and right after the storms, and the snow stabilizes relatively rapidly. Thus avalanche danger is less, usually, than in the Rockies. That doesn't mean that you can ignore it, though. You will find much less TG snow or very light powder, which means that you are less likely to end up slogging up to your hips while climbing or moving horizontally. Lastly, although the U.S. Rockies are higher, the scenery of the Coast Range is far more alpine, with great icecaps punctured by spirelike peaks.

The Spearhead Traverse, of course, doesn't exhaust the ski possibilities of the Coast Range. There is a group of huts in Garibaldi Provincial Park, only 40 miles from Vancouver, that serves a beautiful volcanic region of open forests and gentle glaciers. Farther afield, several traverses have been done in the range that can only be matched in the United States by the

Sierra Crest route. One of these is the traverse of the Monarch Icecap, which takes three weeks. Another one, grandly conceived, is a traverse of the Pantheon, Waddington, and Homathko ranges in one trip. Mt. Waddington, in the center of this traverse, is one of North America's dominant peaks, a massive granite uplift rising directly from sea level to over 13,000 feet and surrounded on all sides by great glaciers. Given the frequency of bad storms in the Coast Range, the difficulty of escaping from the middle of one of these routes, and the difficulty of navigating in storms on the icecaps, the skiers who pioneered these traverses have to be congratulated for their boldness and determination. These trips are certainly much more serious endeavors than the Sierra Crest.

The best source for information on ski touring in the Coast Range is the book *Exploring the Coast Mountains on Skis* by John Baldwin, who was one of the driving forces behind the exploration of the long traverses. Another Coast Range skier worth mentioning is John Clarke, who made several ski trips in the early 1970s—alone—deep into unexplored glacial-wilderness areas of the range. I've heard people say they expected that one day he would go off on one of these wilderness trips and never return, but that never happened. His accomplishments are comparable to Orland Bartholomew's solo Sierra trip.

British Columbia

Durrand Glacier

TOUR   Skiing out of the Durrand Glacier Hut in the Selkirk Mountains of British Columbia.

IN A NUTSHELL   The hut is placed at timberline and is reached via a helicopter ride from the Columbia River just north of Revelstoke, British Columbia. There is a wide range of both glacial and nonglacial slopes above the hut and good tree skiing below it.

WHAT MAKES THE TOUR SPECIAL   The hut makes a very comfortable midwinter base for skiing the wide variety of terrain around it. The Northern Selkirks is a spectacular, heavily glaciated range, which usually has good snow conditions due to the intermediate location between the coastal mountains and the colder, more continental Rockies.

LEVEL OF DIFFICULTY   Moderate to difficult. The hut allows inexperienced skiers to stay comfortable.

BEST TIME TO GO   December to May.

HOW TO GET THERE   Revelstoke is on the Trans-Canada Highway. You must make reservations for the hut and helicopter with Selkirk Mountain Experience at POB 1250, Revelstoke, B.C. VOE 2S0, phone (604) 837-9489.

SPECIAL EQUIPMENT   Ropes and prusiks for glacier travel should be carried. Also have avalanche gear, such as electronic locators and shovels.

MAPS   Durrand Glacier.

INFORMATION ON ACC HUTS   Alpine Club of Canada, POB 1026, Banff, Alberta T0L 0C0, phone (403) 762-4481.

LODGING AND SUPPLIES   Revelstoke, British Columbia.

I f you want to go on a multiday backcountry ski tour in midwinter you have two superior options. One is to go south to the desert-southwest ski tours (described elsewhere in this book) where even though you are camping out, the days are so warm and the situation so comfortable that it's acceptable to the soft-core as well as to the hard-core skier. Or you can stay in the north and center your trip around a high-mountain cabin. Then you can ski powder snow all day and dry out, dine, wash, play, rest, read, and sleep in warm, roomy comfort. If it storms you can stay in the trees, taking advantage of the superior definition they provide. If the day is nice you can climb high above timberline, and, in the good Canadian huts described here, ski on glaciers in spectacular alpine surroundings.

A lot of young skiers who start out winter camping on January ski trips become hut fanatics in later years—enough of claustrophobic tents, dripping snow caves, undriable clothes, 15-hour nights, and constant cold.

There are relatively few high-mountain huts in the western mountains of the United States. In Yosemite National Park there is one at Ostrander Lake. In Sequoia National Park there is one at Pear Lake. Both of these have good skiing around them. There is a hut at timberline on Mt. Shasta, with good alpine skiing above and good, gentle touring below. In Oregon there is a hut in the Wallowa Mountains. In Washington there is a set of huts in the Chiwaukum Mountains near Leavenworth. A hut is to be installed in a particularly beautiful site in the North Cascades near Winthrop in the fall of 1987.

In Idaho for many years now there have been guided tours between luxuriously appointed yurts in the Sawtooth Mountains. A similar yurt-to-yurt system also exists in the Bighole Mountains that directly face the west side of the Tetons. There is a network of huts near Aspen and the beginnings of a hut-to-hut system between Aspen and Vail.

In Alaska there is one of the best of all mountain huts, built by bush pilot Don Sheldon in the Ruth Amphitheater, and I've devoted a whole chapter to it elsewhere in this book. There is also a set of mountain huts running from Girdwood to Palmer Glacier, which allow a 4-day glacial traverse, the Eklutna Traverse.

But I think the best set of huts right now for those not living in Alaska are found in Canada, in the Interior Ranges of British Columbia. There, much of the early climbing, guiding, and skiing was done by European guides who brought with them from the Alps the tradition of comfortable mountain huts. For many years the Alpine Club of Canada has maintained huts placed near the treeline in the Selkirk, Purcell, and Rocky mountains. They all have great peaks and large glaciers above them. Below most of them are open forests—fine for powder skiing. This combination of glacier skiing plus tree skiing plus frequently excellent snow conditions is what sets these huts apart from the other ones. Lately private individuals have been building even more comfortable huts in ideal timberline locations in the Interior

Conrad Icefield, Purcell Range, British Columbia.
Photo by Steve Barnett.

Ranges, both for their own pleasure and for business with rentals and guided trips.

The Interior Ranges consist of the Monashee, Selkirk, Purcell, and Cariboo mountains. They have climates intermediate between the huge, wet snowfalls of the Coast Range and the smaller and colder snowfalls of the Rockies. Thus they get large snowfalls of reasonably light powder snow while having fewer problems with depth hoar and windslab than the Rockies. They are high enough to have extensive networks of glaciers. These ranges are the home of helicopter skiing in Canada because of their consistently good powder skiing. Some of the mountain areas like the Bugaboos are almost household words among skiers. Others such as the Adamant Range in the Northern Selkirks are not so well known but are so beautiful that in the United States they would almost certainly be given National Park status because of their combination of granite walls and spires and large glaciers.

To see what a trip to an Interior Range hut is like let's go to one of the best of the new huts—the Durrand Glacier Hut in the Selkirk Mountains north of Revelstoke, British Columbia.

After a 7-hour drive that actually takes 12 hours we sleepily wobble into Revelstoke at 1:30 in the morning and are picked up by guide Reudi Beglinger, who built the Durrand Hut just that summer. We will fly in tomorrow he says with a group of 17 others.

In the morning we drive up along the Columbia River, past the Revelstoke Dam, to an obscure gravel pit jammed with cars and touring skis. This is the airport. Down here at river level it's a dismal scene. There are just a few inches of very old snow, and low clouds and fog obscure any view of the surrounding mountains. We meet the other skiers. They nonchalantly organize the bottles of wine, scotch, and brandy they're carrying up, the huge pots of already prepared stew and chicken cacciatore, the pans of lasagne, the gallons of ice cream. We sheepishly hide our small sacks of tuna noodle one-pot glop. No question about it, these people are experienced hut skiers.

The helicopter falls out of the sky onto the gravel pit. Skis are lashed on to one skid. Loads are stuffed into the baggage compartment and into the laps of the passengers. How much does this flight cost? Only around $85 for the round trip. The cost is directly proportional to the flight time. Most of the hut flights are in this range. The beautiful, privately owned Battle Abbey Hut in the Southern Selkirks is a much longer flight, as is the ACC hut in the Clemenceau Icefields in the Rockies.

Up we go into the layer of clouds. We pop through and suddenly are in sunshine. It's perfect. What will the snow be like? The pilot follows one creek up and then another one. The glacier comes into view surrounded

The Durrand Glacier Hut. Photo by Steve Barnett.

by tall white peaks. In fact, everything is dazzlingly white. We drop down into the trees and there is the hut, a 2-story Swiss chalet.

Every bit of the hut was flown in by helicopter, obviously a very expensive proposition. Reudi was encouraged to make the investment by the success of another hut in the Revelstoke area, at Blanket Glacier in the Monashee Mountains on the other side of the Columbia. That hut is nearly constantly full. It seems that the more people are exposed to the pleasures of skiing out of a high-mountain hut, the greater the demand grows. Thus at this stage of the game in Canada it seems that exceeding capacity is not a problem since each new hut creates even more demand for future ones.

The group we were with is a perfect example of this. This was the tenth year in succession that they had spent New Year's skiing out of a hut. They were a group of Canadian professionals from Calgary, Jasper, and Vancouver—lawyers, architects, teachers, a dentist, an environmental consultant, a park ranger. Between them they had used just about every hut in Canada and were eager to try the newest ones.

As quickly as possible after we land we get our ski equipment out and start climbing up the vast nonglaciated slope behind the cabin. The idea is to get a good view of the surroundings while the sun is still out. And to get in some good skiing. The snow is much better than I thought it would be. The hut is high enough—6,350 feet—that the snow did not melt and form a breakable crust during the long period of sunny weather the Northwest has had this winter. The highest peak on this slope is about 2,000 feet above the cabin, and the group makes the best of the vertical, repeating the choicest pieces. Only at the very top is there wind-blasted, difficult-to-ski snow. The slopes are moderate enough to be relatively safe from avalanches but still steep enough to be exciting skiing.

Location, of course, is the key to a hut's usefulness to ski tourers. The hut should be near timberline. There should be good terrain both below it in the trees and above it in the alpine zone. In the alpine zone it's good if there is ready access to glaciers and interesting ski mountaineering, including steep mountain descents. At the same time gentler nonglaciated slopes are good to have for more dangerous snow conditions and for freer skiing unencumbered by ropes and glacier equipment. The terrain in the trees is important for stormy days. If you don't have it then you may feel stuck in the hut without being able to do any interesting skiing. For most of these huts skiing out is such a difficult proposition that you would much rather be able to enjoy the stay and fly out as scheduled.

We stay out in the sun, climbing back up and skiing new runs in the powder snow nearly until dark. Back at the hut the Canadian group invites us to share some of their multicourse feast. Their separate personalities start to shine through. The full moon also shines through the windows. Time to go skiing again, under the moonlight, in the powder, in the trees. It's magnificent. A fine run with 400 to 500 feet of drop. Let's do it again. Clouds start covering the moon. A storm is moving in.

The next morning the glacier is socked in and it is snowing. We start exploring the tree runs beyond where we skied the night before. The hut is situated on a rib in a basin. On one side is the big nonglaciated slope. On the other, higher side is the Durrand Glacier and the network of other glaciers it is connected to. We can ski off of either side of the hut's rib. Both sides are forested. One side is very steep, the other side has both steep and gentle slopes. Even though we have a large group we never quite succeed in skiing out the good slopes.

Another morning and maybe the sun will break out. There's a blue hole in the clouds. Acting on the assumption that the day will clear we head up toward the glacier. The slope down from it looks steep from the hut, but there is actually a system of ramps that makes the ascent moderate in grade and not too dangerous from the point of view of avalanches. The snow is much deeper now, deep enough that we might even advance our snow report from powder to deep powder, which means that when skiing down both skis will be flying in the snow, never touching a base. The blue hole turns out to have been a "sucker hole" for as soon as we reach the glacier everything socks in. Down we go. But the trip down is pure delight.

It's like skiing through feathers. Even falling is fun in this perfect snow. A good group of skiers, too, these Canadians, who take such delight in playing with the powder.

The hut is a delight, too. The kitchen area is first class with a propane oven and restaurant-quality utensils. It's well insulated, and the wood stove heats it quickly and for a long time on one charge of wood. The wood is already stacked and split. Light comes from kerosene lamps and one propane lamp. Since this hut was privately built there's a very strong incentive for the owner to keep it in immaculate condition. He plans to have a cook or hutkeeper up there much of the time. He says that if the hut is immaculate when guests arrive then they are much more likely to take good care of it during their stay. The Canadian group says that the ACC and provincial huts are cheaper than the private huts but are not so well maintained, or so well outfitted. Most of them are simpler and smaller. One of the main exceptions, the Fairy Meadow Hut in the Adamant Range of the Selkirks, was also privately built and then expropriated by the ACC. They say that it has deteriorated somewhat in the last few years.

For the next several days it keeps snowing. We are stuck in the trees but we are skiing deep powder and seem always able to find new lines to ski. Amazingly the avalanche hazard seems to be low even though we expected it to be high when so much new snow fell on the thick layers of surface hoar. There has been no wind, and there are no signs of slab formation. One of the good features of this hut's location is that it is sheltered from the wind by the surrounding mountain walls.

The Canadians brought up funny hats and fireworks for New Year's and an endless supply of jokes cunningly inserted into normal conversation. It's been fun to get to know them. Staying in a hut with a large group is inherently a social experience. This may be wilderness skiing, but the experience is not very much one of wilderness solitude, nor do you feel thrown out in the wild with only your own resources to keep you going. Well, if you wanted a hard-core experience you would be out there in your snow cave. This is the charm of hut-based skiing—wilderness skiing with civilized amenities.

Here are capsule descriptions of Interior-Range huts, as well as some of the ones in the Canadian Rockies. I'm only listing those that are best for winter ski trips.

Durrand Glacier Hut. This has the best combination of accommodations, range of slopes above and below the cabin, and reasonable access.

Monashee Hut out of Blue River, British Columbia. This is the most luxurious one. There are moderate slopes around it.

Blanket Glacier Hut. This is in the Monashees west of Revelstoke, British Columbia. The skiing around it is gentler than at the Durrand Hut.

Fairy Meadow Hut (ACC). This is in the Selkirks north of Golden, British Columbia. The hut is in an exceptionally beautiful alpine setting. There is excellent ski mountaineering above it but limited tree skiing below.

Wheeler Hut (ACC). This is just south of the Rogers Pass Highway. There is good skiing above it on Illiciliwaet Glacier and other runs.

Stanley Mitchell Hut (ACC). This is in Yoho National Park. There is excellent ski terrain above the hut.

Battle Abbey. This is a beautiful, privately built hut in the Southern Selkirks administered by Canadian Mountain Holidays. It's hard to get reservations for it, and it's a long flight in. There is good tree skiing below the hut.

Assiniboine Lodge. This private lodge is reached by helicopter but is still very popular. Accommodations are excellent. It has excellent cross-country ski terrain plus good ski mountaineering. The Rockies around it are exceedingly scenic, but the Rockies snow is often not as good as that of the Interior Ranges.

The ACC huts are usually reserved long in advance for such peak-season times as holidays. You may be able to get into them by waiting for cancellations.

Washington

Mt. Olympus

TOUR   Mt. Olympus in Olympic National Park, Washington.

IN A NUTSHELL   A midsummer hike up the Hoh River through rain forest to the Blue Glacier of Mt. Olympus. From there the trip crosses the mini-icecap of Olympus and climbs up almost to the summit.

WHAT MAKES THE TOUR SPECIAL   A fantastic rain-forest hike, the opportunity to ski a small icecap, a beautiful mountain summit surrounded by water on three sides, and the pleasures of summer skiing are all combined in this one trip. Together, these make this one of the most distinctive of ski trips possible in the United States.

LEVEL OF DIFFICULTY   The hike is long (20 miles) but easy. The skiing is moderate and with summer snow shouldn't present any special problem.

BEST TIME TO GO   June, July.

HOW TO GET THERE   Drive on US 101 to Hoh River Road south of Forks. Follow it to the campground. From there hike up the river trail until it gets to Glacier Meadows Camp, the end of the trail. Climb straight up until you get to the moraine of the Blue Glacier. Cross the moraine, cross the glacier, and climb up the obvious slopes on the other side to the Snow Dome. From the Snow Dome the way to the summit is clear.

SPECIAL EQUIPMENT   A light rope and prusiks for glacier travel should be carried. An ice axe is advisable as well. Heavy skis aren't needed in midsummer. Be prepared for rain.

MAPS   USGS Mt. Olympus quadrangle.

LODGING AND SUPPLIES   Forks and Port Angeles, Washington.

There are very few glacial icecap tours that you can do in the lower 48 states. A summer ski ascent of Mt. Olympus in Olympic National Park in Washington is the best of them. It combines skiing and scenic virtues with an extraordinary hike through the nation's lushest rain forest. Together, these features make skiing Mt. Olympus one of the premier ski tours in the United States.

Mt. Olympus receives the heaviest precipitation of any spot in the United States. That is more than 200 inches of water a year, and most of it is in the form of snow that falls almost continuously from November to April. The reason for the heavy precipitation is that Mt. Olympus is situated in the middle of a peninsula sticking out into the stormy North Pacific, and it is the first high peak to intercept every storm. Due to orographic lifting, even in good months (July and August), any stray breeze blowing in from the ocean causes fog and rain. All of that snow and rain cause two phenomena that make this a marvelous ski tour. One is a glacial system that is second in size in the lower 48 states only to Mt. Rainier. It really is a mini-icecap with all the glacial skiing experiences that implies, such as skiing up and over glacial passes and working your way through seracs and crevasses. The size of the icecap (some 24 square miles) is remarkable, considering that the peak is not quite 8,000 feet high (Rainier is 14,000 feet high). It's the enormous snowfall combined with summers kept cool by the proximity of the Pacific that let the glaciers grow so big at such a low altitude. The other weather-induced phenomenon that makes this tour special is the rain-forest hike you must do to get to the glaciers. The hike along the Hoh River is some 13 miles long. The forest is one of the natural wonders of the country. Enormous trees, most among the biggest anywhere of their species, form a canopy above. Moss covers everything, and the light filters down green in tone. The forest floor is alive with new trees, even very large ones growing out in lines where some ancient and giant tree fell.

The best time to ski Mt. Olympus is in July. In winter the weather is too foul, the avalanche danger too high, and the quality of the snow too sketchy for you to have a good chance of having a pleasant trip (though in a "drought" year, a midwinter trip might work out well). In spring the long hike is muddy and the weather still uncertain. In several of the last ten years for example, almost all of June has had poor weather. Olympus is a tour that should be done in good weather to be worthwhile. Mid-July gives you the statistically greatest chance of getting good weather plus dry trails plus corn snow that is both easy skiing and relatively stable and free from avalanche danger. You don't have to worry if there will be snow. In all but the very worst years the glaciers will be completely covered through the month of July.

The tour starts at the Hoh River Ranger Station from where you hike some 20 miles to get to the moraine at the side of the Blue Glacier. The first 13 miles are almost flat, and although the distance is long it is also easy. It's such an interesting hike, due to the rain forest, that it will most likely seem too short. After the lowland forest hike you cross the Hoh River Gorge and start climbing. You pass several campsites along the way and finally break out of the trees just below the moraine of the Blue Glacier. This is likely to be where you'll hit snow in July. To get to the summit of Olympus you cross the Blue Glacier, which is quite broad and flat at this level, and then climb moderate slopes to the dome-shaped peak on the other side of the glacier. This peak is called, appropriately, the Snow Dome. There is a hut on one end of the Snow Dome that houses a summer glaciological research team from the University of Washington. From the Snow Dome

Mt. Tom, Washington, seen from the summit of Mt. Olympus.
Photo by Steve Barnett.

you ski across a broad plateau of snow and then climb the final crevassed slopes to the summit ridge of Olympus. In general the glaciers here are well behaved. The snow bridges are thick and strong, and since there is rarely new summer snow, there are rarely tricky, thinly covered slots. When you get to the summit ridge you must cross to its other side and then climb up to the col between the real and false summits. The false summit can be skied, but the real one is a rock tower. It is a straightforward third-class climb, feasible in vibram-soled ski boots.

Olympus is not a wilderness mountain. Though it's a long hike in you will share it with the university researchers and probably several teams of climbers. (One year a harpsichord was flown in for one of the researcher's wives, a musician. That makes it a civilized mountain, indeed.) But these people will all be concentrated on the main route up the Blue Glacier and the Snow Dome. Ski tourers can enjoy total solitude while exploring the icecap around the mountain. This is one of the real treats of this tour. It's an easy way to get some of the same feel you might get skiing the glacier systems of the Canadian Selkirks or Rockies ranges. For example, instead of crossing the Blue Glacier to the Snow Dome you might head left and go up to Blizzard Pass. A tricky little crossing over a crevasse wall gets you onto the Hoh Glacier, which seems nearly as vast as the Blue. If you were to keep going you could cross yet another pass and get on yet another glacier, and so on. It is possible that Olympus could be circumnavigated with glacier crossings and a little bit of climbing. For me, crossing these passes is tremendously exciting. I'm filled with anticipation to see what I will see on the other side. I also like very much to work my way through intricate glacial features such as seracs and crevasses. It's a kind of skiing that stresses slow-speed precision rather than all-out high speed. The thrill is different, but it's a great one nevertheless.

Olympus is a good example of the joys of summer touring. In the Pacific Northwest it is in many ways the best time to ski. The weather is best, the days longest, and the snow is reliably of good quality for skiing. It's easy to find snow-free areas for campsites, lunch spots, and afternoon snoozes. Access to the highest and most alpine areas is relatively easy, and you don't have to travel with the constant fear that you might get pinned down for days in storm and fog.

What equipment is best for this trip? Because of the long hike, it's a good idea to keep the weight down. Light touring skis, such as Epoke 900s or Karhu Kodiak Edges, should be sufficient. Waxless bases will be in their proper element on the summer snow. Hard ice would be very rare in midsummer. Even at the top of Olympus the altitude is not high enough for the temperature to be below freezing during the day. Medium-weight boots will be sufficient both for the approach hike and for the skiing. Carry a light rope for glacier travel and light mountaineering and an ice axe. You shouldn't have any trouble with the glaciers, but you must be prepared for a crevasse rescue just in case. It wouldn't hurt for everyone to have a 50-foot length of 7 to 8 mm rope. Crampons probably aren't necessary unless you're going to try a more mountaineering-oriented exploit on or around the peak.

There are several other excellent long trips possible in the Olympics. One is the Bailey Range Traverse. The Bailey Range is a subrange that extends in an arc from 7 Lakes Basin above Sol Duc Hot Springs to Mt. Olympus. It is glaciated in part and exceedingly scenic. The start of it, from Sol Duc Hot Springs to 7 Lakes Basin, makes a beautiful shorter trip.

Washington

Ptarmigan Traverse

TOUR Ptarmigan Traverse, Washington.

IN A NUTSHELL This is a multiday traverse that follows the ridgeline running from Cascade Pass to Dome Peak. It stays mostly above timberline and crosses several large glaciers. It includes a ski descent of Dome Peak.

WHAT MAKES THE TOUR SPECIAL The route goes through the glacial heart of the North Cascades, true wilderness from which unplanned escape is difficult.

LEVEL OF DIFFICULTY The trip calls for good mountaineering skills. There is plenty of advanced skiing with steep slopes and possibly difficult snow conditions.

BEST TIME TO GO June.

HOW TO GET THERE Cascade Pass is at the end of the North Fork Cascade River Road reachable from Marblemount, Washington, which is on WA 20, the North Cascade Highway. The other end of the trip, Downey Creek Trailhead, is reached from Suiattle River Road, which is in turn reached from the Mountain Loop Highway out of Darrington, Washington.

SPECIAL EQUIPMENT Metal-edged skis, ice axe, and crampons are all recommended. A tent and clothing really capable of withstanding rain are also advised.

MAPS   USGS Cascade Pass or Green Trails Cascade Pass, available from Green Trails, P.O. Box 1272, Bellevue, WA 98009.

LODGING AND SUPPLIES   Marblemount, Washington.

The North Cascades are the most rugged, the most wild, and the most heavily glaciated mountains in the lower 48 states. Their climate is only a hair drier than that of the nearby Olympic Mountains, which are the wettest of all the lower-state ranges. It's no surprise that until recent years deep explorations on skis into the range were very rare. No Orland Bartholomew crossed their entire length in the dark ages of ski touring, and even now that hasn't been done, though some groups are getting close.

Still, skiing in the North Cascades can be a marvelous adventure. It's the only place in the lower 48 where real glacial traverses are possible, like those commonly done in the Alps. These are trips where you climb one glacier, cross a pass, ski down another glacier, and then climb up yet another one, and so on. Along the way you can climb and ski the great peaks from which the glaciers flow. There's still a strong feeling of wilderness adventure found when doing long trips in the Cascades, created by the isolation of the areas through which you travel, by the tremendous difficulty of escaping from the routes in their middles, by the related difficulty of traveling below the snowline (the horrors of the brush are legendary), and by the sea of lofty white peaks that surrounds you on most of these routes. A small number of enthusiastic ski mountaineers are pioneering these long routes on skis right now.

The classic glacial traverse in the North Cascades is the Ptarmigan Traverse. Until recently it was classic only for mountaineers walking it in midsummer, but the terrain is better for skiers than for mountain hikers and in the last several years the traverse has been gaining recognition as one of the country's premier ski trips.

The Ptarmigan Traverse runs through the glacial heart of the North Cascades, a north-to-south crestline that is the center of the south unit of North Cascades National Park. It starts at Cascade Pass, reachable by 5 miles of foot trail (or a shorter and more direct route on skis) from the trailhead at the end of the North Fork Cascade River Road. It then runs for some 25 miles past Mixup, Sentinel, LeConte, Dome, and Spire peaks, following glacial shelves and passes under these mountains. Finally it tumbles 3,500 feet down from a pass beside Spire Point to a 14-mile-long hiking trail, which takes you back to civilization. While on the trip you're in almost total wilderness, with no easy escape except at the two ends.

The best time to do the Ptarmigan or any of the long Cascade traverses is in late spring or early summer. Mid- to late June is about right. There are several reasons for this. The weather in the Cascades can be frightful even through April and May. Sudden heavy snowstorms can cause extreme avalanche hazards. The terrain around the Ptarmigan is so rugged that there are almost no sections of it that will be safe if there's a lot of new snow. There's little option for any party caught in such conditions other than to find a safe campsite and sit tight. Furthermore, new Cascade snow is notorious for its poor skiing quality. This is a maritime range, and not only is the snow often wet, but it frequently rains at altitudes well above timberline. Let your imagination picture a cycle of several feet of fresh wet snow, followed by heavy rain, followed by a good freeze, followed by wind or hot sun, and then picture yourself skiing in this concoction with a heavy pack. It's not always this way, but it happens often enough that you should not be surprised to find it on a winter or spring trip.

Travel in June or July, and everything will be different. The days are long, and the weather is usually much better. The snow has settled into a reasonably stable corn-snow condition, which is excellent for traveling and also good for fun on the downhill runs. Why suffer? Some have done these trips earlier, but if you want to enjoy yourself, go late.

The nature of the skiing is determined by the peculiar terrain of this part of the Cascades. Due to the heavy glaciation of the Ice Ages, followed by the present lighter glaciation, the central part of the North Cascades is cut into double cirques. There is a lower cirque that usually extends from around 5,000 to 6,000 feet down to below 3,000 feet, then a shelf, and then another walled cirque rising above the shelf to the tops of the peaks, at 8,000 to 9,000 feet. The lower cirque is usually very steep, even cliff-walled at its top, and usually is very brushy, since avalanches clean out the big trees. Travel in these lower cirques is often frustrating (one group I know of tried to take a shortcut in a similar area in the Olympics and took 3 days to go 10 miles), and most folks travel through them only where there are trails. The upper cirque is not brushy (treeline is at about 6,000 feet), but its upper walls are usually steep cliffs and are exceedingly avalanche prone. Occasionally an easier slope or glacier cuts through the cliff bands to a pass in the ridge. The Ptarmigan generally follows the shelf between the cirques, and crosses the ridgecrest at the glacial passes.

I've tried to do the trip three times, and only succeeded on the last attempt. The first time I was with Bill Nicolai, who had done it on foot several times and had told me that it would be a perfect trip on skis. We started in early May just as the weather cleared from a series of heavy storms.

By the time we got to Cascade Pass, we were thoroughly surprised by the amount of new snow—several feet of it. The next section of the trip is a traverse on a steep sidehill called Mixup Arm, from Cascade Pass to the Cache Glacier. There are huge cliffs both above and below the traverse and it is one of the most dangerous parts of the route. We were torn between our desire to do the trip and our fear of avalanches as the spring sun hit the new snow. Even a small avalanche could take a skier over the lower cliffs. In the end we decided to wait. Later that afternoon, and the next day too, we were entertained by the repeated spectacle of monster slides starting from the summit of Mixup Peak, dropping 3,000 feet to the traverse, sweeping it clean, and then plunging another 1,000 feet to the valley floor. It certainly was good that we hadn't tried it!

The second time I tried the trip was in mid-June. The weather forecast wasn't good, but it didn't call for any really large storms. To make a long story short, we ended up sitting out many days in the middle of the traverse, running out of food, and then navigating through the fog with map, compass, and altimeter to the one bailout route available on the whole traverse, the very rudimentary trail that runs down from South Cascade Glacier and that is used by University of Washington glaciologists doing research on the glacier. The ten rainy miles out on this trail are not remembered with a warm glow.

Compared to the two preceding attempts, the final one was uneventful. The weather was perfect. The first night we camped, as we had done before, just above Cascade Pass in the last scraggly trees before timberline. The view from there, as from almost all of the tour, was spectacular, with huge glacier-hung walls all around.

The next morning we crossed the steep and hazardous Mixup Arm traverse on foot, carrying our skis and using ice axes and crampons. It is possible to ski this section of the trip, but it must be done with great care since a slide could carry skiers over cliffs. It's a good idea to carry an ice axe in any case, since it is needed for the Trick Ledge that goes through the cliffs of Art's Knoll, not very far beyond Mixup Arm. In normal June weather it's possible, in theory, to dispense with crampons and cut steps if needed with the axe. I have always taken them with me, however, despite their weight, since they make steep passages on foot much quicker and more sure. For the Ptarmigan, fancy crampons aren't needed. Simple hinged ones will be fine.

From Mixup Arm the route goes over the Cache Glacier and the pass at its top, Cache Col. From there the route down isn't immediately apparent, but we actually had no problems, and the way down opened up into a fine leftward-trending ski slope, which took us to frozen Kool-Aid Lake. From here the route wasn't apparent, and there was something to appearances this time. A rock wall, which is the side of a small peak called Art's Knoll, blocks the way. You can make an end run on it and fight your way up a steep, brushy gully to get around it, or you can take the usual climber's route, the "trick ledge." Head up the snowfield in the middle of the wall, and when you get to its top you'll see a steep snow ledge, partially hidden from below, which takes you to the right to a short snow couloir that goes to the top of the ridge. With crampons and axe this passage is not at all difficult, although it is exposed and adds adventure to the route.

From Art's Knoll a long sidehill traverse brought us to the Middle Cascade Glacier, which is an impressive piece of icy real estate. At its top is the Spider-Formidable Col. The Middle Cascade Glacier is one of the nicer downhill runs on the Ptarmigan, and if you're not rushing it's worth taking some time to ski it. When planning a traverse like this you have to consider how much time you want to spend climbing the peaks and skiing the slopes along the way. If you want to just do the traverse as quickly as possible, three days are sufficient. But it makes more sense to take some extra time so that you can ski the more spectacular runs, like the Middle Cascade Glacier, or the run off the top of Dome Peak. The longer you stay out, of course, the greater your chance of running into bad weather, and the greater your loads. So there's a balance to be achieved that will give you the most fun and the most adventurous trip.

From Spider-Formidable Col we finished the day's travel with a run down to Yang-Yang Lakes. These are set in sparse trees right at timberline, and their location is one of the most beautiful spots in the North Cascades. The huge LeConte Glacier on Sentinel Peak dominates a grand circle of snowy peaks wrapped around you. In late June it doesn't get dark until 10:00 P.M. so late evening skiing is possible, another of the advantages of touring at that time of year. A disadvantage on my last trip there was the layer of pollen that had blown up from the lower forests, making the snow sticky and slow. I had never seen this before, and people who traveled in the area several weeks later said that it had washed off. Is it usual? I don't think so; I think that it was an unusual confluence of botanical and meteorological phenomena.

The route continues with the same combination of glacier crossings, sidehill traverses, and pass crossings. Take the skis off. Climb up a couloir to LeConte Arm. Sidehill traverse to LeConte Glacier. Climb up and over the glacier. Ski Old Guard Peak. Traverse across Upper South Cascade Glacier. Climb over the pass and ski down steep slopes to White Rock Lakes. A steep sidehill traverse leads to a climb up to Spire Glacier. Then camp and after dinner ski up and down from Spire Point.

The next leg contains the high point of this trip, the ski ascent of Dome Peak. Dome is one of the higher peaks of the North Cascade, 8,995 feet. Its bulk and large system of glaciers make it dominant in this area. It's also very wild, with the closest road access at least 20 miles away, and not a very easy trip either. Only the last few feet of rock at the top were beyond the reach of our skis.

To leave the Ptarmigan we skied up and over Spire Col and down 3,500 feet of steep and exciting slopes. From Cub Lake at the bottom of this slope we climbed 500 feet and then headed down forested Bachelor Creek until the snow ran out. At this point, where the snow was patchy and the brush thick, we faced one of the harder parts of such a Cascade trip—finding the trail. Very careful map reading, and perseverance with the brush, finally put us right. The final stretch is 14 miles of downhill trail with a tricky log crossing over Bachelor Creek. (We left a car at Downey Creek Trailhead on the Suiattle River Road.)

Only in the last few years have skiers started doing the Ptarmigan. Some of those who have done it have gone on and explored similar high traverses nearby. One has been done starting from the North Cascade Highway, climbing up Colonial Peak, and then traversing over to Eldorado Peak, which is the center of a small icecap. The section from Eldorado Peak to Cascade Pass probably was done many years ago. Another ski traverse has been done from Glacier Peak, an ice-covered volcano just south of Dome Peak, out along the Dakobed Range to the south and east, ending at the old mine site of Trinity. Thus the pathfinding is almost complete for a ski route covering the entire glacial crest from the North Cascade Highway to south of Glacier Peak. We await our Orland Bartholomew.

For a shorter but still classic introduction to North Cascades skiing the trip up Mt. Shuksan is ideal. Mt. Shuksan is one of North America's most beautiful mountains. Indeed I have seen posters in both Europe and South America claiming it as their own.

The best route up Shuksan for skiers is via the Sulphide Glacier on its south side. This is reached via Shannon Creek Road, which in turn branches off the Baker Lake Highway that connects with the North Cascade Highway, WA 20. The skiing is not difficult and the trip can be done in a day. For a spectacular variation you can circumnavigate the summit on the mountain's interconnected glaciers.

Washington

Ptarmigan Ridge

TOUR   Summer skiing along Ptarmigan Ridge between Mts. Baker and Shuksan in the North Cascades of Washington.

IN A NUTSHELL   From the Mt. Baker Ski Area traverse along the ridge toward Mt. Baker, skiing the bowls, slopes, and small glaciers along the way for either a day trip or an easy overnight trip.

WHAT MAKES THE TOUR SPECIAL   There is almost always good snow cover well into August. This is one of the most beautiful mountain areas in the country. Little climbing is needed to get to the snow. There is a great variety of slopes.

LEVEL OF DIFFICULTY   Slopes range from very easy, even flat, to very steep. None have verticals bigger than 1,500 feet, except Mt. Baker itself. The approach is easy.

BEST TIME TO GO   The end of July.

HOW TO GET THERE   From Bellingham, Washington, drive up WA 542 to the Mt. Baker Ski Area. Continue driving until either you are stopped by snow or you reach the Artist Point parking lot just a few miles beyond the ski area. Take the trail marked Camp Kiser, which goes around the southeast side of flat-topped Table Mountain in front of you. It will take you along the ridge toward Mt. Baker. The skiing lies along the way and then continues beyond the trail's end.

SPECIAL EQUIPMENT   This trip is pure recreation, so bring along the kind of food and drink you like to celebrate with. If you intend to go on the glaciers on Mt. Baker itself, a rope and prusiks may be advisable. You will want sunscreen.

MAPS   USGS Mt. Shuksan and Mt. Baker quadrangles.

LODGING AND SUPPLIES   Glacier and Bellingham, Washington.

S ummer is a great time to go skiing. Hot sun, long days, easy-skiing corn snow, and snow-free islands of grass, ideal for lunch or camping, are strong attractions for diehard skiers. Pardon them for thinking that those who only ski in midwinter are the diehards! Those skiers have to face constant cold, violent storms, and uncertain snow, plus avalanche hazard where it's steep.

The Pacific Northwest is the best place in the United States for summer skiing. It has the heaviest winter snowfalls and the coolest summers. The Northwest is where the overwhelming majority of the glaciers in the United States are found. In this book we have three other late-spring or summer Northwest ski tours—the Ptarmigan Traverse, Mt. Olympus, and Three Sisters. All of these are fairly long, multiday trips. What's needed is a lighter, easier summer ski tour—one that combines summer pleasures along with great skiing. The Ptarmigan Ridge of Mt. Baker is just such a tour. It's a perfect trip for the end of July.

The Ptarmigan Ridge runs between Mts. Baker and Shuksan on the west slope of the Cascades just south of the Canadian border. It is one of the most scenic places in the entire United States. Mt. Baker is a great volcano, 10,778 feet high. It is the most completely ice-covered of all the Cascade volcanoes. To me it is a more beautiful mountain than Mt. Rainier, better shaped, more completely white, standing above a range of great mountains rather than standing alone. Also, Mt. Shuksan can lay a strong claim as the most beautiful of all peaks in the United States. It is such a classic mountain that I've seen pictures of it all over the world being pawned off as local scenes. On the Ptarmigan Ridge both of these peaks are a constant presence.

You can get to the ridge from the road to the Mt. Baker Ski Area, which in summer climbs beyond the ski area to a viewpoint known as Artist Point. In a heavy snow year this will still be snow-covered in August. In other words, you will frequently be able to drive right up to the snow, even in August. Even if the snow is gone from the parking lot at Artist Point, you don't have to gain much altitude to start skiing. Unlike almost all the other good summer ski trips, you don't have to climb much to find solid snow cover on this tour. Instead you traverse along the ridge, getting closer and closer to Mt. Baker. The snowfields gradually get larger until

Ptarmigan Ridge, Mt. Baker, Washington. Photo by Steve Barnett.

they merge into the glaciers of Mt. Baker itself. All along the way, right up to the end of the ridge at Mt. Baker's Rainbow Glacier, there will be grassy meadows melted free of the snow, perfect for lazy lunches, afternoon naps, or evening camps.

What's the skiing like? The verticals are moderate (with the exception of Mt. Baker itself), with a range of 1,000 to 1,500 vertical feet, but the size of the area and the variety of ski slopes are considerable. There is both very steep and very easy, even flat, skiing. There are almost no serious crevasses. The snow will be solid and stable summer corn, which has been baked long enough by the sun that it will stay firm all day, even in mid-July. Sometimes suncups are a problem but usually not, as summer rainstorms seem to flatten them out.

Start the trip from the Artist Point parking lot. Take the trail labeled "Camp Kiser," which runs along the east side of Table Mountain, the flat-

Ptarmigan Ridge. Photo by Steve Barnett.

topped peak above you. Circle above a small bowl (possibly skiable) and come to a small pass. Cross it and take a climbing traverse around a west-facing bowl on the other side. This too will probably be skiable. Your climbing traverse will take you to the ridgecrest, which should be a mixture of flowered meadows and snowfields. At the end of this ridge you have a choice. The trail heads left. Follow it and you'll get to a succession of snow-filled bowls, some very steep. At their end is a flatter meadow area, Camp Kiser. If you take the path forking to the right you get to snowfields that lead to a prominent local peak with a rock pinnacle for a summit. This is Coleman Pinnacle, 6,400 feet high. There is a glacier under Coleman Pinnacle that provides a fun, moderate, 1,400-foot descent. Beyond Coleman Pinnacle is another glacier dropping from a timbered ridge. You can climb this to rejoin the other route and get onto Mt. Baker's endless snowfields. The fact that glaciers here start from below timberline is testimony to the enormous snowfall and moderate summer temperatures of this region. The Mt. Baker Ski Area must have the highest annual snowfall of any ski area in the United States.

The two routes (one north and one south of the ridge) rejoin on the far side of Coleman Pinnacle. There's relatively flat skiing on the ridge. Ahead is an opening onto the massive Rainbow Glacier of Mt. Baker. The opening is framed by two rock towers and is appropriately named the Portals. You can also make an end run to the right around the Portals and get on the Sholes Glacier, which is gentle, beautiful, and nearly crevasse-free.

You can do Coleman Pinnacle as a one-day trip. The whole route out to Rainbow Glacier makes a fine unhurried overnight trip. You will be able to camp on grass, will see few other people, and likely will see wildlife. This tour has become an annual end-of-July event for me, in good snow years and bad. In midwinter Ptarmigan Ridge is accessible from the ski area and is still exceedingly beautiful, but there is strong danger of getting trapped by storm, as well as avalanche danger and navigational difficulties. One very experienced group I know of tried this as a New Year's trip and was caught by a storm. They tried to return but set off a large slide on the way back that buried several of them up to their necks. They had to bail out down Wells Creek instead of making it back to the ski area. Typical for the Cascades, they got only part-way down when the snow turned to sleet and rain, and they had to follow the narrow creek bottom through wet jungle, fighting downed logs and Devil's Club (a wretched spiked plant that grows thickly on the shady Cascade rain-forest floor). They spent the night keeping warm by wringing their clothes out. Summer is a lot more pleasant time to visit this area with skis. In fact, at that time of year this is one of the most pleasant ski tours I know of anywhere—and I'm not alone in this opinion. The area is also a good one for fall trips. Only a few inches of new snow on the permanent snowfields can create excellent skiing in late September or October.

The Ptarmigan Ridge is my favorite area for short summer ski trips, but there are quite a few other popular ones in the Northwest, including those I describe below:

1. **Muir Snowfield, Mt. Rainier National Park.** A climb of 4,500 vertical feet from Paradise Ranger Station takes you to Camp Muir, at 10,000 feet, a staging area for summit climbs. There are always at least 2,700 vertical feet of moderate skiing on the way down. This route is popular with skiers and is always crowded with climbers.

2. **Black Tusk, Garibaldi Provincial Park, British Columbia.** This is a popular summer area for Vancouver skiers. Take the road from Vancouver to the Whistler Ski Area. Ask in the town of Squamish about the "microwave road" and take it to the Black Tusk. Snowfields under the Black Tusk, a volcanic plug some 7,500 feet high, provide runs of up to 1,500 vertical feet.

3. **Mt. Baker, south side, Easton Glacier.** The south-side route is a good way to ski and climb the peak right into August. There is a skiable vertical of up to 6,000 feet in the middle of summer. The skiing is generally moderate, though you do have to keep track of crevasses. The route starts from Schreiber Meadow, which is reached by logging road from Baker Lake and WA 20.

4. **Mt. Hood, Oregon.** There are downhill lifts climbing much of the way up Mt. Hood's south side. The last several thousand feet are still free of contraptions and are all yours for summer skiing. The last part is steep and possibly crevassed.

Washington

Eureka Creek Loop

TOUR   A 7-day circle around the basin of Eureka Creek in the Pasayten Wilderness in the North Cascades of Washington State.

IN A NUTSHELL   The route goes 4 miles up the Lost River Valley outside of Mazama, Washington, and then climbs 5,000 feet to cross Pistol Pass. It then drops into and follows Monument Creek Valley, which is surrounded by several high, skiable peaks. Crossing Shellrock Pass, the route enters Eureka Creek Basin and crosses it at a high altitude. All of the surrounding high peaks are skiable. It then leaves the basin and drops down to the Pasayten River, crosses Robinson Pass, and returns to the road very near the starting point.

WHAT MAKES THE TOUR SPECIAL   This trip combines deep wilderness, wonderful scenery, and lots of excellent mountain skiing. Campsites are superb and, being on the east side of the Cascades, the chances of getting good weather and snow conditions are relatively high.

LEVEL OF DIFFICULTY   You have to be in condition to do a 7-day trip that will be at times strenuous (first day especially). Skiing is difficult at times, but the trip can be (and has been) enjoyed even without a high level of skiing competence. The key is knowing when to quit and walk or sidestep.

BEST TIME TO GO   The last half of April or the first half of May is usually the ideal time to do this trip. It is accessible even in midwinter, and occasionally conditions will be favorable then.

HOW TO GET THERE   Mazama is located on WA 20, the North Cross-State Highway. If Washington Pass is open (usually opens sometime in

April), it is the best way to get to Mazama from Puget Sound. Otherwise take US 2 to Wenatchee, then drive north up the Columbia River and then up the Methow River from Pateros.

SPECIAL EQUIPMENT   Since only the first day is a hard one while carrying full packs, ultralight camping gear is not necessary. My companions on the trip thought it smarter to take a heavier but more comfortable camp, and they seemed to be right.

MAPS   USGS Robinson Mountain, Pasayten Peak, Mt. Lago, and Lost Peak quadrangles. The Washington Pass, Pasayten Peak, and Billy Goat Mountain quadrangles from Green Trails are smaller and easier to handle than the USGS maps. They are available from Green Trails, P.O. Box 1272, Bellevue, WA 98009.

LODGING AND SUPPLIES   Winthrop, Washington.

The North Cascades are not all deep rainforest-filled valleys, cloud-hung glaciers, and impenetrable brush-covered mountainsides. As you head east from the Pacific the weather changes from dripping wet to desert dry. At the same time the peaks stay at about the same altitude but the vertical relief becomes less and less. Thus there is an eastern part of the North Cascades that is totally different in climate and topography from the western part. This eastern part of the range, most of which is part of the Pasayten Wilderness Area, has some of the finest winter and spring wilderness skiing in the nation. There is a sense of spaciousness skiing in the Pasayten that is missing in the western Cascades. The terrain is excellent, and the snow conditions are often favorable, neither too wet, too dry, too dense, nor too dangerous.

In the western nonvolcanic peaks the relief may be as much as 7,000 feet from summit to valley. The peaks farthest to the east, such as Cathedral Peak or Windy Peak, rise only 1,000 to 2,000 feet above their valleys. These valleys are high for the Cascades, 6,000 feet or more. They are above the rain level for all but the very warmest storms. (Even though the North Cascades are in the northernmost part of the United States, the proximity of the Pacific Ocean keeps temperatures moderate.) Because the weather is milder than in the western peaks, the treeline is as much as 1,500 feet higher, up to around 7,500 feet. Even in storms, when the visibility is bad, the trees allow you to see the snow's surface. With this added visibility you can continue both to travel and to enjoy the skiing, whereas the same storm in the western slopes would keep you pinned in your tent. Slopes are generally more moderate than in the western peaks, and snowfall is much less. These factors mean that avalanche danger, though not completely absent, is much reduced. Another factor that makes avalanche prediction easier (compared to the Rockies) is that temperatures are tempered enough by the Pacific that the long periods of extreme cold that create depth hoar and that preserve buried instability in the snowpack are rare.

Because of the isolation of the peaks in the Pasayten Wilderness there are few good short trips possible. Many of the tours that have been done are very long, three to five weeks. These require either careful placement of caches in the fall, that skiers carry enormous packs, or that they use sleds. It seems better to me to do trips of about a week's duration, of which there are several excellent choices in the Pasayten. A week's load is heavy but not so much as to prevent you from enjoying the skiing. A week's trip is long enough to forget the world back home and short enough not to provoke homesickness.

A nearly perfect ski tour of that length is a loop trip around the Eureka Creek Basin in the central part of the Pasayten. It is midway between the rolling highlands of the Cathedral Peak country on the eastern edge of the wilderness area and the deep, jungle-filled holes of the western Cascades. Eureka Basin combines spectacular alpine ski mountaineering with relatively good weather and easy travel. It also is very wild, not well-known to most Washington mountaineers, and little traveled even in the summer. There is no entrance to it from the creek because the creek exits from the basin through a nearly inaccessible gorge. Instead you enter or leave via high passes. There are three high peaks—Osceola (8,600 feet), Carru (8,600 feet), and Lago (8,700 feet)—strung in a line on the basin's northern end and more high peaks—Blackcap (8,400 feet) and Monument (8,600 feet)—on the eastern rampart. The basin is bounded on the south by the massif of Robinson Mountain (8,700 feet). This is one of the greatest collections of high peaks in any one area in the Cascades. What makes it all the better is that all of these peaks are skiable. There is a maintained trail running along the high northern end under Lago, Carru, and Osceola. This trail runs from the unnamed pass near Lake Doris to Shellrock Pass. It connects the Pasayten River Valley on the west to Monument Creek and Lost River on the east. An abandoned trail runs into the basin farther to the south but is little used and is not in good condition.

The first day will be by far the hardest of the trip. After 4 miles of flat trail along Lost River, you climb straight up almost 5,000 feet to Pistol Pass at 7,200 feet. This is one of the biggest trail climbs in all the Cascades and is definitely the exception to the general rule of shorter climbs in the

The view from the summit of Mt. Osceola, Washington.
Photo by Steve Barnett.

Pasayten. It's so steep because of the great cleft of the Lost River Gorge, which drops from peaks of over 8,000 feet to the riverbed at 3,000 feet (the Gorge is an interesting summer wilderness hike in itself). The theory behind doing it in this direction is that all the suffering is in the first day and from then on the traveling is relatively easy. At the end of this difficult day you pull over Pistol Pass and gaze down into the upper end of Monument Creek. The open bowl at the top and the inviting open larch forest below will reward you for the effort to get there.

One of the delights of Pasayten travel is the larch forest that covers the higher slopes. These are conifer trees that lose their needles in winter, are usually spaced well apart, and don't have dangerous projecting branches. They are beautiful trees, often twisted and broken by avalanches and weather but able to survive. The loop trip spends most of its time in larch forests. If you are very lucky you can catch an early October snowstorm in the Pasayten and go skiing through the trees while they are bright yellow.

From camp below Pistol Pass, ski down the general path of the hiking trail as best you can. Eventually it makes a turn and starts climbing up Monument Creek Valley. A clearing below Lost Peak, which is part of a very wild, trailless subrange, makes a good place to set up camp. There may be enough daylight left to climb Lost Peak to its summit (8,400 feet).

On the way to Shellrock Pass, Washington.
Photo by Steve Barnett.

From the top the view is of an endless sea of white peaks. The Cascades are not so well organized as the Sierra or Tetons, and there are high peaks visible in all directions from almost any high mountain viewpoint. The snow for the run down was almost perfect when I was there, corn with a thin layer of new snow on top.

The next day, climb steep slopes to Shellrock Pass and look into Eureka Creek Basin underneath Mt. Lago. The view from the pass is stunning. These peaks are not heavily glaciated (Mt. Lago has the easternmost glacier in the Cascades) and in summer don't look nearly as alpine as their brethren farther west. In winter they stand white and magnificent above the basin. I think it's one of the best views in the Cascades.

Mt. Lago can be skied up its steep south slopes, but you can also go through the narrow col between Lago and Carru, circle under Lago's north face, and ski up a ramp to the northeast that goes to the summit. The col is a spectacular slot in the high mountain walls of Lago and Carru. Leading up to it is a scooped-out bowl, kept warm and bright by its south-facing aspect. Cross the col and you are in a cold, shadowed north-face environment. The snow changes from corn snow to a mix of powder or breakable crust. Behind you are the black walls of Lago and Carru. Ahead is the U-shaped valley of Lease Creek, and on its eastern rampart is Ptarmigan Peak. The run down from Lago's summit is varied and exciting. It can be extended all the way to Lease Lake for a 3,000-foot vertical descent. When I did it there was a sudden electrical storm to dodge on the way up and breakable crust to battle on the way down from the summit. It was thrilling to stand on this peak, possibly never before skied, and look around at the enticing ski mountains surrounding us—Ptarmigan Peak, Mt. Carru, Blackcap Peak, Many Trails Peak, and the peaks extending north from Robinson Peak.

From Lago follow the summer trail westward and set up a camp at Lake Doris under the south side of Mt. Osceola. Osceola's south side is not steep, but it is windblown and rocky. It's a good example of a slope that looks perfect on a map but is far from perfect in reality (a common situation in any mountain range for above-timberline ridges that are exposed to the prevailing winds). On a previous trip in from the west I thought it couldn't be skied. From the east I saw that it might be possible to traverse from the south face to the east face, crossing above a zone of cliffs, and thus find a continuous path of snow to the summit. The route proved to be barely skiable, but it was a fun and interesting descent from a high Cascade summit.

From Lake Doris cross a corniced ridge and ski down a steep bowl to Fred's Lake. From there ski the bobsled run of a trail down to the Middle Fork of the Pasayten River. All three of the high altitude passes you cross—Pistol Pass, Shellrock Pass, and this last high ridge—have potential avalanche danger underneath the cornices that rim them.

The climb alongside Pasayten River is a beautiful, gentle ski-through forest. There are many good campsites. In late May the snow on the valley bottom might be soupy or patchy. Climb over Robinson Pass (6,400 feet) and then ski 9 miles down the Robinson Creek Trail. The point where you reach the road is only 2 miles from the starting point.

Every one of the skiers who went on this route with me was ecstatic about the quality of the skiing, the beauty of the terrain, and the feeling of deep wilderness travel. In years to come, we all thought, this trip might become a popular classic but for now it was all ours to explore. There seemed to be countless other possibilities for multiday ski trips of the highest quality.

The Pasayten is one of the better ranges in the country for very long trips. The long river valleys and gentle terrain permit the use of sleds. They have been used successfully as a sort of moveable basecamp, allowing skiers to carry small loads on their backs and still camp luxuriously. The shortest good trip that I know of is the ski ascent of Robinson Peak, which is reached by the Robinson Creek and Beauty Creek trails. The trailhead is on the Harts Pass Road some 2 miles past the last plowed point. This is still an overnight trip.

One trip of such quality that it deserves to be mentioned in this book is a tour into the Remmel-Cathedral region in the far east of the Pasayten. It's a delightful area of rolling, high-altitude meadows that is perfect for cross-country skiing and is surrounded by high peaks that are all skiable.

Oregon

Three Sisters Wilderness

TOUR   Skiing in the Three Sisters Wilderness in central Oregon.

IN A NUTSHELL   This is a compact high-altitude area with four glaciated volcanoes standing next to each other. A large variety of ski tours are possible around and on the peaks.

WHAT MAKES THE TOUR SPECIAL   This exceptionally beautiful area is compact and easy to travel through. It has an unusual variety of tours starting from comfortable base camps, from beginner-easy to extreme skiing, from excursions a few hours long to traverses of several days, and includes both tree skiing in wide open forest and above-timberline glacier skiing.

LEVEL OF DIFFICULTY   Whatever you want.

BEST TIME TO GO   May is usually best, but good touring is possible from November to July.

HOW TO GET THERE   The town of Bend on US 97 is the base for trips into the Three Sisters Wilderness. Oregon 46, known as Century Drive, heads west from Bend and is plowed to the Mt. Bachelor Ski Area, where there is a Sno-Park lot. A permit must be bought for the right to park there.

SPECIAL EQUIPMENT   Camping gear, ice axes or crampons for the summits, normal avalanche gear.

MAPS   USGS, Three Sisters, Oregon.

GUIDEBOOKS   Both of these books describe easier and more accessible tours in the Bend area than those described in this chapter: *Cross-Country Ski Tours in Central Oregon* by Virginia Meissner, Meissner Books, POB 5296, Bend, OR 97708, and *Cross-Country Ski Routes of Oregon's Cascades* by Klindt Vielbig, The Mountaineers, 715 Pike St., Seattle, WA 98101.

LODGING AND SUPPLIES   Bend, Oregon.

The most developed centers for cross-country skiing in the Cascade Mountains of the Pacific Northwest are the Methow Valley of northern Washington and the Bend area of central Oregon. Both are on the sunny eastern side of the mountains, but that is about the end of their similarities. The Methow Valley extends deep into the North Cascades, a wild and rugged range with an endless expanse of high peaks.

Bend is a town out on the high desert of Oregon, a desert formed by immense lava flows in ages past. A road heads west from the town up to the ski area at Mt. Bachelor. Unlike the Methow, there is no valley extending deep into a range of craggy peaks. What you have instead is a road rising steadily up a tilted highland into an area of once intense volcanic activity. There is no sea of peaks here, just several large volcanic cones rising out of a volcanic highland. Scattered far in the distance both north and south are other high volcanoes. The Oregon Cascades aren't an alpine range in the way that the North Cascades are. They consist of low and gentle timbered ridges completely dominated by the occasional volcanic cone rising thousands of feet higher. The four volcanoes in the Three Sisters Wilderness, though, are close enough together to give you the feeling of skiing in a high mountain range along with the advantages usually found skiing on volcanoes. On the one hand it is possible to put together high traverses or loops going from peak to peak. On the other hand each peak is skiable in every direction and almost everywhere on it.

The view of these volcanoes as they rise white from their spacious highland bases to well above timberline is a beautiful one, and there is ski-touring potential here to match the scenery. It's a perfect place for short (1 to 4 days) mountain tours. Access to the high country is easy since the always plowed ski-area road takes you right into it. The forest is composed of big trees, spaced well apart, with little undergrowth and few low-hanging limbs. The trees climb nearly 2,000 feet above the road (up to about 8,000 feet), which gives you plenty of room to ski in stormy or foggy weather

Three Sisters, Oregon. Photo by Steve Barnett.

(visibility is infinitely better within the forest in such conditions than it is in the open areas above timberline, and the trees protect you from the wind). The snowpack is exceedingly reliable. The Bachelor ski area gets one of the nation's deepest snowpacks, usually in the 15-feet-plus range. Combine that with the fact that the volcanic soil is as smooth and brushfree as a golf course and you can see why in even a low snow year you will be able to find good skiing here from October to July.

Much of the terrain is relatively flat or rolling—perfect for cross-country ski travel. There is plenty of terrain for the beginner. Beyond that there is excellent intermediate mountain skiing on the slopes of the various volcanoes. If you want to find it there is extremely steep and difficult skiing as well off the summits of the volcanoes. By their very nature volcanic cones tend to have nearly perfect ski slopes with long and continuous vertical drops. These treeless slopes wrap completely around the mountains, which allows skiers to choose whichever exposure to the sun or weather they like best. Mt. Bachelor, 9,000 feet high, is the site of a lift-served ski area. Broken Top, 9,600 feet high, lies due north of Bachelor. Beyond Broken Top, to the west and north, are the Three Sisters, a line of three cones, named South, Middle, and North Sister, each rising over 10,000 feet high. Broken Top and the Three Sisters are all administratively contained in the Three Sisters Wilderness Area. Trips to Broken Top can be done as day trips from the parking lot at the Bachelor Sno-Park near the ski area. If you want to climb any of the Three Sisters you must camp out. Trips of 2 to 4 days are sufficient.

Ski trips into the Three Sisters Wilderness can be done safely any time of the winter, but the best time for travel there is usually (as with so many good western tours) in the spring. Spring skiing in this area of heavy snowfall lasts well into July. The problem with midwinter travel is that storms can be so intense that travel, even escaping back to the road, becomes difficult. On a trip into the Three Sisters Wilderness late in December one year, we got struck by a massive storm just after setting up camp at Green Lakes, which are right under the South Sister. So much wet snow fell that going out, downward, was far more exhausting than the climb up the day before. Nothing can be more frustrating to a skier than having to exhaust oneself struggling down what should be the most fun part of the trip.

Another problem with midwinter travel is that the snow above timberline is likely to be difficult to ski. This is a general rule from Mt. Washington, New Hampshire, to the Colorado Rockies to the Sierra Nevada and is due to the ease with which high winds and sun can affect the unprotected surface of the snow when there are no trees. Given all these cautions it has to be admitted that the Three Sisters Wilderness is one of the easiest and most ideal places in the west for short midwinter camping trips. Access is very easy, and escape is usually straightforward. Most important of all, avalanche danger can be kept to a minimum since you needn't cross any steep, open terrain while retreating from the bases of the volcanoes. If there is a persistent storm, the worst you can do is stay at the ski area and ski fresh powder snow every day! There's also a Nordic Center with an exquisitely well-groomed trail network.

The Cascades in Oregon are a soggy range with generally mild temperatures, frequent cloudy days, and lots of wet snow. To some extent the Three

Sisters area escapes these problems since it is east of the Cascade crest. That means the temperatures are lower, the weather sunnier, and the snow somewhat drier. Most important, the altitudes in the area are high by Cascade standards and thus most precipitation will be in the form of snow. Very good snow, powdery enough to be fun to ski and dense enough to travel on, should be common in the trees just below timberline.

The Green Lakes are a good base for skiing the Three Sisters. There are several good routes to get to them. If the weather is good it's most scenic and interesting to go north from the ski area, past Todd Lake to the east, and up to the foot of Broken Top. Then contour around Broken Top to the left to get to the lakes. There is a trail, but the deep snow and open forest mean that it will be hard to find. If the weather is bad, you can go or return by the Fall Creek Trail. This crosses no steep slopes and is very easy to follow. From the ski area, follow Century Drive (snow covered in winter) 4.5 miles. There is a sign and a short spur road heading north that will guide you to the Fall Creek Trail. Four miles farther up the trail are the lakes. This route has the disadvantage of dropping nearly a thousand feet before you start climbing back up to the lakes.

Green Lakes is a good base for many different trips. Just about every part of every mountain in the area can be skied. Only portions of the steeper North Sister are exceptions. A climb on skis up the easy south side of South

South Sister, Three Sisters, Oregon. Photo by Steve Barnett.

Sister is a natural for one day and so is a climb of Broken Top, which gets steeper at its top. A bit longer is a circumnavigation of South Sister, skiing several of its glaciers along the way, or else a ski climb of Middle Sister. A circle around Middle Sister, complete with a ski trip up the area's largest glacier, the Collier Glacier, is another possibility. The variety of possible ski trips and the ease with which you can combine different objectives, combined with your ability to constantly stay high on any route, right at timberline or even above it, are what make mountain skiing in this area so marvelous. If you want to do one of the loops around one or two of the Sisters at an easy level of difficulty, there's no difficulty finding a route. If you want to test your skiing skills to the maximum, the area can also accommodate you. Off the summits there are skiable routes of almost any degree of steepness and difficulty you might desire.

Even longer and more ambitious trips are possible in this compact but rich wilderness. One group of Coloradans took a 14-day holiday one May, traversed the four volcanoes, skied their most extreme slopes, and ended the trip by exiting out to the north via Pole Creek Road, which goes to Sisters, Oregon. They set up one camp after another, spending several days at each one exploring the different possibilities of steep and even extreme skiing that could be reached from that camp. Such a trip has a quite different feel than the other traverses discussed in this book since the skiers were most interested in the downhill skiing (they used alpine touring gear). The carries from camp to camp were easy since the routes between them were short and none went deep into valleys or climbed high passes. But it was still a real wilderness ski trip, with the solitude, isolation, and natural beauty that implies. That's the beauty of the Three Sisters Wilderness for ski tourers—it combines such a richness of skiing with such easy access in a pristine wilderness setting.

There are many other ski tours in the Bend area. Many follow trails marked specifically for cross-country skiers. These are well described in two local guidebooks (see above). Not too far away to the south is the Diamond Peak Wilderness, centered around yet another volcano, which also has excellent ski-touring potential.

Yet further south is Crater Lake National Park. It is centered around the lake that fills the caldera of yet another volcano that blew its top off thousands of years ago. A road, unplowed in winter, runs around the lake. It can be the route of an extraordinarily scenic, but easy, tour of a little over 30 miles length. This trip is said to be particularly good under the light of the full moon with fast light skis.

Oregon

Steens Mountain

TOUR   A traverse of Steens Mountain, Oregon.

IN A NUTSHELL   Steens Mountain is a huge fault-block mountain rising out of the basin and range country of southeastern Oregon. The trip starts from the mountain's south end at Wildhorse Canyon, crosses over the summit plateau, and ends by going down the Kiger Gorge to the north. This is a long trip, which should take about a week for the skiing and several days more for getting there and arranging the car shuttle.

WHAT MAKES THE TOUR SPECIAL   Steens is a unique geological feature. The scenery is weird and magnificent. Wildlife is abundant. The skiing encompasses dead-flat cross-country skiing and steep alpine skiing. This part of the country is extraordinarily remote and empty and is worth the visit.

LEVEL OF DIFFICULTY   Winter camping skills are more important than skiing skills, though those will help. The weather can vary quickly from hot and sunny to arctic cold and high winds.

BEST TIME TO GO   Late April and all of May.

HOW TO GET THERE   Take US 20 or US 395 to Burns, Oregon. From there drive south on either OR 205 or OR 78 to get to the tiny hamlet of Diamond. This is one end of the traverse. To set up a car shuttle at the other end of the traverse, go back north to New Princeton on OR 78 and then south to the junction with the gravel road along the east side of Steens Mountain. Take this to Alvord Hot Springs, the other end of the route.

SPECIAL EQUIPMENT   Winter camping gear. Any type of touring skis will do. Light skis are preferable considering the distance involved, but heavier skis are nice if you want to ski the steep bowls.

MAPS   US Department of the Interior, BLM, Steens Mountain quadrangle is available from BLM, Burns District, 74 S. Alvord St., Burns, OR 97720.

LODGING AND SUPPLIES   Burns, Oregon.

The southeast corner of Oregon is both geologically and culturally more a part of Nevada than of Oregon. It has the basic geology of basin and range country—the rivers drain from the mountains into basins that have no outlets. Around the basins are fault-block mountain ranges, steep on one side and gentle on the other. It's empty country with a population density of less than two people per square mile and very long vistas. You will drive mile after mile with only an occasional ranch or lonely gas pump. There are almost no trees—just endless sagebrush desert. The dominating peak of this region is Steens Mountain. It is an enormous fault block, 30 miles long and almost 10,000 (9,773 to be exact) feet high. On the west side it rises so slowly as to be hardly noticeable. It takes 15 miles to rise 5,000 feet. On the east side there is a precipitous fault scarp dropping 5,000 feet in just a few miles.

Steens Mountain is an outstanding ski-touring objective for several reasons. The view from it in any direction is wonderful. Other fault-block ranges stretch as far as the eye can see. On the east side is the basin of the Alvord Desert, which in the last few years of exceptional snowfall has become a lake. Malheur Lake to the west is one of the nation's premier wildlife refuges. The mountain itself is scarred by huge glacially cut canyons running down the west side and breaking its otherwise smooth profile. These canyons are among the most classic examples of glacial carving to be found anywhere. They almost, but not quite, cut through the rim of the fault block. Had they done so they would have cut Steens into separate peaks. As it is they come just close enough to make a wonderful spectacle for the summit onlooker.

Skiing on Steens Mountain gives the tourer a chance to explore this beautiful and exceedingly remote country. The skiing combines elements of an arctic traverse, of easy cross-country skiing through rolling woodlands, and of classic alpine ski mountaineering with steep long slopes well above timberline. Several routes are possible. None should be done in less than 4 to 5 days, and longer is probably better. The route I'll describe is the one with the most classic dimension, the one that traverses the length of the mountain.

I've tried to ski Steens Mountain twice. Both times I was with Julie Meissner, a mountain guide from Bend, Oregon. The first time we tried to approach the mountain from Frenchglen, a tiny town at the edge of its western slope. From Frenchglen, the Bureau of Land Management (BLM) maintains a road that runs up to the summit ridge. The road is gated in the spring. Because this is the gentle side of the fault block, the road goes for mile after mile with only imperceptible climbing. It's a long, straight, and almost featureless hike. We bogged down and stalled after only a few miles of wallowing in mud, while rain and snow fell on us. We thought then that there must be a better way than this endless road, but we didn't know what it was. Five years later we tried again, fortified by a more interesting plan.

Our idea was to start at Wildhorse Canyon, which is the glacial gorge that runs south from the summit crest, and to proceed up the canyon all the way to its head. From there we would follow the summit crest all the way to Kiger Gorge, the northern glacier-cut chasm. Somehow or other we would drop into Kiger Gorge and ski down it as far as we could. Then we would hike out the rest of the way. To give you some idea of the scale of these gorges, Kiger Gorge is 2,500 feet deep at its top and extends for 25 miles.

This route worked to perfection, even though the weather for our trip was mostly rotten. I think it is the best way to explore Steens on skis since it avoids the long, boring hike up the BLM road, gets to the snowline quickly, visits the most interesting parts of the mountain, and gives you the sense of doing a high-mountain traverse in the middle of a vast desert domain.

The entrances to both the Wildhorse and the Kiger gorges are privately owned and you have to get permission to go through the ranches in the gorge bottoms. Don't take it for granted; it is often not given. There is public access to Wildhorse Canyon that requires no permission and perhaps gives a more interesting hike than starting at the canyon's mouth. The route goes up the steep eastern escarpment and then drops into Wildhorse Canyon. By starting up the eastern slope you quickly gain altitude and get to the snowline. It also has a great view of the Alvord Desert.

Your first problem is shuttling your cars. You want to leave one at the tiny hamlet of Diamond, north of the mountain. Then you have to circle around to your starting point at Alvord Hot Springs. This shuttling will take up the good part of a day. The hot springs are a delight, and a good plan is to spend the night there before starting out.

Start at the road opposite Alvord Hot Springs. Head up the road until just before it reaches the first buildings. From there head straight up the hillside until you reach the jeep road visible high overhead. Follow the jeep road as it climbs and heads northward. You are trying to reach Straw Hat Pass, which is at the head of Indian Creek. At some point you must leave the road and angle up and northward toward the pass. There is good camping in groves of trees just below the pass.

The forest here is very unusual for a mountain ski tour. The highest trees are mountain mahogany and mountain juniper. On all of Steens Moun-

Camping on Steens Mountain, Oregon. Photo by Steve Barnett.

tain there are very few conifer forests. On the western side the highest trees are aspens, with juniper and mountain mahogany found just a little lower. Most of the conifers are concentrated in small groves like that in Fir Canyon on the west side.

The view from Straw Hat Pass is excellent. From here the Steens look like a real mountain range because you are seeing the steep cirque walls of the gorge and the rugged pinnacles of the eastern scarp.

From the pass you drop down into Wildhorse Canyon, a drop of only some 600 feet. The hike up the canyon is beautiful. It's lined with cottonwoods, and you can always see the white, treeless slopes ahead dropping down from the rim. The top of the canyon is a steep, alpine bowl. Great caution for avalanche danger is necessary for the final climb up to the rim. There is a cornice around most of it but there should be some gaps that will let you through to the top with only a little bit of struggle.

When you pull over the rim you enter a completely different world. It is reminiscent of being on an arctic icecap rather than on a western desert mountain. There's a long plateau of pure white, and it's not unlikely that the wind will be howling over it.

Over the eastern edge of the plateau there's a straight drop right down to the desert. To the west the land drops very gently, except for the gorges cutting into the plateau. These gorges are rock-rimmed with steep snow slopes leading to the nearly flat U-shaped bottoms. When I stood on that plateau I would have liked dearly to try descending into the gorges, to attempt to ski their steep slopes, but as luck would have it this pleasure was not to be. As we climbed up in the morning from Wildhorse Canyon the sun was out and there was no wind. Our whole group was as happy and self-satisfied as any group of sunbathers on a tropical beach. As soon as we pulled over the rim a strong wind started blowing and clouds started building up out of nowhere. Soon there was a full-scale gale with an attendant ground blizzard of wind-blown snow. It was all we could do to grope our way 5 miles along the rim to the head of Kiger Gorge, Steen's northernmost gorge. It was the beginning of May but the summit rim was now arctic in weather as well as appearance.

This is always a possibility on Steens Mountain. There are no other large mountains around it, and once you are on the summit you are totally exposed to any scrap of weather passing through. Some of our group had packed for a typical spring ski trip in sunshine and corn snow. Others had prepared for an arctic expedition (heavy down jackets and warm overboots). It could have gone either way, but this time the pessimists were right.

Our plan was to descend into Kiger Gorge, ski out as far as we could, and then hike the rest of the way. But the wind was so strong from the south that it was likely building up cornices and dangerous avalanche conditions in the bowl at the top of the gorge. Furthermore we wanted to explore the top of Steens. We skied west, almost blind, down the sloping plateau, until we found wind-sheltered campsites in the first groves of aspens. Due to the wind and the general dryness, there isn't any large forest on Steens, but there are instead groves of trees in sheltered areas. Skiing along the rolling west side means going up and down from one gentle timbered drainage to another, with open slopes on the hills between.

Kiger Gorge is impressive. The bowl at its head falls 2,500 vertical feet in a rush. Its top is rimmed with cliffs and there was no easy way into it that we could see through the fog and blizzard. From the bowl the gorge runs over 20 miles without a break in its high walls. For a long way it's a perfect example of a U-shaped, glacier-cut canyon. With good snow conditions it would be exciting skiing. In the conditions we had to deal with we skied down a gentle drainage running parallel to Kiger instead and then crossed into it a long way downslope.

The final day was entirely spent hiking down the gorge. Lower down it is private property, and cows were grazing there. If you can't get permission to travel through it before the trip or if you just want to get out of the gorge and enjoy a longer view, you can climb out its west bank at various points and traverse over to a BLM road that runs northward down the mountain. Either way it's a long trip. You should allow a week for this trip. That gives you a little margin for storms, for leisure, or for exploring the canyons.

This is one of the most interesting long ski trips you can do in the West. Geologically it's a fascinating and different region. In the spring the nearby Malheur Wildlife Refuge hosts one of the greatest varieties of birdlife in the United States and Steens Mountain itself is rich in wildlife, including wild horses. It has every sort of skiing, including steep, open, alpine slopes and excellent natural cross-country skiing. There is an exceptionally strong sense there of being in the middle of nowhere—of a spaciousness that is hard to find anymore in the lower 48. That sense of place, more than anything else, is what makes the long trip to Steens worthwhile.

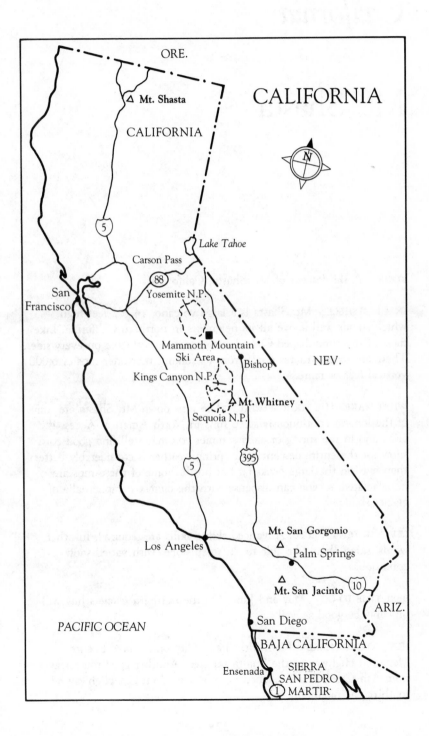

California

Mt. Shasta

TOUR   A ski descent of Mt. Shasta, California.

IN A NUTSHELL   Mt. Shasta is a large volcano, 14,162 feet high, which stands well above all its neighbors in northern California. Like most of the cone-shaped Cascade volcanoes, it is skiable on every side. There are several routes down from its summit that offer runs of 6,000 vertical feet or more.

WHAT MAKES THE TOUR SPECIAL   The runs down Mt. Shasta are some of the longest continuously steep runs in North America. Access is easy, and in the spring or early summer you may well find good corn snow for the entire descent. The spring weather is considerably better than it is on the large peaks farther north. Some of these runs are nonglaciated, so you can dispense with the clumsy paraphernalia of glacier skiing.

LEVEL OF DIFFICULTY   Advanced skiing skills are required. In other words, skiers should be able to ski steep slopes with varied snow conditions.

BEST TIME TO GO   May and June. On the northern glaciers July will probably be good as well.

HOW TO GET THERE   From Mt. Shasta City on I-5 take Everitt Memorial Highway to the Shasta ski area. Another good route leaves from Ash Creek Road, reached from McCloud on CA Highway 89 south of the mountain.

SPECIAL EQUIPMENT   This is a good ski tour for alpine touring equipment. Telemark equipment should include boots offering good support and downhill-oriented telemark skis. Ice axe and crampons should also be carried.

MAPS   USGS Shasta quadrangle.

LODGING AND SUPPLIES   Weed, California.

I t's the dream of every downhill skier turned ski mountaineer to find a mountain with a straightforwardly skiable slope of nearly infinite length running down it and of a steady steepness without level or uphill interruptions. "Nearly infinite" may be interpreted to mean 5,000 vertical feet or more. To put that in perspective, a large downhill ski area in North America will typically have a vertical drop of 3,000 feet, and a few exceptional ones have drops of 4,000 feet. Even then few of these areas have slopes that run continuously downhill from top to bottom at a steady steepness.

There are not many mountains in the United States that offer such a run. Few mountain ranges rise high enough, fast enough, over their bases. The eastern scarp of the Sierra is big enough and steep enough, and there is at least one run on it that drops 7,000 feet vertically in a steep, continuous, skiable swoop—Elderberry Canyon on Mt. Tom outside of Bishop, California. You won't find any such run, as far as I know, in the Colorado Rockies, in the Wasatch, or in the nonvolcanic North Cascades. It certainly won't be found in the east. The eastern fronts of some of the Teton peaks may offer such long runs, although at a steepness that borders extreme. Mt. McKinley's Wickersham Wall is probably the ski run with the greatest vertical drop in the world, 14,000 icy feet, but it is a slope of such difficulty that it has not yet been successfully skied. Mt. Sanford in the Wrangell Mountains has a 10,000-foot drop and is occasionally skied. Mt. Logan in Canada offers at least a 10,000-foot drop, but its ascent is a considerable expeditionary effort.

As you can see these kinds of runs are not common. Most of those in the United States are found on the Cascade volcanoes that stretch along the Pacific coast from Mt. Shasta in the south to Mt. Garibaldi in British Columbia, Canada. The Cascade volcanoes are ideal for ski descents. They typically have very long verticals from their bases and uniform slopes that run from top to bottom at just the right angle for downhill skiing enjoyment. Fortunately all of the Cascade volcanoes get heavy snowfalls and usually have excellent spring and summer skiing. These peaks are naturals for ski descents, so pardon us if we express a bit of pity for the thousands of climbers we see every spring and summer wallowing up their snowfields in boots without skis. What a waste!

Mt. Baker's south side offers a descent of 6,000 to 8,000 vertical feet, mostly of moderate steepness, mostly over glaciers, and frequently good until mid-August. Glacier Peak stands out as a wilderness volcano, with ski runs ranging up to 7,000 vertical feet.

Mt. Rainier is undoubtedly the largest mountain in the lower 48 states in terms of bulk and vertical rise (it's only 85 feet short of Mt. Whitney's height). It rises about 12,000 feet from its base, and it's quite feasible to ski about 10,000 feet of that. The Emmons Glacier is the best ski route from the summit, and the first 4,000 feet of it are steep. The next 4,000 feet down Interglacier are more moderate, and then there is a 2,000-foot run down a trail to the trailhead. It's a rare day when you can find good snow conditions down the whole slope. You should wait for a very hot (90° + F.) June day on the coast with no wind whatsoever. Then, with luck, you might have corn snow all the way down. I must admit to never having had such luck.

Mt. Adams, 12,000 feet high and just north of the Columbia River, is one of the best of the volcanoes for skiing. The normal climbing route up its south side offers a 6,000-vertical-feet run of modest steepness that is mostly unglaciated. A trip there in mid-July can be a tremendous thrill, and for those who are hooked on sailboarding it doesn't hurt that the Columbia Gorge, the best spot in North America for the sport, is only a few miles away.

The best of all the volcanoes for skiing is arguably the southernmost one in the Cascades, Mt. Shasta in California. It is 14,162 feet high with a base of about 6,000 feet. Though it is nearly as high as Mt. Rainier, it is actually much less massive and is glaciated only down its north-facing slopes. Shasta is easily accessible from the San Francisco Bay area, and a plowed road runs to the base of the skiing. There is a hut on it at 8,000 feet, and it is frequently possible to ski from the summit down to the hut as late as the Fourth of July. The run is not glaciated so skiers can climb unencumbered by ropes. Most importantly, the spring weather is much better than it is on the volcanoes farther to the north. You have a very good chance of spending a hot, cloudless June day skiing corn snow down the side of Mt. Shasta. On Rainier, in many years, your chances of finding either good weather or good snow for the whole run down are not so good.

Shasta stands alone in its northern California location, absolutely dominating the landscape for a hundred miles in any direction. It is natural

Skiing the north side of Shasta. Photo by Gary Brill.

for the ski mountaineer upon sighting this imposing but skiable-looking peak to want to climb to its summit and launch himself downward. Fortunately it can be done with few obstacles.

As on other volcanoes, there are many routes since there are uniform slopes in almost all directions from the summit. The most popular route on Mt. Shasta is the Avalanche Gulch route from the south. A plowed road, the Everitt Memorial Highway, runs from Mt. Shasta City on I-5. At Bunny Flat there is a turnout for parking at 7,100 feet altitude. From here you ski north-northeast through open forest and small meadows to reach the Shasta Alpine Lodge, which is a hut built long ago by the Sierra Club. The hut is right at timberline at 7,900 feet on the left bank of Avalanche Gulch, which will be the route to higher altitudes.

Climb up the modestly steep slopes of the gulch to Lake Helen at 10,400 feet. This is a good place to rest but not so good for camping. I personally witnessed a tragedy when a camper at Lake Helen got up in the middle of the night to relieve himself and was blown off the lake's shelf and down the gulch where he died. More of a problem than such a bizarre accident is the danger of avalanches from the steep slopes above. There's a reason this route is called Avalanche Gulch. The main lift for the downhill ski area on Mt. Shasta, situated just a short way to the east of this standard climbing route, was destroyed by an avalanche just a few years ago. Continue up the gulch for 800 feet more and then climb the much steeper slopes under the cliffs called the Red Banks. Head to the right under the Red Banks and then climb up leftward (north-northwest) alongside Thumb Rock. If these very steep slopes are icy, you might elect to leave your skis behind and continue on with ice axe and crampons, which you should have with you. You might climb the slope with crampons early in the morning and carry your skis in the hope that the sun will soften the slope by the time you are ready to descend it. This is a dangerous place. Skiers have fallen and been killed here. There is a much better chance on the Fourth of July than in April to descend from the summit on soft corn snow. Even so, sometimes even as late in the season as Memorial Day these slopes will have treacherous, icy surfaces.

When you get to a saddle, head left to the north-northeast to a false summit (Misery Hill) and then the real one. It's a long way, but that is the idea—to get a long, steep run, high above every other mountain in sight.

The route described, the standard climbing route on Shasta, is not necessarily the best ski route. It is the most popular route principally because the access to it is so good and because of the hut. There are other routes that frequently have better snow conditions and less danger, are more direct, and are very much less crowded than the standard route. On a big weekend that route will be a circus, where skiers will have to do a slalom around living human gates. One very good alternative is the ridge between the Hotlum and Wintun glaciers, which runs to the east-northeast directly from the summit for a run of over 7,500 vertical feet. Since it is an east-facing route, it gets morning sun and often gets softened to just the right consistency by the time skiers get to the summit. It is steadily steep with a headwall right under the summit. To get to it take the Ash Creek Road from McCloud, south of Shasta, and turn off on the Forest Service road that goes to Brewster Creek. The end of the road is at about 6,500 feet, lower than the trailhead for the standard route, but since this is on the east rather than the south side of the mountain the snow will continue on down to a lower elevation. This run should be good through June in a year of normal snowfall.

Other good runs on Shasta include skiing the northern glaciers in midsummer. These have the longest and best summer skiing runs in California. Since they are active glaciers, summer skiers should carry ropes, prusiks, ice axes, and enough hardware to rescue someone from a crevasse. The subsidiary cone of Shastina (12,330 feet) on the west side of Shasta is also perfectly shaped for ski descents. One good route, the most continuously steep one on Shasta, goes from Shastina down to Whitney Glacier. Another goes straight west from Shastina down Diller Creek. It is steep, wide, and steady for thousands of feet. The view from Shastina is exceptional because it's the one place on the mountain where you stand far enough away from the summit of Shasta to see it.

Mt. Shasta is a perfect mountain for the ski mountaineer to whom the downhill run is paramount. It is a wilderness area since 1985, but the feel of skiing on it is different than it is for the several other wilderness traverses in this book. The point isn't to spend days out of sight of any sign of mankind. Instead it is to work hard to stand on a summit that is way above everything else in sight, natural or man-made, and then to enjoy an hour or two of blissful concentration skiing down those seemingly endless slopes you just spent six hours climbing up.

California

Sierra Crest Traverse

TOUR   A 250-mile-long traverse of the crest of the Sierra Nevada.

IN A NUTSHELL   How can you put a 250-mile trip in a nutshell? As closely as is reasonable, without creating undue mountaineering difficulties, the route follows the crest of the range as it goes from north to south from Carson Pass to south of Mt. Whitney.

WHAT MAKES THE TOUR SPECIAL   What about it isn't special? The Sierra has a perfect mix, unique in the world, of beautiful alpine mountain scenery, reliable snow, reliable sun, excellent ski terrain, open forest, easy access, and an unbroken high crest for hundreds of miles.

LEVEL OF DIFFICULTY   You will cover the whole range of skiing difficulty from easy cross country to steep alpine. It's always possible to take the skis off for a particularly bad section. As with most long ski traverses navigation, camping, and general mountaineering skills are more important than particular expertise with skis.

BEST TIME TO GO   April and May.

HOW TO GET THERE   The route parallels US 395 from Carson Pass, California, to Lone Pine, California.

SPECIAL EQUIPMENT   Crampons, ice axes, and a short rope are useful for some sections. The best in lightweight camping equipment will make the skiing as well as the camping that much more enjoyable.

MAPS   USGS quadrangles: Markleeville, Sonora, Tower, Matterhorn, Tuolumne, Devil's Postpile, Mt. Morrison, Mt. Abbott, Mt. Tom, Mt. Goddard, Big Pine, Mt. Pinchot, Mt. Whitney, Kearn Peak, and Olancha.

GUIDES   Some are available from Alpine Expeditions, P.O. Box 1751, Bishop, CA 93514, (619) 873-5617, and from Alpine Skills Institute, P.O. Box 8, Norden, CA 95724, (916) 426-9108.

GUIDEBOOK   *Ski Touring in California* by Dave Beck, published by Wilderness Press of Berkeley, California.

LODGING AND SUPPLIES   Markleeville, Yosemite Village, Mammoth Lakes, Bishop, and Lone Pine, California.

T he Sierra Nevada is a perfect range for ski touring. It combines ideal terrain, heavy snowfall, sunny weather, breathtaking scenery, easy access, and a large area of wilderness. There are so many beautiful trips in the Sierra that it's hard to pick out just a few to mention. Those desiring information about a wider variety of tours should read Dave Beck's excellent guide, *Ski Touring in California.* I've selected several trips that have the greatest scenic and skiing values and that also are grand enough in concept to strike a chord in our imaginations.

An obvious possibility for an immensely long tour on skis is to ski along the Sierra Crest, roughly following the John Muir Hiking Trail. It's one trip that is unique to the Sierra—there's no other range in North America that could let you do such a high-level traverse for so long. The construction of the range is what makes it natural. A huge piece of the Earth's crust has been tilted upward by geological forces, leaving a 400-mile-long ridge with one side sloping very gently and the other a jagged precipice ripped over 2 miles straight up out of the surrounding landscape. The scarp is so dramatic that the highest point of the Sierra, Mt. Whitney, stands within sight of Death Valley, the lowest point in the entire United States. To the skier this means that there is a continuous high crest hundreds of miles long that is surrounded by fine mountain scenery. Access from the east is usually short, while most obstacles can be circumvented on the more gradual western slope. It's hard to imagine a more perfect situation. Combine this with a generally sunny and warm climate punctuated by occasional intense storms that lay a deep cover of snow on the range and you have a ski tourer's paradise. Avalanche danger is usually high only during storms, since the fair weather rapidly settles and stabilizes the snow. In the spring the hot sun transforms the snow into corn snow, one of the easiest and most fun of all snow conditions to ski. Spring is the time to go out on the Sierra Crest Traverse.

There is a long history to the Crest Traverse. In 1928 Orland Bartholomew set out alone to ski the Muir Trail. This feat is singular in the history of American skiing. It stands as the single greatest ski-touring feat done on this continent. It wasn't until 1970 that Doug Robinson and Peanut McCoy repeated the trip. In 1978 Bill Nicolai and Pam Kelley did the longest version of the traverse yet done, taking 55 days to go all the way from Carson Pass (north of Yosemite) to Whitney. They were interested not in speed but in savoring living in the snow-covered mountains. Only a couple of years later Bela and Mimi Vadascz did several long sections of the trip in just a few days, showing how fast a competent, lightly equipped party could move in good corn-snow conditions. In 1983 Allan Bard, Tom Carter, and Chris Cox did an extreme mountaineering-oriented version of the traverse, sticking close to the absolute ridgeline and climbing and skiing many of the highest peaks. Since it followed the red line they drew on their map connecting the highest peaks, they called it the Redline Traverse. In the last few years the Sierra Crest Traverse described in this chapter has become relatively popular and is being done several times each season. Even more popular is for parties to do shorter sections of it and over a few years to complete the whole trip.

A key strategy in making such a long trip possible is the placement of caches along the way. The relatively short access from the east all along the crest makes this feasible. "Relatively short" however isn't so short that putting in the caches isn't a major ski expedition on its own. Bill Nicolai put in six caches on his very long version of the Crest Traverse and took a full two weeks to do so. The more caches there are the less you have to carry and the more you can enjoy the skiing. Most groups nowadays put in four to six caches along the way from Mammoth to Whitney. Their locations are pretty much governed by the accessible roads into the east slope of the Sierra. Popular spots are Sonora Pass, Tioga Pass, Mammoth, Rock Creek, Piute Pass, Bishop Pass, and Kearsarge Pass. One problem with caches is how to package them to be safe from animals and the ravages of the weather. Another is how to mark them so that you can find them even after heavy snows. Hanging them from trees insures that they can be found and to some extent protects them. Some people have used wooden boxes that could be burned after the cache is recovered.

Which direction to go, north to south or south to north, depends largely on when you are doing the trip. If you go in April and head north to south you will be skiing down moderate south-facing slopes on good corn snow. That's a delightful combination. Climbing, you will usually be on steeper north-facing slopes that will still have wind-packed powder and breakable crust on them. Since you are climbing up you don't have to worry about whether or not the snow is difficult skiing. Later in May these northern slopes will be transformed into corn snow runs and the south-to-north option will become more attractive. Earlier than April, it's possible that the north-facing slopes will have powder and that south to north will be the better way to go. It's by no means to be taken for granted that there will be powder, though. The snow above timberline in any mountain range is subject to wind and sun, and breakable crust is the normal snow condition. In the Sierra this will be true in the winter months. Groups have gone both ways and then have stoutly defended their choice as the only one possible. Probably the easiest is to go north to south, and that's the way we'll describe the tour. Bill Nicolai topped off his arguments for that direction by saying that the southern part was the scenic climax of the Sierra and that it was most satisfying to reach it at the end of a long trip.

The following is Bill Nicolai's route from Carson Pass to Whitney. It does not follow the Muir Trail all the way, since that route drops deeply into valleys along the way while Nicolai's route stays continuously high along the crest. It is, however, much less demanding of mountaineering and skiing skills than the Redline Route done by Cox, Carter, and Bard. The Nicolai Route is longer than the routes anyone else has done. Most parties start at Yosemite and head south from there. Many segments of this route can be done as excellent shorter trips. I'll point out those that have special merit of their own. After the title to each section is the name of the USGS map quadrangle or quadrangles that include it. I'll also point out where caches were left. Each cache had nine days worth of food for a planned seven days of traveling. The extra was added in case a long storm had to be sat out.

Carson Pass to Sonora Pass
Maps: Markleeville, Sonora quadrangles

From Carson Pass the route goes to Ebbets Pass and then to Sonora Pass where Nicolai's first cache was located (actually a few miles east of the pass at the junction of the Sonora Pass Road and the Leavitt Creek Road). The terrain along here is easy, flat, and open timbered. It's cross-country touring rather than ski mountaineering. The trip to Lake Winnemucca just 2 miles south of Carson Pass is a scenic, easy, and short tour, good for someone just starting out touring in the Sierra.

Sonora Pass to Tuolomne Meadows (Yosemite National Park)
Maps: Tower, Matterhorn, Tuolomne quadrangles

This is a particularly nice section. The gentle touring in the forest gradually changes to a High Sierra tour above timberline. The route goes from Grizzly Meadow to Piute Meadow to Buckeye Pass to Rock Island Pass to Burro Pass. At that point it is just west of the Sawtooth Range that towers above. This is "an ultimate scenic leg of the trip," according to Nicolai. From Buckeye Pass to Tuolomne is one of the trickier parts of the trip in terms of navigation. Many canyons in this area lead skiers in the wrong direction and dump them into Hetch Hetchy Reservoir. There is a summer trail that goes the right way, but it is hard to follow in the winter as the route crosses and recrosses the crest, circumventing the rocky, spectacular peaks. Burro Pass leads to the upper part of Matterhorn Canyon. But instead of dropping into it, the route climbs up again; crosses to Virginia Canyon; then up, out, and over to Cold Canyon, which leads to the summer camp at Glen Aulin. From there the trail follows the Tuolomne River to Tuolomne Meadows. Despite the complexity of the route the skiing is always easy. Nicolai had a cache at Tuolomne Meadows, put in via the Tioga Pass Road.

There's an alternate route to start a shorter version of the whole tour or for a short tour on its own. Start at Conway Summit on US 395, ski up to Summit Lake, over to Cold Canyon, down to Glen Aulin, and then either continue on your way to Whitney or go out if you are doing a short tour. On the east side of the Sawtooth Range there is road access from US 395 to Twin Lakes that is kept plowed all winter and is just a short distance from excellent and steep ski mountaineering on Matterhorn Peak.

Yosemite to Mammoth
Map: Devil's Postpile quadrangle

The route goes from Tuolomne up the Lyell Fork of the Tuolomne River. Then it crosses Donohue Pass. From Donohue to Thousand Island Lake is "sublime terrain," according to Nicolai. It's beautiful and open with scattered groves of trees. From Thousand Island Lake the normal route goes directly down the bottom of the North Fork of the San Joaquin River to a road coming up from Mammoth. A good variation is to go via Garnet Lake to Iceberg Lake, right under the spectacular Minarets of the Ritter Range.

This is the only place in the entire trip where the definite crest disappears. The Ritter Range is the temporary end of the High Sierra. Mammoth Mountain, which has one of the country's largest downhill ski areas on its slopes, is where the high country starts again.

The Yosemite-to-Mammoth leg of the Crest Traverse is a very popular one as a trip on its own. If it wasn't included in the longer tour I would have included it separately as a classic tour. It can be done in one day with light touring gear and good spring snow, but usually it is done as a several day trip where the skiers take their time and enjoy the many good side trips along the way. It is the easiest and most popular of the trans-Sierra trips and is a good introduction to the longer Sierra traverses.

Mammoth Mountain to Little Lakes Basin
Maps: Mt. Morrison, Mt. Abbott quadrangles

The route now goes over Mammoth Pass to the east side of the Sierra Crest behind Bloody Mountain (most of the rest of the route is actually west of the Crest). Up to this point it has mostly followed the Muir Trail, but it leaves it here. The Muir Trail becomes boring for skiers as it goes deep into west-side valleys. Nicolai went by Mt. Hopkins and followed Fish Creek to get to Red and White lakes and then Grinnell Lake. An unmarked pass from Grinnell Lake leads to Hopkins Creek. This terrain is all above timberline. The next stop is Mono Pass. Slopes lead down from there to Rock Creek and Little Lakes Valley, which the famous Sierra mountaineer Norman Clyde thought had the best skiing terrain in all the Sierra. He climbed out of Rock Creek via an easy pass on the north side of Bear Creek Spire. Since there is a road up Rock Creek, it's also a good place for a cache.

Little Lakes Valley is one of the best basins in the eastern Sierra to set up a comfortable base camp for an easy ski trip of several days. From a camp at one of the upper lakes there's a tremendous variety of skiing possibilities in every direction. Access is easy from Rock Creek.

Rock Creek to Bishop Pass
Maps: Mt. Tom, Mt. Goddard quadrangles

The first pass, located at the side of Bear Creek Spire, is an easy one. The next pass east of the peak is another crux of this route. It can be circumvented, but much distance is saved if you do it following the Nicolai Route. A steep snow slope leads to a 40-foot-high rock wall that is fifth-class climbing. Nicolai used his rope to haul up the packs and then to aid his wife. It wasn't difficult, he says, but it was exposed for a few moves. Other possible routes are to drop down Morgan Creek or to go around to the west via Lake Italy.

The route then goes up over Pine Creek Pass and over Desolation Lake in Humphreys Basin. "Now it gets really interesting," comments Nicolai. It goes down into Evolution Valley and up to Muir Pass where there is a hut. From there it descends toward the huge Le Conte Canyon, but instead of dropping it climbs back up and traverses its top. This is a second key to the trip. It probably had never been done on skis before Nicolai's trip, but it saved him a lot of vertical travel and also avoided some serious avalanche danger. The route then crosses a col between Mt. Gilbert and Mt. Johnson and arrives at Bishop Pass.

Saddlerock Lake just below Bishop Pass is another area that is excellent for a base camp for several days of skiing. Access is easy from the east, and there is a lot of good terrain nearby ranging from easy alpine wandering to the ski descent of a major peak, Mt. Goode.

Bishop Pass to Mt. Whitney
Maps: Big Pine, Mt. Pinchot, Mt. Whitney, Kearn Peak, Olancha quadrangles

From Bishop Pass Nicolai passed right under the sheer faces of the Palisades, the most alpine of all the mountains of the Sierra. This area was a scenic high point of a trip that had been continuously spectacular since Mammoth. From the Palisades the route rejoins the Muir Trail, which stays high from here on to Whitney. Nicolai had a cache at Kearsarge Pass.

There is another crux at Forester Pass. For Nicolai it was trivial, a piece of cake. For Doug Robinson it was "one of my most gripping moments in a long life of mountaineering." It depends on the snow conditions. It can be circumvented via Junction Pass. Forester Pass leads to the Bighorn Plateau, the huge above-timberline tableland at the head of the Kern River. The Sierra here splits into two ranges, the Kaweahs, which go to the west, and the main crest, which is followed by the Muir Trail. The Sierra High Route, a popular multiday traverse, takes advantage of this split to cross the range from east to west without ever going low. It's a classic route, well-described in Dave Beck's book, and an excellent preparation for the longer Sierra Crest traverse described here.

The Nicolai Route follows a natural bench around the huge peaks of the crest, including Mt. Whitney. You can exit at Whitney Pass, but Nicolai continued on and exited at New Army Pass, south of Mt. Whitney. He skied down Cottonwood Creek, eventually ran out of snow, and was finally forced to take off his skis for the first time in two months and 275 miles. It was an epic journey but it distinguishes itself by its lack of privation, pain, and struggle. There was definitely a touch of Californian hedonism to the trip—great skiing, lots of sun, beautiful mountains. That's what

Sierra Crest. Photo by Chris Cox.

makes the Sierra stand out among all U.S. ranges as the place to do long trips.

It needs to be said after all this praise that it isn't unusual for there to be severe storms in the spring. Frequently a lot of snow falls in March and April. There are still long sunny periods, but it isn't unlikely that you could be pinned down for a greater percentage of the time than Bill Nicolai was on his trip (4 days out of the 55-day trip). Late April and all of May are said to have steady good weather.

The trip doesn't have to end at New Army Pass. It would also be possible to continue southward for another 60 to 100 miles to the actual end of the Sierra. It would be delightful skiing through less spectacular scenery than in the land of the high peaks. I don't know of anyone who has yet skied this section of the crest, but some experienced Sierra skiers think that this very unexploited part of the range contains great skiing.

That's a long description of a long route—the longest continuous ski traverse in North America. It's not the hardest one; the Redline Traverse in the Sierra is harder, and the Ha-Iltzuk and Waddington traverses in the British Columbia Coast Range are much more serious mountaineering affairs. But no other long traverse has the perfect combination of commitment and hedonism that this one possesses.

The Sierra Crest Traverse stands apart from other long North American traverses in that portions of it are regularly done in the spring by professionally guided parties. The names and addresses of guides that lead trips on the route are found at the head of this chapter.

California

Mt. San Gorgonio and Mt. San Jacinto

TOUR Ski descents of Mt. San Gorgonio and Mt. San Jacinto near Los Angeles, California.

IN A NUTSHELL Mt. San Gorgonio is a piece of the Sierra placed right next to the land of the surfboard. It has excellent alpine ski mountaineering on it. Nearby Mt. San Jacinto has gentler touring terrain. San Gorgonio is a two-day ski trip. San Jacinto can be done as a day trip due to the aerial tram from Palm Springs.

WHAT MAKES THE TOUR SPECIAL What is special is the proximity of such refreshing alpine environments to the smoggy tangle of Los Angeles. The forests on both San Gorgonio and San Jacinto are especially beautiful. The weather is usually excellent.

LEVEL OF DIFFICULTY The slopes of Mt. San Gorgonio range in difficulty from moderate to advanced. Those of Mt. San Jacinto are easy or moderate.

BEST TIME TO GO February to April.

HOW TO GET THERE The trailhead for Mt. San Gorgonio is reached from Redlands via CA 38. The Mt. San Jacinto tram is located on the west side of Palm Springs, California.

SPECIAL EQUIPMENT Metal-edged skis should be used for San Gorgonio, as well as climbing skins and the other paraphernalia of the ski mountaineer. Light touring gear is fine for most of the San Jacinto skiing.

MAPS   USGS San Gorgonio Mountain and Palm Springs, both California quadrangles.

LODGING AND SUPPLIES   For San Gorgonio: Redlands, California. For San Jacinto: Palm Springs, California.

Southern California is a land of surfboards, beach cruisers, and endless shopping centers—not a land of ski tourers. Thousands will drive 300 miles for a weekend of downhill at Mammoth Mountain but relatively few stay close to home for cross-country skiing.

It's not that there are no opportunities. Snow-covered mountains may not be such an overwhelming reality as the beaches, but there are plenty of them within two to three hours of Los Angeles. Running parallel to the coast all the way from Santa Barbara to the middle of Baja California are a set of discontinuous mountain ranges, rising from near sea level to above timberline.

Highest and most alpine of these mountains is Mt. San Gorgonio, 11,510 feet. It's as refreshing as a piece of the Sierra dragged into the home of smog. Mt. San Gorgonio is the center of a small wilderness area some three hours from Los Angeles. It is the place for multiday ski-mountaineering trips away from the lifts, cars, and crowds of the ski areas and above the smog of the Los Angeles basin.

The mountains of the Peninsular Ranges, such as Mt. San Gorgonio and its near neighbor to the southeast, Mt. San Jacinto, should not be taken lightly as mountains. San Gorgonio's above-timberline summit stands white above Los Angeles on those rare, really clear winter days. San Jacinto drops straight down from its 10,804-foot summit to an altitude of 1,200 feet on its north side in a distance of only 5.5 miles. That's a bigger drop than you can find in the U.S. Rockies. Of course, what's important to skiers isn't the absolute vertical drop but the vertical drop above the snowline. The climate of southern California is such that that distance of skiable vertical may range from many thousands of feet to zero in those occasional times when there is no snow at all. The snow is highly variable. Powder is rare. Wet snow and corn snow are common. So is ice. The temperatures are generally warm so the snow stabilizes rapidly and avalanches are rare, except during and just after heavy storms. Conditions are not just variable with the year, of course, but with the altitude and exposure to the sun.

To get to Mt. San Gorgonio take CA 38 from Redlands east through Camp Angelus and on to the turnoff to Jenks Lake. The basic touring trail

Mt. San Gorgonio, California. Photo by Steve Barnett.

to the peak starts from the Jenks Lake trailhead (6,860 feet), follows a sometimes snow-covered road for 4 miles, and then climbs gently up through forest and meadows some 4 more miles to break out of the timber at Dry Lake at 9,100 feet. This is a good spot for a camp below the long wall of chutes and cirques dropping from the summit ridge of San Gorgonio. This alpine wall stays above 11,000 feet for some 2 miles. It's impressive. If you want steep skiing, and the snow permits it, simple. Just keep going straight up one of the chutes. The gentler approach is to the right, west of the San Gorgonio summit, to the col between Jepson Peak and Charlton Peak. A steep climb of 400 feet gets you to the ridgeline, and from there you can traverse around to San Gorgonio's summit. Usually this is a good two-day trip from the road. Charlton Peak is a good alternative climb to San Gorgonio if conditions are too icy for a safe ski ascent.

Skiing the highest peak by the main trail far from exhausts the possibilities in this beautiful wilderness area. The forest is composed of large, well-spaced trees and is skiable virtually everywhere. Hence, there are many possible ascents and descents of up to 3,000 vertical feet that cover the full range of steepness.

One trip that looks particularly interesting to me is a traverse of the whole San Bernardino crest. San Gorgonio is only the highest point of a long chain of 10,000-foot-plus peaks. One could gain the crest from Camp

Angelus (5,780 feet) and then stay high all the way past San Gorgonio, some 12 miles.

The peaks east of Dry Lake, such as Grinnell Mountain (10,250 feet), look as though they would provide a good and much easier ski ascent than San Gorgonio and thus would be good for beginning mountain ski tourers.

Mt. San Jacinto also has good ski touring on it. Its nature is a bit different from that of San Gorgonio, and the two complement each other well. Whereas San Gorgonio is alpine and skiing on it is really ski mountaineering, San Jacinto is well suited to gentler ski touring.

Skiing out of Palm Springs, that desert resort best known for its golf and its wealth, should be a joke, but it's not. There's a tram that rises 6,000 feet from the desert floor to a station at 8,516 feet on the rim of Mt. San Jacinto. Step onto the tram with the hordes from Los Angeles and San Diego dressed in shorts and t-shirts and you may feel a bit clownish in your ski clothes. The tram rises over a vertical mile, and then the tables are turned. The hordes shiver, but you can put on your skis and go. And you will find great touring.

Much of the terrain on San Jacinto is perfect for cross country. There are gentle slopes and flat meadows. The forest is a beautiful one, wide open with big, well-spaced sugar and Jeffrey pines. Several miles away is the peak of San Jacinto (10,800 feet). To get there, follow the trail to Round Valley. This is a moderate climb and fun on the way back down. From Round Valley, aim for the obvious col between two peaks on the surrounding ridgeline, San Jacinto and Jean peaks. The final slope is steep. Check different exposures to see where the easiest going is. Northern exposures might still have powder on them; southern ones may be softened by the sun. Once on the ridge follow it north past the lesser summits to the main summit. If you like the extreme, the northern slopes are precipitous.

The terrain west and south of San Jacinto also looks good for ski touring, and it may have more snow on it than the terrain on the Palm Springs side since west slopes usually get more precipitation than east slopes and since the crest of the mountain may protect the slopes from desert winds.

The terrain on Mt. San Jacinto is perfect, and there is a small touring center near the tram station. Why then are there no set trails? Touring-center personnel say that no matter what they do they cannot keep the hordes from the tram from walking on the trails and ruining them. Hence, there are no trails close to the tram. Farther away from the tram, Mt. San Jacinto is a wilderness area, and no set tracks are permitted. What does the touring center do without trails? First, they rent about as many sleds as they do skis. Then they rent skis and boots and give lessons. It's only a small touring center, but if it can protect trails it has the potential to be a very good one.

What kind of snow conditions can you expect to find in the southern California mountains? As with the Sierra, there's tremendous variation from year to year. The highest areas, such as San Gorgonio and San Jacinto, almost always have sufficient snow for skiing. Temperatures in the middle of winter are not so high, however, as to insure corn snow at the highest altitudes. This is the fly in the ointment. Winter conditions at the top of San Gorgonio or San Jacinto are often wild mixtures of ice, breakable crust, and patches of south-facing soft snow. When I skied each of these peaks, the descents of the steeper upper slopes were extremely difficult and were just short of being scary. In the spring, of course, it's a different story, and easy-skiing corn snow is the rule. San Gorgonio is tall enough that you can expect good skiing to last there through May.

The Los Angeles area has big mountains as well as big population, basketball, and smog. The presence of the Sierra, one of the world's best ski-touring ranges, has diverted attention from these mountains, but by any other standard they would be major. The terrain is good and the forest as beautiful for skiing as you can find. The weather, of course, is generally excellent. It's the rare luck of southern Californians to be able to travel on a moment's notice from a beachside culture to an oasis of alpine ski mountaineering just a few hours away.

Baja California

Sierra San Pedro Martir

TOUR   Skiing the Sierra San Pedro Martir plateau in Baja California, Mexico.

IN A NUTSHELL   From a basecamp on the plateau (8,000 feet altitude) skiers can ski cross-country for miles or ski the peaks on the rim of the plateau (over 9,000 feet high).

WHAT MAKES THE TOUR SPECIAL   Ski under a hot sun in the middle of January in an extraordinary location between the Gulf of California and the Pacific Ocean. Enjoy both spectacular desert canyon scenery and perfect cross-country terrain with open forest.

LEVEL OF DIFFICULTY   Easy skiing on a plateau. Peaks may be much more difficult depending on snow conditions.

BEST TIME TO GO   January and February.

HOW TO GET THERE   80 miles south of Ensenada take the turnoff to the left to Rancho Meling and Observatorio Nacional. The road is plowed all the way to the snow-covered plateau.

SPECIAL EQUIPMENT   Sunscreen.

MAPS   Use the maps in the guidebook by John Robinson, *Camping and Climbing in Baja* (La Siesta Press, Glendale, CA). Good Mexican topographic maps exist and can be ordered from Centenal, San Antonio Abad, No. 124, Mexico 8, D.F. The quadrangles you want are Santa Cruz H 11 B 55 and San Rafael H 11 B 45. These are in the 1:50,000 series.

LODGING AND SUPPLIES   Ensenada, Baja California, Mexico.

January is a good month for downhill skiing and cross-country running on groomed tracks. But it's usually a bad month for backcountry touring. If you live in deep snow country, you have to deal with short and cold days, long and colder nights, and deep, unconsolidated snow. Add high avalanche danger and it's easy to see why most tourers wait for spring for their serious trips. If you don't want to wait for spring to find hot days and grand touring, there is an alternative. Go south! Go to those places that aren't deep snow country—that only get snow for a short part of the year—where you can enjoy springlike weather and snow in the middle of January in some of North America's most spectacular spots. Here we'll talk about the southernmost of all tours in this book—Baja California, Mexico.

When I first thought of skiing down in Baja, most of my skiing friends laughed. Where could there be skiing in Baja? Going all the way down there with skis would be the height of fanatical excess. In this case, skiing well was the best revenge; the trip to Baja was a wonderful one.

The place to go is the Sierra San Pedro Martir, about 140 miles south of San Diego. This range is the highest in Baja California. It is a plateau some 70 miles long, 25 miles of which are above 8,000 feet (high enough to have snow most years). There is only one real peak separate from the plateau in the whole range. That one peak, though, is a great one, the Picacho del Diablo, 10,152 feet high. It is a white granite pyramid rising more than 9,000 vertical feet from the San Felipe Desert on the east side of the peninsula.

The San Pedro Martir happens to have some of the finest January ski touring imaginable. Days are warm, the weather usually good, and the snow well consolidated by the hot sun. The terrain is both good for skiing and scenically spectacular. There are also a multitude of other winter activities you can do on a trip to Baja. That's why it is the kind of trip that should become an annual event.

To get to the plateau you must drive down the Coast Highway some 83 miles south of Ensenada, which is itself some 60 miles south of San Diego. There will be an intersection on the left with a dirt road marked "Observatorio Nacional" and "Rancho Meling." Follow that road for many miles along the San Telmo River and continue with it as it climbs up a small ridge. From the top of the ridge you will see the huge mass of the San Pedro Martir Plateau running south to north across the horizon. The range is bounded on both the west and the east by fault scarps. The eastern one is the radical one; it drops 8,000 feet in just a few miles. The western scarp isn't so dramatic, but it clearly demarcates the plateau. The road drops back down to the San Telmo River at Rancho Meling, an idyllic spot that is both working ranch and resort. The road up to here is rough but not extreme. There are ruts big enough to swallow the wheels of a small car but we were, with care, able to sidestep them. A pickup truck or car with good clearance would be best.

Continue on the main road, crossing the river. This is where the road is likely to wash out following heavy rains. Because this road serves the Mexican National Astronomical Observatory it is, however, quickly repaired following damaging storms. Now the road climbs in earnest. At around 7,000 feet you come to Corona de Abajo, a station of the San Pedro Martir National Park. There is a shelter here as well as buildings for the park staff. This is where we first encountered snow on our trip, in what we were told was a normal season. By now you have entered the forest zone. There are delightful groves of yellow pines along with patches of scrubby and almost impenetrable desert chaparral.

This is also where we found one of the most pleasant surprises of the trip. The road is plowed. It must be the only plowed road in all of Mexico. The road is kept open to serve the National Observatory. We had expected to have to walk a long distance with skis, or at least to wish we had a 4-wheel-drive vehicle. As it turned out, chains were sufficient.

The road climbs up from Corona de Abajo to a pass, Cima de Corona, at 8,200 feet. This is the rim of the western scarp. From it you can see the plateau and its eastern rim. Hanging above all that will be the granite top of the Picacho del Diablo, impressive even at this distance. The ridge that marks this western rim can be skied for a considerable distance. It is over 12 miles long above the 8,000 foot level and it has a nice open forest with little underbrush. It seems to get heavier snow than the higher eastern rim, presumably due to the normal rainshadow effect as you go from west to east. The Picacho, despite its altitude, has the skimpiest snowpack of all. We didn't get to explore this western scarp edge very thoroughly, but it does have some possibilities for good downhill skiing through open forest on the slopes that head down from it to the plateau. We saw particularly good-looking slopes a few miles to the south of the road. These slopes had a northeast orientation. If weather or road conditions kept you from continuing on to the eastern side of the plateau, you could spend a few days profitably exploring this part of the San Pedro Martir.

The road drops 600 to 800 feet from Cima de Corona. Then it climbs at a moderate pace as it heads across the plateau. This whole region is covered with a beautiful forest of sugar and Jeffrey pines, very much like the forest that covers the upper reaches of the southern California mountains. The trees are widely spaced with almost no undergrowth. In fact it's probably as smooth as your new-mowed lawn. Consequently only a little snow is needed to turn it into perfect cross-country ski terrain.

If you are familiar with the southern California ranges, you will feel at home. The forest is just the same. The white granite is the same. The San Pedro Martir can be considered to be just the southernmost extension of these mountains. But none of the other peaks, even San Gorgonio, are so dominant as the Picacho. None of the others are so close to salt water. None of the others have such an expanse of high-altitude plateau.

Five miles from Cima de Corona the road goes through a large meadow called Vallecitos. This is just before the final ridge that marks the eastern scarp of the plateau. When we were there it contained several delightful spots for camping, out of sight of the road, free of snow under the trees, with running streams alongside, and with plenty of firewood. (Don't let the delightfully clear running streams fool you into using the water untreated. Cattle graze here in the summer and, just as bad, there's a garbage dump for the observatory just a little upstream, right on the banks of the stream.)

From Vallecitos there is a lot of ski terrain in all directions. The road climbs up to the observatory, which is set on a nubbin on the east rim at 9,200 feet. Here are wonderful places for viewing the scarp face and the Picacho and good slopes for skiing off to the north. Start at the Cabaña Azul just a short way down the road from the big observatory tower at road's end. (It would be best to ask permission at the observatory to climb up to the upper portion of the road.) These northern slopes continue for a long way out to the small peaks known as Venado Blanco.

You can probably also reach Venado Blanco from Vallecitos, cutting cross-country northward. We didn't get to explore this rather vast chunk of plateau, but it all looked good for skiing.

We did spend time exploring to the south of Vallecitos. That's where the Picacho and the highest parts of the rim are. The Picacho is separated from the rim of the plateau by a thin rocky ridge, which takes fifth-class climbing to follow. An enormous canyon rising from the desert, the Cañon del Diablo, cuts the Picacho from the plateau. Most people climbing the Picacho climb up the canyon to get to the peak. It is possible to get there from the plateau, but, despite the seemingly small distance, it's a hard trip. You must first get to the high point of the plateau, a peak known, ingloriously, as Blue Bottle (Botella Azul). It's variously listed as 9,400 and 9,600 feet high. Then you drop from its summit down a steep gorge into the Cañon del Diablo. That's a drop of over 3,000 feet. Then you climb up another steep set of chutes some 4,000 vertical feet to get to the summit. These chutes (the Slot Wash route) are the only nontechnical route to the summit.

The rolling meadows and ridges south of Vallecitos are as good a cross-country terrain as you could hope to find. The trees are both beautiful and widely spaced. There is no underbrush. The snow is quickly hardened by the sun to form a fast surface. When we were there in January, it froze hard every night (down to about 5°F.). The sun was hot enough to allow us to throw most clothes off by mid-morning but never got high enough in the sky to turn the snow into soup. It was a perfect combination of luxurious warmth for midwinter plus fast skiing.

Several miles to the south the meadows of Vallecitos are closed in by a system of rocky ridges, known as La Tasajera. Skirting these eastward and climbing, you go up excellent north-facing slopes to a small peak on

Skiing Baja California on the plateau near Vallecitos.
Photo by Steve Barnett.

the east rim of the plateau, directly opposite the Picacho. With a truly spectacular view, it's easy to spend hours lolling around on this nubbin. The scarp drops 8,000 feet and the Sea of Cortez gleams in the not-so-great distance. To the west you can see the gleam of the Pacific. The Picacho itself, a twin-summited pyramid of white granite, is imposingly large, climbing straight out of the desert.

The forest on the way down is surprisingly northern. It is largely lodgepole pine and a local variant of white fir. The most sheltered pockets of trees have moss hanging down from their branches, looking for all the world like something right out of the Pacific Northwest. On the other side of the ridge, at the same altitude, you will find manzanita thickets and desert vegetation.

Scouting out the route to the Picacho, if not actually climbing it, turned out to be less trivial than thought. We hoped we could traverse easily via the rim described above from the peak over to Blue Bottle. This is probably possible but seemed like it would be difficult going. There is supposed to be an easy summer trail from Vallecitos to Blue Bottle. It goes below the rim, into the rocky Tasajera Ridge and then up to the peak. Easy on foot in summer doesn't translate here to easy on skis in winter. We not only couldn't follow the trail, but we kept getting hung up in steep-walled stream beds and snow-covered rockpiles that made travel extremely slow and frustrating. Maybe there is an easy route, but at this time I can't tell you what it is.

We did get a good look at Blue Bottle's northern side, and it seems like there will be excellent open skiing there. I'm also curious to know if the gully down to the bottom of Cañon del Diablo is skiable in a good snow year. It looks like the route from there up to the Picacho's southern summit (lower by 2 feet than the northern one) would be mostly skiable. There is much less snow on the Picacho than on equivalent exposures and altitudes farther west due to the desert winds that blow up the eastern slopes, but in a very good snow year it might be fun to try it. There is another set of large meadows like the Vallecitos meadow south of Blue Bottle, and these should be good for cross-country skiing, too.

What kind of snow can you expect in the San Pedro Martir? Workers at the observatory told us that 1 meter would be about average. In a very good year there would be 2 meters, and in a very bad year there would be nothing at all. Going by the records of southern California, you might expect decent snow three out of four years. The workers told us that the snow usually lasted through March. The best times would probably be January and February—as much for the contrast with the blustery weather up north as for the best snow conditions. None of those I talked to had ever seen skiers up there before, though I know that there have been a few. They must be rare.

You can change that. This is one of the most enjoyable trips in this book. Not only can you ski on a midwinter trip to Baja, but you also can hike amidst palms and waterfalls in the eastside canyons of the mountains, windsurf on the Pacific coast, and kayak along the Sea of Cortez shore. It's easy to get there and cheap to stay. So why isn't there a crowd? I don't know—maybe most skiers don't look south toward the Tropics when they think of ski vacations, but what they don't know will only help you if you are one of those who wants to give skiing Baja in January a try.

Glossary

alpine skiing Skiing on boots and skis specialized for descending lift-served slopes. The bindings do not permit the heels to be lifted from the skis.

altimeter An instrument that indicates the altitude of its location above sea level.

angulation The bending done by skiers so that they edge against the pull of gravity, i.e., knees and hips leaning into the hill but not the upper body.

ascenders Mechanical devices that allow a climber to climb up a rope.

avalanche The sudden downward release of a large quantity of snow.

avalanche cord A long (40 feet or more) brightly colored cord left dangling behind the skier. If the skier is buried by an avalanche, a piece of the cord may be exposed at the surface. It can be followed to the victim.

bail The steel clip on the front of a Nordic 3-pin binding that holds down the toe of the boot on the pins of the binding.

belay A belay is the act of putting oneself in a fixed position from which one can suddenly stop the motion of a rope tied to a skiing or climbing partner and thus prevent a dangerous fall.

carabiner A strong metal oval used by climbers with a gate that allows a rope to be clipped through the oval.

cirque A semicircular basin cut by the erosive action of a past or present glacier.

climax slide An avalanche in which the entire snowpack, not just an upper layer, slides.

climbing skins Strips of special material strapped or glued to the bases of skis for long ascents. The strips have hairs or scales that permit skiers to climb steeply uphill by preventing backsliding.

col A slotlike opening in a high mountain ridgeline that can act as a pass from one side of a ridge to another.

compression parallel A parallel turn used for heavy snow that uses a low, compressed position to weight the skis (not unweight) at the start of the turn, pressing their centers into the snow and making them carve into the fall line.

cornice The wall of snow formed by the wind on ridgelines or summits in high mountains. The wall always faces away from the prevailing wind. The cornice may overhang, and since it is easy to mistake it for the actual ridgetop it poses a danger to the curious skier straining for a look at the other side of a ridge.

corn snow Grainlike chunks of ice, formed during the spring when the snowpack is subject to a succession of above-freezing days and sub-freezing nights and snow crystals are transformed, losing their points and gaining size. While corn snow is thawing in the morning it makes a near-perfect skiing surface.

couloir A narrow slotlike gully cut into a steep mountain wall. Filled with snow it may form a ski route of exceptional steepness and difficulty.

counterslope turn A turn where the slope is banked outward from the turn, making it harder to avoid slipping outward.

crampons Frameworks of steel points that strap to a climber's boots, facilitating climbing on steep ice.

crevasse A deep slot cutting through the surface of a glacier, formed by the motion of the glacier over an uneven surface.

cross-country skiing Skiing on prepared tracks over gentle horizontal or rolling terrain with exceptionally lightweight skis and boots.

declination The variance between magnetic north (indicated by a compass needle) and true north (defined by the axis of rotation of the Earth).

depth hoar Another name for TG snow, which forms at the bottom of the snowpack early in the season and may act as the sliding layer for climax avalanches.

diagonal stride The classic style of running on cross-country skis with the poles alternately touching the snow.

double poling The technique of cross-country skiing in which skiers propel themselves by using both poles simultaneously.

edging (the ski) Using the ankles, knees, and hips to control the angle that a ski's edges make with the surface of the snow.

fall line   On any slope, the steepest, straightest line down, the line of maximum descent.

glissade   The skilike descent of a snow slope done by sliding down on either the soles of the boots or on the seat of the pants.

hard-slab avalanche   An avalanche caused by the sudden cracking loose of a thick, wind-hardened slab at the surface of the snowpack. These are particularly difficult to predict.

headwall   The very steep uppermost slopes of a glacier-cut bowl.

hydrographic apex   The geographic point from which precipitation drains to more than one river drainage, for example, the Continental Divide.

massif   A compact group of mountains clustered around a dominant peak.

moraine   The ridges of rocks and debris left by a receding glacier at the line of its former maximum advance.

neve penitentes   Sharp spikes of snow created by differential melting at high altitudes under an intense summer or tropical sun.

nordic skiing   Skiing with soft-soled boots and toe bindings that leave heels free to rise.

open turn   A form of parallel turn using some pressure on the uphill ski at the end of the turn (*see* scissors turn).

orographic lifting   The action by which storm clouds carried by winds reach the frontal slopes of a mountain range, are forced to rise over the range, and are cooled, causing more precipitation than would otherwise fall.

parallel position   Basic ski position with the skis parallel to each other, the uphill ski slightly ahead of the downhill one and the body facing somewhat downhill.

parallel turn   A turn on skis in which both skis move together approximately as a single unit.

pole glissade   Sliding down a snow slope, controlling the speed not with the skis but with the ski poles held tightly into the snow as brakes.

powder snow   New-fallen snow with a temperature well below freezing, a low density, and little cohesion between the snow crystals. A skier literally flies through the snow, which parts for his turns with the wish. It's a skier's dream for downhill runs.

prusiks   Special knots used by glacier travelers that are used to help someone unfortunate enough to fall into a crevasse to climb out by climbing up the rope.

rappeling Descending a rope fixed at the top of a slope or cliff.

scarp The near perpendicular mountain wall formed as a vertically moving fault raises a mountain out of the earth.

schuss To run straight down a hill without turning, letting gravity take its course.

scissors turn A turn where the uphill ski is advanced slightly and allowed to fork uphill at the end of a parallel turn, helping pull the turn to a finish in difficult snow.

serac A tower of glacial ice, often teetering over the heads of passing skiers, formed by the motion of a glacier.

sidecut The arc built into the sides of many skis to promote ease in turning. The tips and tails are wider than the middles of the skis, making them narrow-waisted. When a ski a tipped on its edge and weighted, it will try to turn while following the arc of the sidecut.

single-cambered skis Skis with a uniform longitudinal flex. When they are pressed together bottom to bottom, the bottoms touch simultaneously all along the skis' length.

skating Skating on skis as done on ice or roller skates. A fast and efficient way to travel over hard-packed or frozen surfaces.

ski mountaineering Skiing through high mountains with some of the goals and techniques of the mountain climber (e.g., summit bagging, glacier travel, rock climbing, and rappeling).

ski touring The art of being a tourist on skis, of traveling under your own power on skis over prepared tracks or over untracked snow.

snow bridge A bridge of snow or ice extending over the open mouth of a crevasse and offering a route across it for the skier. Most are safe for skiers, but not all.

step telemark A telemark turn started by stepping sharply downward with the downhill ski.

step turn Turning while skiing by stepping with the skis in the desired direction.

suncups Fields of small hills and hollows on the snow surface, formed by the differential melting action of the spring or summer sun.

surface hoar A thin layer of TG snow that forms on the surface of the snowpack in regions that combine intense solar radiation and intense night-time cold, such as the San Juan range in southwestern Colorado. It can act as a sliding layer for subsequent layers of snow, and thus poses a potential avalanche danger.

swami belt   A belt of nylon webbing used by climbers to connect themselves to climbing ropes.

telemark turn   A skiing turn done with free-heeled boots by placing one ski well ahead of the other and turning it slightly with respect to the other. Just as a bicycle turns when the front wheel is turned in relation to the rear one and the whole bike is banked into the turn, so does the telemarking skier turn.

TG snow   Snow crystals that are changed from stellar-like crystals into delicate cup-like and scroll-like shapes. As the season advances and snow accumulates above them, TG snow may act as a weak layer that can cause the whole snowpack above to avalanche. The changes in the crystal's form are caused by a strong temperature gradient in the snowpack, caused by cold air at the snow's surface, warmer temperatures at the bottom of the snowpack, and a relatively thin snowpack.

3-pin equipment   Boots and bindings joined by 3-pin bindings and the middle-weight skis that go with them. The 3-pin boot and binding is an internationally standardized system that holds the boot by the toe in the binding and leaves the heel free to rise.

topo map   A map that shows the three-dimensional shape of the land by elevation-indexed contour lines.

traverse   A route that stays high in the mountains for several days as it goes from a starting point to an ending point many miles away.

unweighting   Rising up or sinking down on skis to momentarily take weight off them, making it easy to move them across the snow's surface in turns.

whiteout   A condition on a snowy, treeless slope in which fog or blowing snow can so whiten the air that the snow and the sky can't be distinguished and depth perception disappears in a featureless sea of whiteness.

wind-blasted   A condition in which the wind carries away the snow lying on a slope on the windward side of a ridge. By mechanically working what snow remains, the wind turns it into an uneven and very hard surface.

wind-loaded   A condition in which a high wind picks up snow from the windward side of a ridge and then deposits it on the lee slope as it crosses the ridge.

windslab   A slab of denser snow in which the grains are strongly bonded to each other, created as the top layer of a powdery snowpack is moved about by a high wind and hardened. A windslab may slide as a unit on the weaker snow beneath it.

Bibliography

Abbey, Edward. *The Monkey Wrench Gang*. Dream Garden Press, 1985.

Bach, Orville E. *Hiking the Yellowstone Backcountry*. San Francisco: Sierra Club Books, 1980.

Baldwin, John. *Exploring the Coast Mountains on Skis*. Vancouver, BC: John Baldwin, 1983.

Barber, John F. *Yellowstone Ski Tours*. Yellowstone National Park, WY: Rocky Mountain Trading Co., 1979.

Barnett, Steve. *Cross-Country Downhill*. Seattle: Pacific Search Press, 1983.

Beck, Dave. *Ski Touring in California*. Berkeley, CA: Wilderness Press, 1980.

Daffern, Tony. *Avalanche Safety for Skiers and Climbers*. Seattle: Alpenbooks, 1983.

Dawson, Louis W. *Colorado High Routes*. Seattle: The Mountaineers, 1985.

Gillette, Ned. *Cross-Country Skiing*. Seattle: The Mountaineers, 1979.

Goodwin, Tony. *Northern Adirondack Ski Tours*. Glens Falls, NY: Adirondack Mountain Club, 1981.

Johnson, Randy. *Southern Snow: The Winter Guide to Dixie*. Appalachian Mountain Club Press, 1986.

Kals, W. S. *Land Navigation Handbook*. San Francisco: Sierra Club Books,

Kelner, Alexis and David Hanscom. *Wasatch Tours*.

LaChapelle, Ed. *The ABC's of Avalanche Safety*. Seattle: The Mountaineers, 1985.

Lentz, Macdonald and Carline. *First Aid*, 3rd ed. Seattle: The Mountaineers, 1985.

Meissner, Virginia. *Cross-Country Ski Tours in Central Oregon*. Bend, OR: Meissner Books, 1984.

Messick, Tim. *Crosscountry Skiing in Yosemite*. Denver: Chockstone Press, 1985.

Mitchell, Dick. *Mountaineering First Aid*, 2nd ed. Seattle: The Mountaineers,

Noren, Elizabeth and Gary Noren. *Ski Minnesota.* Minneapolis: Nodin Press, 1985.

Peters, Ed, ed. *Mountaineering: The Freedom of the Hills,* 4th ed. Seattle: The Mountaineers, 1982.

Robinson, John. *Camping and Climbing in Baja.* Glendale, CA: La Siesta Press,

Tejada-Flores, Lito. *Backcountry Skiing.* San Francisco: Sierra Club Books, 1981.

United States Geological Survey. USGS maps. Denver, CO, and Reston, VA.

Vielbig, Klindt. *Cross-Country Ski Routes of Oregon's Cascades: Mt. Hood and Bend.* Seattle: The Mountaineers, 1984.

Wilkerson, James, ed. *Medicine for Mountaineering,* 3rd ed. Seattle: The Mountaineers, 1985.

Index